EPSON GP 3500

Introduction to Application Software Using Open Access

Robert A. Szymanski

Donald P. Szymanski

Norma A. Morris

Donna M. Pulschen

MERRILL PUBLISHING COMPANY
A Bell & Howell Information Company
Columbus Toronto London Melbourne

Published by
Merrill Publishing Company
A Bell & Howell Information Company
Columbus, Ohio 43216

This book was set in Times Roman and Helvetica.

Library of Congress Catalog Card Number: 87-63186
International Standard Book Number: 0-675-20823-8
Printed in the United States of America
2 3 4 5 6 7 8 9 -- 92 91 90 89 88

Preface

This workbook provides a hands-on tutorial that guides students through the basic functions of Open Access. The text is geared to the first-time user.

Contained in this workbook are information and exercises to get started on DOS and on Open Access. There are numerous hands-on exercises within each chapter as well as study questions and additional exercises at the end of each chapter.

The material in the chapters is arranged so that the hands-on practice can be started and stopped at specific points. The "TO QUIT" and "RESTART" instructions are interspersed throughout the chapters to allow the student to quit an exercise if the length of that lab session does not permit completion of the entire chapter. Instructions provide the steps to restart and begin where the student quit during the preceding lab session.

The data diskette for use with this workbook contains all the files needed to do the chapter hands-on exercises and the exercises at the end of the chapters.

Contents

Chapter 1
Getting Started On the MS-DOS Operating System

Introduction

Every computer requires an operating system to start and manage its operations. An operating system can be thought of as a "behind the scenes" manager. Two of its primary responsibilities are managing the devices attached to the computer and helping other programs to run.

MS-DOS (Microsoft-Disk Operating System) is an operating system developed by Microsoft Inc. for use on many personal computers. MS-DOS is currently the operating-system standard for the IBM/PC/XT/AT series and IBM compatible microcomputers. It is used on about 68 percent of the microcomputers sold for business. IBM distributes a version of MS-DOS called PC-DOS.

We've used MS-DOS Version 3.1 in developing this chapter. The topics covered in this workbook apply equally to all versions 2.XX and higher, although there may be some differences in the wording of prompts and error messages. For simplicity, we will refer to only MS-DOS.

Once MS-DOS has been loaded into a computer, it takes care of all the details necessary to perform the requested tasks such as managing the attached peripheral devices (printers, keyboards, disk drives, monitors, modems) and running other system and application programs.

Throughout the hands-on exercises on MS-DOS, entries that you are to type will be enclosed in brackets ([]). Type what is inside the brackets but do not type the brackets themselves. Names of the keys that you must press will be boldfaced. For example, "Press the **Return** key." Note that the Return key is marked "Enter" on some keyboards. MS-DOS uses both names; they are interchangeable. The Return key, or Enter key, is used to enter a command, that is, to send the command to the computer for processing.

MS-DOS Filenames and Filename Extensions

All data, text, and programs used by a microcomputer are stored in the form of a file on either a floppy diskette or a hard disk. A file is a collection of related data.

MS-DOS requires that each file be identified by a unique name, which may consist of two parts: a filename and a filename extension. A filename may be from one to eight characters long and may consist of the special characters $#&@!%()-_{}' and numbers and letters. Spaces cannot be used between characters in a filename. The letters in a filename may be typed in either uppercase or lowercase, but they are automatically stored by the computer in uppercase. Although you can name a file almost anything (not over eight characters), MS-DOS reserves a few names, called reserve filenames, for its own use that you cannot assign to other files. These include AUX, COM1, COM2, CON, LPT1, LPT2, LPT3, LST, NUL, and PRN. Your MS-DOS reference manual gives more information about their use.

A filename extension is optional. It can be from one to three characters long and is used to identify a file's type. It is separated from the filename by a period (.). The same characters that are valid for a filename are also valid for a filename extension. Letters may be typed in uppercase or lowercase, but they are automatically stored by the computer as uppercase. A good filename and filename extension tells the nature of a file according to any scheme you choose. For example, if you have separate files to keep track of monthly living expenses, you might name them FOOD.EXP, RENT.EXP, CAR.EXP, and ENT.EXP for food, housing, transportation, and entertainment expenses. A particular category might be subdivided further into several files. For example, car expenses might be divided into two files called CAR.REP and CAR.GAS, for repair and gas expenses.

Drive Names

A disk-drive name tells MS-DOS where to find or where to put a file. A drive name consists of the drive letter and a colon (:). Some computers have two floppy-diskette drives, referred to as drive A and drive B. If they are stacked one on top of the other, drive A is usually on top and drive B is on the bottom. If the disk drives are side by side, drive A is usually on the left side and drive B is on the right side.

Other systems have a hard-disk drive that is usually referred to as drive C. A system that uses a hard disk always has at least one floppy diskette drive, which is usually referred to as drive A.

A drive name can be placed before the file being referred to. For example, B:FUN.TXT would tell MS-DOS to look for the file FUN.TXT on the diskette in drive B. If a drive name is not specified, MS-DOS looks for the file on the current, or default, drive. The current drive is one on which MS-DOS will put, or look for and execute, any commands or files specified unless it is instructed to check another drive. The current drive is indicated by the MS-DOS prompt, which is discussed later in the chapter.

Loading MS-DOS

In order to use a computer, you must load the operating system into the computer's primary storage (memory). The process of starting the computer and loading the operating system into primary storage is called "booting" the system. We will look at loading MS-DOS from both a floppy diskette and a hard disk.

Loading from a Floppy Diskette

Each time the computer is turned on, the booting process must be repeated. Follow the sequence of operations in the hands-on exercise to boot the computer with MS-DOS from a floppy diskette (drive A).

Hands On

1. Insert a copy of MS-DOS into drive A and close the door.
2. Turn on the computer. Most systems perform some internal tests, and after a few moments the computer begins to read from the diskette and displays the message:

   Current date is Day xx-xx-xxxx
   Enter new date (mm-dd-yy):

3. Enter a new date in the format of mm-dd-yy (for example, 01-23-88) or mm-dd-yyyy and press the **Return** key, or just press the **Return** key to accept the default entry if it is the correct date. A default entry is a value that the computer uses if no other value is supplied. In this case, the default entry is displayed on the screen following the message "Current date is." Then the following message appears:

   Current time is xx:xx:xx.xx
   Enter new time:

4. Enter a new time and press the **Return** key, or just press the **Return** key to accept the default entry if it is the correct time. The system is now booted and ready to use, and you may now enter an MS-DOS command at the prompt A>. Some commonly used MS-DOS commands are described later in this chapter.

Loading from a Hard Disk

We will assume the hard disk has been prepared and contains the system files necessary to boot MS-DOS. The necessary files include two hidden files, IO.SYS and MSDOS.SYS, for the version of MS-DOS we are using. These files may have different names and be different sizes for different versions of MS-DOS.

A hidden file is one that will not be displayed when you request a listing of the files on a disk. Any file can be hidden by setting the appropriate file attribute. See your MS-DOS manual for more on file attributes. The third necessary file is called COMMAND.COM. This file *is* displayed when you request a listing of the files on a disk. These three files are necessary to boot a computer system from either a hard disk or a floppy diskette.

To boot the computer from a hard disk, drive A must not contain a diskette. Drive A door should be open. If drive A contains a diskette when the computer is started, the system will try to load DOS from drive A. If the diskette in drive A contains DOS, it will be loaded; but, if the diskette in drive A does not contain DOS, the following message will be displayed:

Non-System disk or disk error
Replace and strike any key when ready

To boot MS-DOS from a hard disk (drive C), make sure drive A does not contain a diskette and use the instructions in the following hands-on exercise.

Hands On

1. Turn on the computer. Most systems perform some internal tests, and after a few moments the computer checks drive A to see if it contains a diskette. If it does not, the computer begins to read from the hard disk (drive C) and displays the message:

   Current date is Day xx-xx-xxxx
   Enter new date (mm-dd-yy):

2. Enter a new date using the format of mm-dd-yy or mm-dd-yyyy and press the **Return** key, or just press the **Return** key to accept the default entry if it is the correct date. Then the following message appears:

   Current time is xx:xx:xx.xx
   Enter new time:

3. Enter a new time using the 24-hour format (you only need to enter hours; however, entering minutes is recommended for precision) and press the **Return** key or just press the **Return** key to accept the default entry if it is the correct time. The system is booted and ready to use, and you may now enter an MS-DOS command at the prompt C>. Some commonly used MS-DOS commands are described later in this chapter.

MS-DOS Prompt

The MS-DOS prompt consists of the current drive letter and the symbol >. For example, the MS-DOS prompt A> means the current, or default, drive is drive A. Remember, the current drive is the drive on which DOS will put or look for and execute any commands and files specified unless it is instructed to look elsewhere.

If at any MS-DOS prompt you decide to change the current drive, simply enter the new drive name (letter of the new drive followed by a colon). For example, to change the current drive from A to B on a two-diskette drive system, make sure drive B contains a diskette and follow the procedure in the hands-on exercise. (This and the remaining hands-on exercises in this chapter assume that DOS is already loaded and that the system prompt is A> for a dual-diskette system and C> for a hard-disk system.)

Hands On

1. Type [B:] at the prompt A>.
2. Press the **Return** key. The new default drive is now drive B. Note the system prompt is now B>.

To change the current drive from C to A on a hard-disk drive system, make sure drive A contains a diskette and use the following procedure.

Hands On

1. Type [A:] at the prompt C>.
2. Press the **Return** key. The new default drive is now drive A. Note the system prompt is now A>.

Special Keys Used with MS-DOS

The computer keyboard contains the standard typewriter keys as well as some other keys with special functions. These keys and their functions in MS-DOS are described now.

1 and 0

If you usually type on a standard typewriter, you may be in the habit of using a lowercase L to mean "one" or an uppercase O to mean "zero." That may have been OK on a typewriter, but it is definitely wrong on a computer. The computer distinguishes between a one and a lowercase L and between an uppercase O and zero, so make sure you type the correct letter or numeral when you specify a filename or give a command to MS-DOS. You must type the numeral 1 to mean "one" and the numeral 0 to mean "zero."

Cursor Movement

The cursor moves one space to the right each time a character is entered. The cursor may also be moved to the right with the Spacebar key.

As you enter commands, you may make mistakes. The following hands-on exercise shows how to correct mistakes before the Return key is pressed by using the Back Space key and the <-- (left arrow) key.

Hands On

1. Type the word [mistake] at the system prompt.
2. Press the **Back Space** key once. Notice the cursor moved back one space and erased the letter "e."
3. Press the **<--** (left arrow) key six times. The left arrow key works in the same way as the Back Space key.

Numeric Keypad

To enter numbers from the keyboard, you can select either the numbers at the top of the keyboard or from the numeric keypad (usually on the right side of the keyboard). The Num Lck key toggles between the numbers function and the cursor movement functions of the keypad as this next hands-on exercise demonstrates.

Hands On

1. Type [a].
2. Press the **Num Lck** key once. This toggles the keypad to its numeric function.
3. Press the <-- (left arrow) key once. Notice that instead of backing over the letter "a," the number "4" was entered.
4. Press the **Num Lck** key once. This toggles the keypad back to its cursor movement function.
5. Press the <-- (left arrow) key twice. Notice that this time the cursor moved to the left erasing the "4" and the "a."

Combination Keys

Some keys, such as Ctrl (Control), Alt (Alternate), and Shift are used in combination with other keys. For example, pressing Ctrl-S means that the "Control" key is pressed and held down and then the "S" key is pressed to access a function. Table 1-1 lists some common control-key combinations.

TABLE 1-1 Control Key Combinations

Key Combination	*Key Function*
Ctrl-PrtSc Ctrl-P Ctrl-N	These three key combinations allow you to toggle echo printing on and off. Echo printing means that whatever you have typed on the screen is printed immediately upon entering it by pressing Return.
Ctrl-S Ctrl-Num Lck	These two key combinations stop the scrolling of the screen display. Pressing any key resumes the scrolling.
Ctrl-Break Ctrl-S	These two key combinations will cancel the current operation and return you to the system prompt.
Ctrl-H	This key combination moves the cursor to the left, erasing characters as the cursor backs over them.

The Shift key is used in combination with the letter keys to type capital letters. The Caps Lock key, when pressed, causes all letters to be typed as uppercase letters. Caps Lock does not affect the keys with two labels. For example, to type a question mark with the Caps Lock on, you still need to press the Shift key first. When Caps Lock is on, the Shift key when used in combination with letters will cause the letters to be typed as lowercase letters. The Shift key is also used in combination with the top row of number keys and other special keys to activate the characters shown on the top portion of those keys. For example, pressing the Shift key and the number "1" key from the row of numbers at the top of the keyboard will produce an exclamation point (!).

A hard copy of current screen contents can be made by pressing the Shift and the Prt Sc (print screen) keys at the same time. Make sure the printer is on and ready first, however.

It is possible to restart the computer, that is, reload DOS, without turning it off and on. By pressing and holding down the Ctrl and Alt keys and then pressing the Del key, the computer will be restarted. This is called a "warm boot," because the computer is being reset from an "on" state. To warm boot from drive A, make sure that a system diskette (a disk containing the COMMAND.COM file) is in drive A. To warm boot from a hard disk, make sure drive A does not contain a diskette.

MS-DOS also uses several keys for editing. When you type a command or file name and press Return, the command or file name is automatically sent to the computer for execution. In addition, a copy of what was typed is also sent to a buffer, or temporary storage area. The buffer holds only one item at a time; so when you type a new item and press Return, the old item is erased and the new item is placed in the buffer. The MS-DOS editing keys allow you to recall or modify the item currently in the buffer. Table 1-2 lists the MS-DOS editing keys and their functions.

TABLE 1-2 MS-DOS Editing Keys

Key	*Function*
-->	Copies one character at a time from the buffer to the screen.
F1	Copies one character at a time from the buffer to the screen.
F2	Copies characters up to a specified character. For example, if the buffer contains the command PRINT TEST1.TXT and you pressed F2 and then typed 1, all characters from the buffer up to, but not including, 1 are copied onto the screen at the system prompt.
F3	Copies all the characters in the buffer to the screen.
F4	Skips over (does not copy) the characters in the buffer up to the character specified.
F5	Allows you to edit a line before you press Return.
F6	Types an end-of-file character (^Z). See the MS-DOS reference manual for more information on the end-of-file character.
DEL	Skips over (does not copy) a character in the buffer.
INS	Allows you to insert characters in the buffer.
Esc	Erases what you've just typed at the system prompt, but leaves the contents of the buffer intact.

Organizing Files on a Diskette or Hard Disk

A disk directory holds files and lets you organize files into convenient groups so that they can be easily located on a disk. Because disks can hold many files, a number of directories can be created. The main, or root, directory is created when you format a hard disk or diskette. Additional directories (subdirectories to the root directory) can also be created. A subdirectory is a directory contained within another directory. These subdirectories can also have subdirectories.

A multilevel directory structure can be viewed as an upside down family tree. Figure 1-1 shows an example of a multilevel directory structure. The root directory is at the top. Under the root are two directories (subdirectories to the root): WORD, for a word processor, and SS, for a spreadsheet. Under the WORD directory are two directories (subdirectories to the WORD directory): LETTERS, for letters created with the word processor, and REPORTS, for reports created with the word processor. Under the SS directory is the directory EXPENSES (a subdirectory to the SS directory) for spreadsheet files detailing expenses.

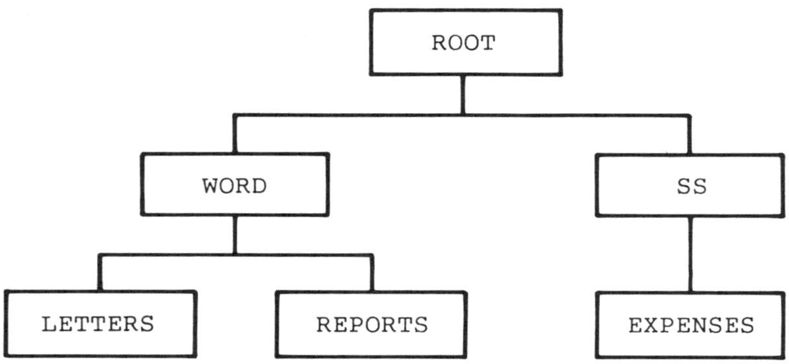

FIGURE 1-1 A Multilevel Directory Structure

Each directory can hold numerous files and subdirectories. The same rules apply for naming directories as for naming files. The directory that you are in at any time is called the current, or working, directory. Any operations or commands you give to MS-DOS affect only the current directory unless you specifically direct otherwise. When there is only a root directory, any operations or commands that you give affect the entire diskette or hard disk.

In a multilevel directory structure, you can move from the root directory down or move down from the directory you're in, or you can move from the directory you're in up to the root and then move downward.

You can move around in a directory structure by telling MS-DOS where you want to go by designating a path. A path is a sequence of directory names, sometimes followed by a filename, each separated by a backslash character (\). For example, look at Figure 1-1. If you are currently in the REPORTS directory and you want to type to the display screen the text file MOM.TXT contained in the LETTERS directory, you would enter the path after the TYPE command at the system prompt: TYPE\WORD\LETTER\MOM.TXT. When a path begins with a backslash character (\) (as in this example), MS-DOS begins the search at the root directory; otherwise, it begins at the current directory and searches downward.

MS-DOS Commands

MS-DOS commands are actually small programs that instruct the computer to perform certain operations. There are two types of commands: internal commands and external commands.

Internal Commands

Internal commands are part of the COMMAND.COM file and are not listed when you ask for a directory listing. Each time MS-DOS is booted, the file COMMAND.COM is stored in primary storage. Because internal commands are stored in primary storage after MS-DOS is booted, they execute immediately after you type them and press the Return key. Even if the MS-DOS diskette is removed after booting, the internal commands remain in memory and are available to you. The MS-DOS internal commands are listed in Table 1-3. See your DOS reference manual for a full explanation of each command.

TABLE 1-3 MS-DOS Internal Commands

BREAK	DIR	PATH	SHIFT
CHDIR	ECHO	PAUSE	TIME
CLS	EXIT	PROMPT	TYPE
COPY	FOR	REM	VER
CTTY	GOTO	REN	VERIFY
DATE	IF	RMDIR	VOL
DEL	MKDIR	SET	

External Commands

External commands are contained in separate files and must be read from a diskette or a hard disk to be executed. These commands are loaded into primary storage only when they are requested. The MS-DOS external commands are listed in Table 1-4. See your DOS reference manual for a full explanation of each command.

TABLE 1-4 MS-DOS External Commands

ASSIGN	DISKCOPY	LABEL	SHARE
ATTRIB	EXEBIN	LINK	SIZE
BACKUP	FDISK	MODE	SORT
CHKDSK	FIND	MONO	SUBST
CHMOD	FORMAT	MORE	SYS
COLOR	GRAFTABL	PRINT	TREE
COMMAND	GRAPHICS	RECOVER	VDISK
COMP	JOIN	RESTORE	XASSIGN
DISKCOMP	KEYBxx	SELECT	XTREE

Commonly Used Commands

A few of the most often used commands are briefly described below. See your DOS reference manual for full explanations of their functions and all available options. If, for any reason, you want the computer to stop executing a command, press the Ctrl-Break or the Ctrl-C key combinations.

DIR. Use the internal command DIR (directory) to view a list of all the files contained in the active, or current, directory of a disk. A directory listing displays the filenames, extensions, file sizes in bytes, and the dates and times the files were last updated in the current directory.

To view the contents of the current directory, give the command DIR. For example, to view a list of files contained in the current directory on drive A, enter the command DIR at the A> prompt.

You can also add several optional parameters after the DIR command. To view the files on a drive other than the current drive, enter the drive name after the DIR command. For example, to get a listing of files on drive B from the prompt A>, type DIR B:.

If a disk contains more files than will fit on the display screen, the list will scroll off the screen. You can stop the scrolling at any time by pressing either the Control-S or the Control-Num Lock key combinations. To resume the scrolling of the file list, press any key.

To display a directory listing one page, or display screen, at a time, you can use the /P option. For example, if the listing is longer than one display screen, type DIR B:/P to stop the scrolling when the display screen is full. Pressing any key continues the scrolling.

Another option displays a large number of files in a column format across the screen. More files can be seen in the same amount of screen space because only the filename and extension are listed. Type DIR B:/W at the A> prompt.

The following hands-on exercise demonstrates the DIR command and some of its options. If you have a dual floppy-diskette system, put the working copy of DOS into drive A and set the system prompt to A>. Also, insert the data diskette in drive B. If you have a hard-disk system, the current directory should be the root directory, and the system prompt should be C>; then insert the data diskette in drive A.

Hands On

1. Type [DIR] at the system prompt and press the **Return** key. The list of files may scroll off the top of the display screen if there are a lot of files stored. Go to step 2a for a dual-diskette system and to step 2b for a hard-disk system.
2. (a) Type [DIR B:] at the system prompt and press the **Return** key. Make sure drive B contains the data diskette.

   (b) Type [DIR A:] at the system prompt and press the **Return** key. Make sure drive A contains the data diskette.
3. Type [DIR/P] at the system prompt and press the **Return** key. Notice the directory listing stops scrolling when it fills the display screen. Press any key to continue the listing.
4. Type [DIR/W] at the system prompt and press the **Return** key. Notice the difference in the way the directory listing is displayed.

The root directory is automatically opened when a hard disk or diskette is formatted. All files will be stored in the root directory if no additional directories are created. But, as the number of files you save increases or as the topics become diverse, you may want to organize th files more efficiently. To do this you can create, delete, and move between directories.

MKDIR. To help organize and locate files stored on a disk or diskette, you can create a new directory with the internal command MKDIR (make directory), or MD. All directories created are subdirectories of the root directory. Each of these directories can also have subdirectories. The directory structure resembles an upside down tree with the trunk (root directory) at the top and then branches downward into subdirectories.

For example, let's say a root directory contains many files, three of which are related. These files are called RED.TXT, BLUE.TXT, and GREEN.TXT. A directory called COLOR could be made by entering the command MD COLOR at the system prompt.

After making the new directory, the files RED.TXT, BLUE.TXT, and GREEN.TXT could be moved from the root directory using the COPY command to place them into the new directory. The DEL command can then be used to remove the original files from the root directory after they are copied. (Both the COPY and DEL commands are discussed below.) This would place the three similar files into a directory with a descriptive name, making them easier to locate.

CHDIR. To change, or move, from one directory to another, use the internal command CHDIR (change directory), or CD. For example, to change from the root directory (labeled as \) to the subdirectory called LETTERS, enter the command CD LETTERS at the system prompt. If you are not currently in the root directory and want to change to a directory on the same level or above, you must always start with the root directory symbol (\). For example, if you are currently in the directory called LETTERS and want to change to the directory EXPENSES, which is on the same level as LETTERS, you would enter the command CD\EXPENSES. The CHDIR command can also tell you what directory you are currently in. Do this by entering the CHDIR command without any parameters. The PROMPT command discussed later can also be used to identify the current directory.

RMDIR. Before you can erase a directory, all files must be removed. This is MS-DOS's way of preventing accidental erasure of files stored in a directory. To erase a directory that contains no files, use the internal command RMDIR (remove directory), or RD. For example, entering the command RD DATA at the system prompt will remove the subdirectory DATA from the root directory--if it contains no files. If the directory contains files, the following message appears:

```
Invalid path, not directory,
or directory not empty
```

If this message appears, it usually means that all the files have not been deleted from the directory or the directory name has been incorrectly typed.

FORMAT. Before you can use either the hard disk or a floppy diskette, you must format it, or make it ready, for use. The ~~internal~~ command FORMAT prepares a hard disk or floppy diskette to store files. Extra caution should be taken when formatting or reformatting a disk because all files currently on a disk are destroyed when it is formatted. This is especially important with a hard disk, which may contain twenty, thirty, or more megabytes of data. If you have a hard disk, *do not* attempt to format it without the permission and guidance of your instructor. In most cases, the hard disk will already be formatted and may contain needed files. We will explain how to format a floppy diskette only.

When formatting a floppy diskette, you will not receive any warning messages; so make sure you are formatting the correct diskette--not one that contains needed files. There are two ways to format a floppy diskette: (a) as a nonbootable data diskette and (b) as a bootable diskette.

e does not contain any system files and cannot be used to start the . bootable diskette does contain the system files and can be used to DOS. To format a floppy diskette as either bootable or nonbootable, tem, follow the steps in the next hands-on exercise.

... of the MS-DOS diskette into drive A.

2. Insert a blank diskette into drive B. To format a diskette as a nonbootable data diskette, follow step 3a. In this case, no DOS system files are transferred to the diskette. This leaves more space for data storage, approximately 362,496 bytes on a dual-sided, double-density disk. To use a nonbootable disk MS-DOS must already be booted. To format a diskette as a bootable data diskette, follow step 3b. This places the system files, including COMMAND.COM, onto the diskette. This leaves less space for data, approximately 297,984 bytes on a dual-sided double-density disk.
3. (a) Type [FORMAT B:] at the A> prompt and press the **Return** key. The diskette in drive B is formatted for use as a nonbootable data diskette.
   (b) Type [FORMAT B:/S] at the A> prompt and press the **Return** key. The diskette in drive B is formatted for use as a bootable diskette. This puts the two hidden system files and the file COMMAND.COM onto the diskette. When the diskette is formatted, the following message appears:

   Format another (Y/N)?

4. Type [N]. The system prompt A> is then displayed and you can enter other MS-DOS commands. Remember that external DOS commands reside on the MS-DOS diskette, which must be in a drive in order to use them.

To format a diskette in drive A on a hard-disk system, make sure the MS-DOS file FORMAT.COM (may be FORMAT.EXE in some systems) is on your hard disk and is in the current directory, or supply the appropriate pathname. Now do the following hands-on exercise.

Hands On

1. Type [FORMAT A:] at the C> prompt to format the diskette in drive A as a nonsystem (nonbootable) diskette <u>or</u> type [FORMAT A:/S] at the C> prompt to format the diskette in drive A as a system (bootable) disk.
2. Press the **Return** key. The prompt "Insert new diskette for drive A: and strike ENTER when ready" appears. When the diskette is formatted the following message appears:

   Format another (Y/N)?

3. Type [N]. The system prompt C> is displayed and you are ready to enter other MS-DOS commands.

LABEL. You may assign a volume label, or disk name, to a diskette with the external command LABEL, as well as change or delete the volume label of a disk. The following hands-on exercise explains how to do this for a two-diskette drive system. As with all external commands, you can precede LABEL with the drive and path on which it is located, for example,

A>C:\DOS\LABEL

Hands On

1. Insert an MS-DOS diskette in drive A and a formatted diskette in drive B.
2. Type [A:] to set the system prompt to A> if it is not already.
3. Type [LABEL B:] and press the **Return** key. The following message appears:

   Volume in drive A has no label
   Volume label (11 characters, ENTER for none)?

   You can choose to give the diskette (volume) a name or press the **Return** key for no name.
4. Type [MYDISK] and press the **Return** key. The label will be displayed when the contents of the diskette are displayed on the screen. Labels can help identify the files on a diskette.

COPY. The internal command COPY creates a duplicate of an existing file. The duplicate file can be stored on a different disk, in a different directory, or in the same directory under another name. If your purpose is to create a backup of the original, it should be copied to another disk. If you keep the backup on the same hard disk or diskette as the original and something happens to it, both your original and the duplicate could be lost or destroyed.

The disk from which you copy is the source disk and the disk on which the copy will be placed is the target disk. The target disk must already be formatted to use the copy command.

When copying a file, make sure there is not an existing file on the target disk with the same filename as the one to be copied. If the file has the same name, the existing file on the target disk will be replaced by the copied file from the source disk. For example, if you enter

COPY RECORDS.TXT B:

at the A> prompt, the text file RECORDS located on the source disk in drive A is copied to the target disk in drive B using the same filename. If a file already exists on drive B with the name RECORDS.TXT, it will be written over.

The typed command,

COPY RECORDS.TXT B:ALBUMS.TXT

when entered at the A> prompt, copies the text file RECORDS.TXT from the source drive A to the target drive B and stores it under the filename ALBUMS.TXT.

Wildcards may also be used. A wildcard is an MS-DOS character that can be entered to represent a character or characters. The wildcard (?) represents one character in its position in the filename. The wildcard (*) may stand for one or more characters in the filename. For example, entering

COPY *.TXT C:

at the A> prompt copies all files from drive A to drive C that have the file extension .TXT, regardless of the individual filename. For example, if a drive contains the text files A.TXT, TEST1.TXT, B.TXT, TEST2.TXT, and ALBUMS.TXT, they would all be copied to drive A by this command. But, if the COPY command were entered as

COPY ?.TXT C:

only A.TXT and B.TXT from the above files would be copied.

Wildcards may also be used with any of the other MS-DOS commands where filenames or extensions are entered.

DISKCOPY. When the contents of an entire diskette are to be copied onto another diskette, the external command DISKCOPY can be used. This command cannot be used to copy to or from a hard disk.

DISKCOPY requires a source diskette and a target diskette. Entering the command

DISKCOPY A: B:

copies the entire contents of the source diskette in drive A to the target diskette in drive B. The same command can be used on a single floppy-diskette system, in which case you are prompted to swap between the target and source diskettes in drive A to complete a disk copy. This command will automatically format the target diskette if it is not already formatted.

DISKCOMP. If the target diskette is defective in any way, the copy made with the DISKCOPY command may be unusable or not exactly the same. With the external command DISKCOMP (disk compare), the target and source diskettes are compared after copying to verify that they are exactly the same. The command

DISKCOMP A: B:

compares the content of the diskettes in drives A and B. If the disks are alike, this message appears:

Diskettes compare ok

If an error message appears, you need to recopy the diskette. Continued error messages when performing a DISKCOMP suggest that you should recopy the original diskette using another target diskette.

DISKCOMP does not work with a hard disk or on a diskette if COPY *.* was used to copy the entire diskette. To determine if those copies were made correctly, enter /V with the COPY command. This verifies that the original and copied files are the same. For example, if

COPY RECORDS.TXT B:/V

is typed at the A> prompt, the text file RECORDS is copied from drive A to the disk in drive B and is then verified (/V) that the contents are the same. This procedure takes a bit longer than simply copying files.

PROMPT. The MS-DOS prompt is indicated by the letter of the default drive followed by the (>) symbol. By using the internal command PROMPT, you can change the prompt to anything you wish. For example, entering

PROMPT Get to work

at the system prompt causes the words "Get to work" to appear as the prompt.

A common use for the PROMPT command is to show the current directory in which you are working. This is very helpful when you have multiple directories and must keep track of where you are in the system. Follow this hands-on exercise to change the prompt to reflect the current directory.

Hands On

1. Type [PROMPT pg] at the system prompt.
2. Press the **Return** key. The $p represents the default directory and $g the symbol (>).

After executing the command PROMPT PG, the prompt for the directory COLOR (a subdirectory of the root directory) on a diskette in drive A would appear like this:

A:\COLOR>

The PROMPT command must be executed each time the system is turned on.

CHKDSK. At any time you can check the status of your disk and system with the external command CHKDSK (check disk). For example, to check the disk in drive A, enter the command CHKDSK A: after the system prompt. CHKDSK is an external command; so remember it must be stored in the current directory, or you must use a pathname to specify in which directory it is stored for it to be activated. The following hands-on exercise assumes CHKDSK is stored in the current directory, and drive A contains a formatted diskette.

Hands On

Type [CHKDSK A:] at the system prompt and press the **Return** key. A message similar to this is displayed:

```
xxxxxx bytes total disk space
xxxxx  bytes in 2 hidden files
xxxxxx bytes in xx user files
xxxxx  bytes available on disk
xxxxxx bytes total memory
xxxxxx bytes free
```

The information supplied is measured in bytes. The total disk space is the amount available when the disk was formatted. The space used by any hidden files is listed. Next appears the amount of space used and number of files that are on the disk. The total space remaining in which to store a file is given next. The next listing displays the total system memory, followed by the amount of space in memory that is available for use.

The CHKDSK command also reports any errors found in the directory but does not fix them unless you use the /F option, for example CHKDSK/F.

DEL. To erase a file or files, use the internal command DEL (delete). The command ERASE does the same task as DEL and can be used instead of DEL. At the A> prompt, type

DEL B:TAPES.TXT

to erase the text file TAPES from the diskette in drive B. When a file is deleted, it is permanently deleted as far as DOS is concerned. However, there are some utility programs available that can recover deleted programs under certain circumstances.

RENAME. If for any reason you want to change the filename, filename extension, or both, you can use the internal command RENAME or REN.

To rename the file H.TXT with the more descriptive name HOUSELST.NEW to indicate that the file contains listings of new houses, type

RENAME H.TXT HOUSELST.NEW

Be careful when renaming files because some application programs require specific filename extensions for the file to be recognized and used.

PRINT. The contents of a text file (that is, a file containing only the letters, numerals, and/or special characters contained in the ASCII code) can be sent, or "printed," to a printer using the external command PRINT. For example, suppose the system prompt is A>, and you want to see a listing of all the new houses contained in the text file HOUSELST.NEW stored on drive B. To print the contents of the text file, make sure the printer is on and ready; then enter the following at the A> prompt:

PRINT B:HOUSELST.NEW

After pressing the Return key, the text file HOUSELST.NEW located on the disk in drive B is printed. This provides a hard copy of the data stored in the file.

TYPE. You may want to view the contents of a text file without making a hard copy. To view the contents on the display screen, use the internal command TYPE. The TYPE command displays text files only. For example, to browse through the text file HOUSELST.NEW on drive B to see if a particular house is listed, enter the following at the system prompt A>:

TYPE B:HOUSE.NEW

The contents of the file are displayed on the screen. If there are many files, the display will scroll off the screen. The Control-S or the Control-Num Lock key combinations stop the scrolling. Press any key to continue the scrolling.

Study Questions

1. What is the purpose of a filename?
2. What is the purpose of a filename extension?
3. How many characters can a filename contain? What are the valid characters?
4. What does the drive name consist of? What is the drive name's function?
5. What does it mean to "boot" a system?
6. Describe the types and locations of the drives for your system.
7. What is meant by the phrase "a bootable diskette"?
8. What does the MS-DOS prompt tell you?
9. How would you change the default drive from drive C to drive A?
10. What is the difference between a source diskette and a target diskette?
11. What is the function of the Num Lck Key?
12. What is a "warm boot" and how is it executed?
13. What is a root directory?
14. What is a subdirectory?
15. What is the difference between an MS-DOS internal command and an MS-DOS external command?
16. What does it mean to "format" a disk or diskette?
17. What will happen if you attempt to format a disk or diskette that already contains data?
18. Which command will display a listing of the files stored on a disk?
19. Which command would you enter at the prompt A> to copy the file TEST.DOC located on drive A to drive B?
20. Which command is used to copy the entire contents of a diskette in drive A to a hard disk (drive C) from the A> prompt?

Chapter 2

Getting Started on Open Access II Publisher's Version

Introduction

The Open Access II Publisher's Version (referred to hereafter as OA) is a set of state-of-the-art software programs developed by Software Products International Inc. These programs, or modules, contain the tools necessary to meet both business and personal needs. They include the following: (1) a utilities module for setting or changing parameters, (2) a desk-accessories module with features such as a calculator, an electronic note pad, appointment scheduler, and business card filer, (3) a word processor module for producing documents, (4) a spreadsheet module with graphics capabilities for manipulating and analyzing numbers and graphing the results, (5) a relational database module for organizing, manipulating, and retrieving data, (6) a programmer module, which contains a command-driven database programming language, and (7) a communication module to access other computers or computer services.

The seven OA modules and the OA installation program are contained on six diskettes. There is also a diskette that includes data you will need to run OA. The seven diskettes are labelled as follows:

- OA_Utilities
- OA_Spreadsheet
- OA_Analyzer

- OA_Database
- OA_Word/Comm
- OA_Install/Drivers
- Sample Data Files

Each OA program is a "module." This means that it may be used independently of the other OA programs, or it may be integrated with the other programs to function together as an integrated set of programs. For example, this modularity allows a file to be created in the database module and then transferred directly to the spreadsheet module for use there.

This workbook provides detailed step-by-step, hands-on experience with the functions of each program module. By working through the hands-on exercises, you will gain the knowledge and experience to apply the concepts of each module to more complex applications.

What Do I Need To Run OA?

A microcomputer with the appropriate primary storage and DOS software, the six OA diskettes, and the sample data diskette are needed to complete the exercises in this workbook. One of the following two IBM PC or compatible microcomputer setups is needed.

1. A computer with a primary-storage capacity of at least 256 kilobytes, a monitor, and two floppy-diskette drives, each with a storage capacity of 360 kilobytes or more. A printer is recommended but not necessary to complete the hands-on exercises.
2. A computer with a primary-storage capacity of at least 256 kilobytes, a monitor, a fixed-disk drive, and one floppy-diskette drive with a storage capacity of 360 kilobytes or more. A printer is recommended but not necessary to complete the hands-on exercises.

The operating system must be either MS-DOS or PC-DOS and must be version 2.0 or higher. To see what version of DOS you have, do the following hands-on exercise. Note that the operating system must already be loaded.

Hands On

1. Type [VER] at the system prompt.
2. Press <ret> **Return**. The computer responds by displaying the version of DOS currently loaded, for example, MS-DOS Version 3.10.

Guidelines for starting and running OA are presented for both a diskette-based system and a hard-disk system later in this chapter.

What Is the "Publisher's Version"?

Open Access II Publisher's Version is based on the commercial version of Open Access II 2.05. It is limited *only* by the size of a file and *not* in the functionality of the package. The purpose of the Publisher's Version software package is to teach the user the features of an integrated software package. It is not intended for use in business and for this reason the file size has been limited. These limitations are explained in Table 2-1.

TABLE 2-1 Publisher's Version Limits

Program	*Limits*
Utilities	Some utilities, such as the file conversion utilities, are not included because this version of the software is intended only for instruction.
Desk Accessories	Up to 50 database records can be created for appointment and business card files.
Word Processor	Files up to 10 kilobytes in size are permitted. Also, printing files from within other files (includes) of .TXT or .DOC files are not allowed.
Database	Fifty database records can be generated. You may join up to eight files that contain up to 50 records each. The joined file may then contain 400 records; but because there is a 50-record limit, a joined file of more than 50 records cannot be saved.
Spreadsheet	A worksheet contains 90 rows by 60 columns (5400 cells). The spreadsheet database files are also limited to 50 records.
Graphics	Graphics information can be contained in a 90-row by 60-column size. The top graphics title is user definable. The bottom and side titles contain the software publisher's labels.
Communications	All features are present except bulletin board options. Files created to send or files being received are limited to 10 kilobytes.

If you exceed the limitations of any feature, the Publisher's Error Window appears (Figure 2-1). To maintain the identity of the Publisher's Version, all printouts display the following line at the top of each page:

Copyright 1987 Software Products International Inc.

Another line at the bottom of the page says

Publisher's Version

```
                  Open Access II Limited Version Communications
   (c) Copyright 1984,1985,1986,1987 Software Products International, Inc.
                            All rights reserved

        PUBLISHER'S VERSION - This feature is Limited or not
        Supported.  Please call Software Products International
        at (619)450-1526 to order full featured Open Access II
                    Press <do> or <undo> to Continue
```

FIGURE 2-1

Conventions and Terms

There are references in each module to function keys, cursor movement keys, windows, menus, commands, and prompts. Conventions used throughout the rest of the workbook to identify entries and keys are explained in the following sections.

Workbook Key Conventions

In the remainder of the hands-on exercises in this workbook, the square brackets [] will continue to represent entries that you are to type on the computer keyboard. For example, "Type [BUDGET] as the filename." tells you to physically type the word BUDGET. Do not type the brackets. However, when the entry between the brackets is underlined, it indicates that you are to substitute the appropriate information. For example, opening bracket name and then the closing bracket means to type your own name. You may enter letters in either uppercase or lowercase unless otherwise instructed.

Words inside angle brackets < > represent a function, and you are to press the associated function key or key combination. For example, "Press <menu> **F2**." instructs you to to press the function key F2 in order to display a menu on the screen; "Press <line_del> **Ctrl-BckSpc**." instructs you to press and hold down the Ctrl key and then press the Back Space key to delete a line.

Function Keys

Function keys access certain functions within OA. The function keys may be used individually or in combination with other keys. For example, "Press <macro> **Alt-F8**." means that you should press the Alt key and hold it down and then press the F8 function key in order to access the macro function.

The first time you are instructed to use a function in a hands-on exercise, the directions will read, for example, Press <do> **F10**. You are given the name of the function (in angle brackets) and the name of the key (in boldface). If that function is repeated later in the same exercise, the directions will simply say "Press <do>."

```
                                                      Options

                                                      Spread_Sheet
          Open Access II Limited Version Communicat   Communications
(c) Copyright 1984,1985,1986,1987 Software Products In  Database
                          All rights reserved         Programmer
                                                      Word_Processor
                                                      Utilities
                                                      Operating_System

                                                       <arrows> <do>
                                                      <search> <undo>
```

FIGURE 2-2

Cursor Movement Keys

The cursor movement keys include the arrow keys, which are used to place or position the cursor. The arrow keys are located on the numeric keypad to the right of the standard keyboard. The direction of cursor movement the key controls is indicated by the direction of the arrow shown on the key. When movement to select a command or option requires using one of the arrow keys, the exercise will say "Use <arrows> to select..." without specifying each time which direction is to be taken.

Windows

A window is a specifically defined area of the display screen and may consist of the entire screen display or a section of it. A window is defined on the screen by a border, and it usually displays a menu, an option screen, or a help screen. Figure 2-2 shows the Options menu superimposed over the OA headings.

Menus

A menu is a window that contains either commands or other user options from which the user can select while using the program. At the start of each module, a main menu is displayed. There may be one or more submenus under the various items in a menu. Figure 2-3 shows the Database Main menu.

Commands

Commands specify the instructions to be performed and are selected from the menu. You can select commands from the menu two ways.

One way is to simply type the first letter of the command. Most command menus have only one command that starts with a given letter. If more than one command starts with the same letter, type the first two letters to make the appropriate selection.

The second way is to use <arrows> to highlight the command and then press <do> F10.

```
                Open Access II Limited Version Database
   (c) Copyright 1984,1985,1986,1987 Software Products International, Inc.
                          All rights reserved



                          Database Main Menu
                 Retrieve   Browse   Enter_Data   Print
                 Design     Macros   Options
                              <do> <undo>
```

FIGURE 2-3

Prompts
A question asked on screen by the computer is called a prompt. A prompt requires a user response. The response may be a simple yes or no, or it may require data or other entries such as a filename to be entered. Responses to prompts that are already entered on the screen by the program are called default values. By pressing <ret> Return or <do> F10, you tell the computer to accept the default value as the response to the prompt. If you would like to respond with other than the default value, you must enter a new value.

Modular-Independent Function Keys

A few keys in OA have the same meaning in all the modules. These keys and their meanings are described in the next sections.

<help> F1
If at any time you forget which key is used for a particular function, press <help> F1 to display a help window such as the one in Figure 2-4. The top half of the help window contains the function name associated with the appropriate function key(s). The lower half of the help window provides explanations. The function keys listed in the help window vary and will depend on where you are currently working in a module.

<do> F10 and <undo> Esc
The <do> F10 key tells the program to accept an entry or to select from a menu, or it indicates that the data on the screen are ready to process or perform another instruction. The <undo> Esc key cancels an entry, removes a help window from the screen, or returns to a previous menu.

```
                              Function Key Setup
<do>          =      F10 |<jump_right>    = Ctrl-End    |<halt> = Ctrl-Break
<undo>        =      Esc |<jump_left>     = Ctrl-Home   |
<help>        =       F1 |<home>          =      Home   |<rec_fwd> =      F5
<menu>        =       F2 |<end>           =       End   |<rec_back>=      F7
<print>       =       F3 |<line_ins>      = Ctrl-Ret    |<select>  =      F9
<search>      =       F4 |<line_del>      = Ctrl-BkSp   |<eval>    = Alt-F10
<change>      =       F6 |<word_fwd>      = Ctrl-Right  |
<desk>        =       F8 |<word_back>     = Ctrl-Left   |
<macro>       = Alt-F8   |<pg_up>         = PgUp        |
<ascii>       = Alt-F4   |<pg_down>       = PgDn        |
<prt_scr>     = Alt-F3   |<user1>-<user8>= Shift F1-F8  |

                              Database Operations
Retrieve      Retrieve record data meeting conditions.
Enter Data    Enter record data into file using screen form.
Print         Start a printing summary to specified printer or file.
Browse        Examine a file's record data and index values.
Design        Design new databases or modify existing files.
Macro         Start macros, Password Pre-Set and Clear.
Options       Return to Options window.

         Help Window: <up><down> to scroll help text,  <undo> to quit
```

FIGURE 2-4

<menu> F2
This key causes a menu to be displayed on the screen. A menu is a special window that provides a choice of options or commands. The particular menu accessed with this key will depend on where you are currently working in a module.

<prt_scr> Alt-F3
The print screen function is a useful key combination that can be used at any time to make a hard-copy of the contents of the screen. The print screen function in OA can be used not only to print the screen contents but also to copy them to a file on disk. This file can then be later manipulated or edited by the OA word processor or text editor. When <prt_scr> Alt-F3 is pressed, a window appears listing all the output devices available, including the option to output a file on a disk. Use <arrows> to select the appropriate printer or select FILE to output to a disk. Figure 2-5 shows the Output Device Selection window listing some of the devices.

<search> F4
The <search> function displays a listing of the available files when OA calls for a filename to be entered. The first time <search> F4 is pressed, the files are displayed in alphabetical order according to their file extensions. If <search> F4 is pressed again, the files are alphabetized according to their filename. If the <search> F4 key is pressed from the Options menu, all the files that are available for the highlighted module are displayed in a list. A typical search window is seen in Figure 2-6.

When OA requires that a device name be entered, press <search> F4 to view a list of the available devices. To select a printer, the console, or file, use <arrows> to highlight the selection and then press <do> F10.

At the bottom of the file search window is a list of some functions that can be performed within this window. These are <home>, <end>, <pg_up>, <pg_down>, <change>, <line_ins>, and <line_del> and are described in Table 2-2.

```
                                 Output Device Selection
                      Open             C:INFOE.PRT              abase
  (c) Copyright 1984,1   CONSOLE                                s International, Inc.
                         FILE
                         PRINTER
                         CITOH 1550
                         CITOH 8510A
                         COLORMASTER
                         DATAPRD 8052/72
                         DATAPRD DP-20
                         DATAPROD 8070
   [C:BILLING.PMK]       DIABLO 630                                      [Inserting ]
  FROM BILLING           DIABLO C150
                         EPSON EX-800
                         EPSON FX-86E
                         EPSON GQ-3500
                         FUJITSU DL
                           <home><end><page_keys>
                             <up><down><search>
              <do> <und                                         h> <print>
```

FIGURE 2-5

```
                      A:\
                                                                abase
  (c) Copyright 19     C                                        s International, Inc.
                       A
                       DATA          LOAN       DF
                                     LOAN       IF
                                     STUDENT    DF
                                     STUDENT    IF
                                     GRADE      DF
                                   -> GRADE     IF           <-
                                     CUSTOMER   DF
                                     CUSTOMER   IF
                                     ORDERNO    DF
                                     ORDERNO    IF
                                     ITEMS      DF
                                     ITEMS      IF

     Database file:     <up><down><home><end><search>
                        <select><undo><pg_up><pg_down>
                       <change><line_ins><line_del><do>
```

FIGURE 2-6

TABLE 2-2 Search Window Function Keys

Function	*Key*	*Description*
<home>	Home	Moves cursor to top of search list.
<end>	End	Moves cursor to bottom of search list.
<pg_up>	PgUp	Moves the cursor to the previous directory and displays those files.
<pg_down>	PgDn	Moves the cursor to the next directory and displays those files.
<change>	F6	Changes the filename without necessitating a return to the operating system.
<line_ins>	Ctrl-Return	Copies one file to another.
<line_del>	Ctrl-BackSpace	Deletes a file.

The <change>, <line_ins>, and <line_del> functions do not appear in every search window. Pressing the <change> F6 function key makes it possible to change the name of a file without returning to the operating system. Figure 2-7 shows the change window for changing the name of a file. You must press <do> F10 after entering the new filename for the change to take place. Pressing the <line_ins> Ctrl-Return function key allows the highlighted file to be copied to a file with a different name. Pressing the <line_del> Ctrl-BackSpace function key starts the delete process by highlighting a file in the search window. It is not enough to simply press <line_del> Ctrl-BackSpace to complete the deletion of a file or device; you must then respond to the prompt "Delete xxxxx.xxx?" by pressing <do> F10. This prompt helps prevent accidental deletions by requiring you to verify your decision.

```
                    A:\
                                                 abase
(c) Copyright 19    C                            s International, Inc.
                    A
                    DATA
                               LOAN       DF
                               LOAN       IF
                               STUDENT    DF
                               STUDENT    IF
                            -> GRADE      DF       <-
                               GRADE      IF
                               CUSTOMER   DF
                               CUSTOMER   IF
                               ORDERNO    DF
                               ORDERNO    IF
                               ITEMS      DF
                               ITEMS      IF

   Database file:
                         Change "A:GRADE.DF" To
                    A:GRADE.DF
```

FIGURE 2-7

```
                 Open Access II Limited Version Database
   (c) Copyright 1984,1985,1986,1987 Software Products International, Inc.
                           All rights reserved

        Current Time              October                            1988
         01:35:16 PM              Wk  Sun Mon Tue Wed Thu Fri Sat
                                  40                               1
                                  41   2   3   4   5   6   7   8
   Los Angeles       Chicago      42   9  10  11  12  13  14  15
    10:35:16 AM   12:35:16 PM     43  16  17  18  19  20  21  22
                                  44  23  24  25  26  27  28  29
                                  45  30  31

                        Desk Accessories
         Calculator   Time   Alarm   Date   Value_Converter
         Stop_Watch  Appointments  Business_Cards  Note_Pad
                      <search><page_keys><desk>
```

FIGURE 2-8

<desk> F8

You can access the Desk Accessories module from anywhere in any of the other modules. Desk Accessories includes many handy features such as an electronic appointment scheduler, business card file, note pad, conversion table, calculator, clock, and even a stopwatch. Figure 2-8 shows the Desk Accessories window.

<macro> Alt-F8

It is sometimes necessary to repeat a sequence of keystrokes when performing certain procedures, such as long, complex calculations or accessing different files. A macro is a function that stores the sequence of keystrokes in a file that can be accessed by a single keystroke or by calling up the macro file. With a macro, you can automatically repeat a sequence as often as required. Macros are examined in more detail in each module where appropriate.

<ascii> Alt-F4

Pressing the <ascii> Alt-F4 combination displays the ASCII Table window with a list of the ASCII values and the characters represented by these values. You can scroll through the list using <arrows> and see that these characters include letters, numbers, and many other symbols. There are some instances where you can copy (<paste> F7) a highlighted character from the ASCII list into the module in which you are working. Some of these characters can be used as simple graphics, such as lines to create a box.

Installing OA on a Dual-Diskette System

This section pertains to a two-diskette drive system, where each diskette has a capacity of at least 360 kilobytes.

To run the OA software, first load the operating system, either MS-DOS or PC-DOS version 2.0 or higher. Refer to Chapter 1 for instructions to load the operating system from a floppy diskette.

OA programs have been designed to run with many types of printers, monitors, and graphic cards. The program disk that configures OA to work with various hardware and installs the programs is called OA_Install/Drivers. The installation program runs and queries you about your particular hardware. You must tell OA which printer, monitor, and graphics card you are using. This process is called configuring the computer. The following hands on exercise will show you how to run the installation program. The operating system prompt should appear as A> before you start.

Hands On

1. Insert the OA_Install/Drivers diskette into drive A.
2. Type [A:] and press <ret> **Return**; if the system prompt on the screen is not already A>.
3. Type [IN] and press <ret>.
4. Follow the instructions given on the display screen. If you do not have a printer, select "Console" to have the output appear on the screen, or "File" to have the output saved to a file on disk. Also, if your computer supports graphics, you are prompted to select a graphics driver program. However, if your computer does not support graphics, this part of the installation is automatically skipped. If you're not sure of the type of printer, graphics card, monitor, or other hardware that your computer system uses, consult the class instructor. When you are asked to set the time settings, simply press <do> **F10** to accept the default time settings. (Installing OA on a two-diskette drive system takes some time while the program checks drive B. Be patient.)

It is also possible to change these configurations to accommodate a new printer, graphics card, or different monitor at any time from the Utilities module by selecting the Configure option. This procedure is discussed in the next chapter.

Starting OA on a Dual-Diskette System

Make sure the computer is on, DOS is installed, and the DOS prompt A> is displayed. To access the various modules, follow the steps in this hands-on exercise.

Hands On

1. Insert the OA_Utilities diskette into drive A.
2. Insert the Sample Data Files diskette into drive B.
3. Type [SPI] and press <ret> **Return**. The Date Screen appears.
4. Type a new date using the format mm-dd-yy or mm-dd-yyyy, or simply press <do> **F10** to accept the date shown. The Options menu now appears from which you can select one of the program modules. These modules are stored on separate diskettes.
5. Select "Spreadsheet" from the Options menu. You are prompted to insert the OA_Spreadsheet diskette.
6. Insert the OA_Spreadsheet diskette into drive A.

7. Select "Options" to return to the Options menu. Steps 4, 5, and 6 can be used to select any module by simply substituting the desired module name. You will be prompted to insert the appropriate diskette.
8. Select "Operating System" from the Options menu to return to DOS.

Installing OA on a Hard-Disk System

To run the OA software, first load the operating system, either MS-DOS or PC-DOS version 2.0 or higher. Refer to Chapter 1 for directions to load the operating system from a hard disk.

OA programs have been designed to run with many types of printers, monitors, and graphic cards. The program disk that configures OA to work with various hardware and installs the programs is called OA_Install/Drivers. The installation program runs and queries you about your particular hardware. You must tell OA which printer, monitor, and graphics card you are using. This process is called configuring the computer. The following hands on exercise will show you how to run the installation program. The operating system prompt should appear as A> before you start.

Hands On

1. Insert the OA_Install/Drivers diskette into drive A.
2. Type [A:] and press <ret> **Return**.
3. Type [IN] and press <ret>.
4. Follow the instructions given on the display screen. A suggested path name for installation to a hard disk is C:\OA. If you do not have a printer, select "Console" to have the output appear on the screen, or "File" to have the output saved in a file on disk. Also, if your computer supports graphics, you are prompted to select a graphics driver program. However, if your computer does not support graphics, this part of the installation is automatically skipped. If you're not sure of the type of printer, graphics card, monitor, or other hardware that your computer system uses, consult the class instructor. When you are asked to set the time settings, simply press <do> **F10** to accept the default time settings.

It is also possible to change these configurations to accommodate a new printer, graphics card, or different monitor at any time from the Utilities module by selecting the Configure option. This procedure is discussed in the next chapter.

It is a good idea to create a separate directory for your data files other than the one on which OA programs are stored. To locate your files, you must specify a searching order (tell the computer where to look for files). This can be done from the Utilities module (see next chapter) accessed from the Options menu.

Transferring the Sample Files to a Hard Disk

You can create a subdirectory within the OA directory that can contain all the OA data files. In fact, you can create several subdirectories to help organize your data files. Right now, create one called FILES. The following hands-on exercise describes the procedure.

Hands On

1. Type [CD \OA] at the system prompt C> and press <ret> **Return**.
2. Type [MD FILES] at the system prompt and press <ret>. This creates a subdirectory called FILES for your data files.
3. Type [CD FILES] at the system prompt and press <ret>. This makes FILES the active directory.
4. Insert the Sample Data Files diskette into drive A.
5. Type [A:]. This changes the current drive to drive A. Since the files for each chapter are stored in separate directories, you will have to execute several copy commands as follows.
6. Type [CD\UT] and press <ret>.
7. Type [COPY *.* C:] This copies all the sample data files from the directory UT on the diskette in drive A to the subdirectory FILES in drive C. Using the wildcard *.* copies all filenames and all file extensions.
8. Type [CD\WP] and press <ret>.
9. Type [COPY *.* C:].
10. Type [CD\DB] and press <ret>.
11. Type [COPY *.* C:].
12. Type [CD\SS] and press <ret>.
13. Type [COPY *.* C:].
14. Type [CD\GR] and press <ret>.
15. Type [COPY *.* C:].
16. Type [CD\DI] and press <ret>.
17. Type [COPY *.* C:].
18. Type [CD\PR] and press <ret>.
19. Type [COPY *.* C:].

In order for OA to find and use these files, a searching order must be defined with the Searching_Order command in the Utilities module. This is described in the next chapter on utilities.

When using a hard-disk system, you can also insert the Sample Data Files diskette into drive A instead of copying the files to drive C.

Starting OA from a Hard Disk

Make sure the computer is on, DOS is loaded, and the DOS prompt C> is displayed. Now you are ready to start by following the steps in this hands-on exercise.

Hands On

1. Type [CD \OA] and press <ret> **Return** to change to the directory in which OA is stored.
2. Type [SPI] and press <ret>. The system date is displayed.
3. Enter a new system date or press <do> **F10** to accept the present date. The Options menu is displayed and you can now select a program module.
4. Select "Operating System" from the Options menu to return to DOS.

In this chapter you learned how to install and start OA from both a dual-diskette system and a hard-disk system. Subsequent chapters show you how to use the various OA modules.

Study Questions

1. Briefly describe the main function of each of the seven Open Access modules introduced in this chapter.
2. Describe one of the microcomputer setups necessary to run OA.
3. What is the minimum version of DOS required for this program? Which version does your system have?
4. What is a window?
5. What is a menu?
6. What is a command?
7. Explain two ways of selecting a command from a menu in Open Access.
8. What is a prompt?
9. How is a help screen accessed?
10. Describe the function of the <do> F10 function key.
11. Describe the function of the <undo> Esc key.
12. Describe the function of the <menu> F2 function key.
13. What is the function of the <prt_scr> Alt-F3 key combination?
14. What is the function of the <search> F4 function key?
15. How is the Desk Accessories module accessed?
16. What is a macro, and which key or key combination will execute the macro?
17. Describe the function of the <ascii> Alt-F4 key combination.
18. What does it mean to configure a computer?
19. Which module is used to configure a computer after OA is installed?
20. Describe the process that starts OA on the system you are using.

Chapter 3
Utilities

Introduction

The Utilities module contains several useful selections. The first, called Configure, has several options:

- *Misc-Parameters* changes system defaults parameters
- *Time_Parameters* changes system time parameters
- *Function-Keys* assigns strings of characters to function keys
- *Searching_Order* tells the system where to find data files
- *Default-Files* changes default file names
- *Printer-Parameters* adds, deletes, or changes printer configurations
- *Options* returns you to the main Options menu

The second utility, Macro_Edit, allows you to convert an existing Macro Command to a text file so that the text can be edited. Then it lets you convert the text file back to a Macro Command.

The third utility in OA is the Graphics_Drivers, which allows you to install a new graphics driver if you upgrade your system with a graphics card or change the current card.

The commercial version of Open Access II contains several other utilities, including powerful data conversion and data recovery programs, that are not available in this Publisher's Version.

Accessing the Utilities Module

The Utilities module appears on the Options menu and can be chosen by doing the following hands-on exercise.

Hands On

1. Load Open Access. The Options menu should appear.
2. Select the Utilities module by highlighting "Utilities" with <arrows> and pressing <do> **F10**; or select it by entering [U]. This displays the Utilities menu shown in Figure 3-1, p. 34.

The function keys used in the Utilities module and a brief description of each is contained in Table 3-1.

TABLE 3-1 Utilities Function Keys

Name	*Key*	*Function*
<help>	F1	Displays help menu.
<menu>	F2	Accesses command menus.
<print>	F3	Prints areas or reports.
<search>	F4	Accesses search windows.
<copy>	F5	Copies a printer record from another file.
<change>	F6	Changes data type, input, or menu.
<test>	F7	Prints sequence test lines.
<desk>	F8	Selects Desk Accessories.
<count>	F9	Counts the number of printer record currently in use.
<do>	F10	Accepts the command sequence.
<undo>	Esc	Rejects the command sequence.
<prt_sc>	Alt-F3	Prints display screen.
<macro>	Alt-F8	Accesses macro chmmand window.
<ascii>	Alt-F4	Accesses ASCII table window.
<line_ins>	Ctrl-Return	Inserts a row/file/parameter.
<line_del>	Ctrl-Backspace	Deletes row/file/parameter.
<jump_left>	Ctrl-Home	Jumps one page left.
<jump_right>	Ctrl-End	Jumps one page right.
<word_fwd>	Ctrl-Right	Moves to next word.
<word_back>	Ctrl-Left	Moves to previous word.
<home>	Home	Moves to first row on screen.
<end>	End	Moves to last row.
<pg_up>	PgUp	Moves up one screen.
<pg_down>	PgDn	Moves down one screen.
<user1-user8>	ShiftF1-F8	Describes user-definable keys.
<tab>	Tab	Moves to the right preset length.
<ret>	Return	Accesses command or moves to next line.

```
                                                                     Options

                                                                  Spread_Sheet
                           Open Access II Limited Version         Communications
   (c) Copyright 1984,1985,1986,1987 Software P
                                All rights reserve        Utilities          er
                                                                             cessor
                                                       Configure             s
                             Today's Date:    9-22-1   Macro_Edit            g_System
                                                       Graphics_Drivers
                                                                             > <do>
                                                                               <undo>
                                                        <arrows> <do>
                                                       <search> <undo>
```

FIGURE 3-1

Configure

The Configure option allows you to set up, or configure, a number of parameters so the program or hardware meets your needs. Begin by looking at the Configuration Setup menu in the following hands-on exercise.

Hands On

Select "Configure" from the Utilities menu. This displays the Configuration Setup menu (Figure 3-2, p. 36).

The Configuration Setup menu offers seven choices. Let's look at each of these.

Misc-Parameters

The Misc-Parameters command allows you to select the default printer, date field format, type of decimal character, screen type, scratch volume name for work files, and default file extensions for the spreadsheet and word-processing document files. You will look at Misc-Parameters in the following hands-on exercise. The Configuration Setup menu should still be on the display screen.

Hands On

1. Select "Misc-Parameters." The Miscellaneous Parameters window appears (Figure 3-3, p. 36). The cursor is on the Default Printer ID field.

2. Press <search> **F4** to view a list of the output devices available. The Output Device Selection window now appears.
3. Select the output device you will be using. Ask your instructor for the proper entry. Select "PRINTER" for a generic printer driver if you are using a parallel printer that is not one listed in the Output Devices Selection window. If you do not have a printer, select "CONSOLE," which "prints" a file to the screen, or "FILE," which "prints" a file to a disk as a text file that can later be used by the word processor or text editor.
4. Press <do> **F10** to return to the Miscellaneous Parameters window.
5. Press <arrows> to highlight "Format for date fields" to configure the date fields.
6. Press <search> and select from any of the nine different date formats listed in the Date Formats window. (Optional: Press <change> **F6** as an alternative method to select the date format. Each time you press <change> the date format will change. Continue to press <change> until the desired date format appears then go to step 8.)
7. Press <do> to return to the Miscellaneous Parameters window.
8. Press <arrows> to highlight "Decimal character." OA uses either a period (.) or a comma (,) as a decimal point.
9. Press <change> twice. Notice that <change> toggles between displaying the period and the comma.
10. Press <arrows> to highlight "Screen Identification."
11. Press <search> to display the Screen Identification Defaults window. This window lists the available screen configurations. OA should already be appropriately configured so leave this window as it is.
12. Press <undo> **Esc** to return to the Miscellaneous Parameters window.
13. Press <arrows> to highlight "Scratch Volume Name." Some commands such as "Select" in the spreadsheet module prompt the program to make a backup of the file on which you are working. Other commands create working files that must be temporarily stored on disk. The location of this "scratch" space for backup and working files is set with this option.
14. Press <search> to display the Volumes Available window. The selections shown in this window are volume "nicknames." The nickname is a short-hand way of expressing the volume (drive) and path(s) (directories) in which the files will be saved. See the section on Searching_Order later in this chapter to see how to define a nickname.
15. Press <do> to accept the current scratch volume name and return to the Miscellaneous Parameters window.
16. Press <arrows> to highlight "Default SS extension." This option sets the default file extension names for the spreadsheet. The standard format is .FMD (Financial Model Data) and the compressed format is .CMP (Compressed Data). When the default extension is set to .FMD, you need only enter a filename, for example, [BUDGET], (the extension is automatically added) to label your spreadsheet BUDGET.FMD. If the default had been set to .CMP, you would enter the .FMD extension along with the file name to store the file in standard format.
17. Select the .FMD extension. The function <change> is used to switch between the two extensions.
18. Press <arrows> to highlight "Default WP extension." This option sets the default file extension for the word processor as either a text file (.TXT), which saves in an ASCII format, or a document file (.DOC), which saves in a binary format. The binary format is faster loading and saving because there is no need to translate it for the computer. If a particular word processor extension is set as the default, there is no need to enter it after a filename in the word processor module.
19. Select the .DOC extension using <change>.
20. Press <do> to return to the Configuration Setup menu.

```
               Open Access II Limited Version Configure
 (c) Copyright 1984,1985,1986,1987 Software Products International, Inc.
                          All rights reserved



                          Configuration Setup
   Misc-Parameters   Time_Parameters   Function-Keys  Searching_Order
             Default-Files  Printer-Parameters  Options

                        <do> <undo> <arrows>
```

FIGURE 3-2

```
                  Miscellaneous Parameters

 (c) Copy       Default Printer ID    IBM QUIETWRITER          Inc.
            Format for date fields    mm-dd-yyyy
                 Decimal character    .
             Screen Identification    Monochrome 1
               Scratch Volume Name    C
              Default SS extension     .FMD  .CMP
              Default WP extension     .TXT  .DOC

         <do> <undo> <menu> <up> <down> <search>

                          Configuration Setup
   Misc-Parameters   Time_Parameters   Function-Keys  Searching_Order
             Default-Files  Printer-Parameters  Options

                        <do> <undo> <arrows>
```

FIGURE 3-3

Time_Parameters

The Time_Parameters command sets the time by time zones, tells how the time will be displayed, and sets the time increments in the Appointment Scheduler (accessed through the Desk Accessories module). Set these time parameters in the following hands-on exercise.

```
                                                                   re
                   Time Default Parameters                         ternational, Inc.

              Time zone #1     MUNICH
       Offset time zone #1        9
      Time zone #1 display     12-Hour  24-Hour
              Time zone #2     LONDON
       Offset time zone #2        8
      Time zone #2 display     12-Hour  24-Hour
       Other time displays     12-Hour  24-Hour
      Appointment interval     15   30   60  minutes

            <up> <down> <do> <undo> <menu>

                          Configuration Setup
   Misc-Parameters   Time_Parameters   Function-Keys  Searching_Order
              Default-Files  Printer-Parameters  Options

                          <do> <undo> <arrows>
```

FIGURE 3-4

Hands On

1. Select "Time_Parameters" from the Configuration Setup menu. The Time Default Parameters window appears as in Figure 3-4.
2. Type [Munich] or the name of any city or country for which you would like the time displayed. The Time Default Parameters listed here pertain to the clock used by several commands in the Desk Accessories module except the "appointment interval" parameter. That parameter pertains to the appointment book activated by the Appointments command in the Desk Accessories module.
3. Press <ret> **Return** to accept the entry and move to "Offset time zone #1." This field sets the number of hours from the current time where you live and the city selected in step 2 above. A positive number, 3, for example, denotes three hours later. A negative number, -3, for example, denotes three hours earlier. If you live in the Eastern Standard time zone, the time in Munich would be 6 hours later.
4. Type [6] or the appropriate hour difference for your location.
5. Press <ret> to accept the entry and highlight "Time zone #1 display." This sets the time to a 12-hour clock using AM and PM designations, or to a 24-hour clock, often called military time where, for example, 2:30 p.m. is displayed as 1430. Use <change> **F6** to select between the 12- and 24-hour options.
6. Select the 12-hour option and press <ret>. The Time zone #2, Offset time zone #2, and Time zone #2 display fields can be set by following the procedures in steps 2-6. For now, accept the default values.
7. Press <ret> three times. "Other time displays" is now highlighted.
8. Press <ret> to accept the default value "12-Hour" for "Other time displays". This establishes how the time will be displayed by the current clock in other portions of OA. "Appointment interval" should now be highlighted.

9. Press <change> to highlight "15" as the time interval for the divisions in the appointment book. If 15 is selected, for example, the appointment book will have 15 minute intervals like 7:00, 7:15, 7:30, 7:45, 8:00. If 30 is selected, then the appointment book will have 30-minute intervals like 7:00, 7:30, and 8:00. The appointment book is activated by the Appointment command in the Desk Accessories module.
10. Press <do> **F10** to accept any changes made, or press <undo> **Esc** (which displays the Abandon Changes? window) and then <do> to abandon any changes. Either way returns you to the Configuration Setup menu.

Searching_Order

The Searching_Order command sets the sequence and defines the volume and pathway (directories) in which OA searches for files. In the following hands-on exercise, you will set one search path, but check with your instructor as to the actual paths needed for your system. Open Access will display an error message if you enter a volume and pathway that does not exist.

Hands On

1. Select "Searching_Order" from the Configuration Setup menu. Notice that the default searching order is already set up for this workbook. The right side of the window shows the proper DOS name for the volume (drive) and path (directories, or subdirectories). The left side of the window is for a nickname, a shorthand name, that you choose to identify the volume and pathway. (Figure 3-5). This nickname is what appeared in the "Volumes Available" window when <search> **F4** was pressed from the "Scratch Volume Name" field of the "Miscellaneous Parameters" window.
2. Press the down <arrow> twice. The cursor is on #3.
3. Press <line_ins> **Ctrl-Return** and enter [DATA] as the nickname.
4. Press <ret> **Return** to accept the entry.
5. Type [C:\OA\FILES]. This defines the path to search for a file in drive C in the directory FILES that we created in Chapter 2 to hold the sample data files on drive C. The paths entered must be valid directory paths for your system. If you have a dual floppy diskette system or did not create the directory file in Chapter 2 go to Step 6a. If you have a hard-disk system and created the directory FILES, go to step 6b.
6. (a) Press <line_del> **Ctrl-Back Space.** Go to Step 7.
6. (b) Press <ret> to accept the entry.
7. Use <arrows> to move the cursor to highlight nickname #1.
8. Press <line_ins>. You may insert additional volume (drive name) and pathnames (directions to the file) in the searching order.
9. Type [WP] and press <ret> and then type [B:\] as the pathway where word-processor files might be stored.
10. Press <line_del> to delete the entry since this was entered only as an example and is not valid for the current setup.
11. Press <do> **F10** to accept the change and return to the Configuration Setup menu.

```
                                  Volume\Pathname Searching Order
  Nickname       Volume:\  Pathname\
-------------------------------------------------------------------
 #1:C         C:\OA\
 #2:A         A:\

-------------------------------------------------------------------
            <menu><up><down><tab><back_tab><line_ins><line_del>
-------------------------------------------------------------------
                          Configuration Setup
     Misc-Parameters    Time_Parameters    Function-Keys   Searching_Order
                Default-Files   Printer-Parameters   Options

                          <do> <undo> <arrows>
```

FIGURE 3-5

Function-Keys

The Function-Keys command allows you to program any one of seven programmable function keys to execute commands or print a string of characters when they are pressed. These user-definable keys are accessed by pressing Shift-F1 through Shift-F7. Table 3-2 gives a complete list of the command sequences for the User Definable Function Keys. When typing, use uppercase or lowercase letters as indicated in the table.

TABLE 3-2 Command Sequences for User-Definable Function Keys

Function	*Sequence*	*Function*	*Sequence*
<help>	\?	<menu>	\M
<print>	\H	<prt_sc>	\#
<scr_off>	\k	<search>	\/
<copy>	\G	<window>	\G
<cut>	\g	<change>	\-
<justify>	\U	<paste>	\S
<place>	\s	<graph1>	\S
<graph2>	\s	<desk>	\R
<macro>	\"	<select>	\L
<edit>	\L	<deselect>	\l
<query>	\l	<do>	\!
<ss_macro>	\%	<ret>	\N

<undo>	\X	<up>	\^
<down>	\v	<left>	\<
<right>	\>	<word_fwd>	\W
<word_back>	\w	<home>	\V
<end>	\&	<jump_left>	\{
<jump_right>	\}	<pg_up>	\p
<pg_down>	\P	<tab>	\T
<back_tab>	\t	<ins>	\i
<del>	\d	<backspace>	\B
<line_ins>	\I	<line_del>	\D

The hands-on exercise that follows demonstrates how to program a function key to automatically execute a macro. A macro is a series of keystrokes that are stored in a file, which can be "replayed" by pressing the macro key.

Hands On

1. Select "Function-Keys" from the Configuration Setup menu. This displays the User Definable Function Keys window (Figure 3-6).
2. Press <arrows> to highlight "User F-Key 7 Return String". In Step 3 you will define a new User F-key 7 Return String that will be used when the Shift-F7 key combination is pressed. A string is a series of alphanumeric characters.
3. Type [\"etest1.mon\N]. (Be sure to type an uppercase N.) This string will execute the macro file named TEST1.MON. In this example (\") means the <macro> key, the (e) means to execute the macro, TEST1.MON is the macro file name, and (\N) means the <ret> key.
4. Press <do> **F10** to accept the entry and to return to the Configuration Setup menu.
5. Press <User F-Key 7> **Shift-F7**. You defined this key to execute a macro. In this example, the macro TEST1.MON displays a help screen and displays the message "Pause mode, Press <macro> to leave."
6. Press <macro> **Alt-F8** to return to the Configuration Setup menu.

Now let's look at a way to enter various ASCII characters as a part of the Return Strings. The procedure in the next hands-on exercise can be used to enter characters not on the keyboard, such as graphics characters that can be used to draw windows or boxes around items.

```
                    User Definable Function Keys
  (c) Copyrigh  User F-Key 1 Return String  ═══              tional, Inc.
                User F-Key 2 Return String  ║
                User F-Key 3 Return String  ╔
                User F-Key 4 Return String  ▣
                User F-Key 5 Return String  ⁞
                User F-Key 6 Return String  \"eauto.mon\N
                User F-Key 7 Return String  ╟╩╩╦╦╢

                   <menu><up><down><line_ins><line_del>

                          Configuration Setup
      Misc-Parameters   Time_Parameters   Function-Keys  Searching_Order
                Default-Files  Printer-Parameters  Options

                          <do> <undo> <arrows>
```

FIGURE 3-6

Hands On

1. Select "Function-Keys" from the Configuration Setup menu.
2. Press <ascii> **Alt-F4** to display a list of ASCII characters from which you may choose characters to use in the Return Strings.
3. Press <arrows> until you are at ASCII character number 155. This is the "cent" symbol.
4. Press <paste> **F7** to enter the character in the User F-Key 1 field. This returns the "cent" symbol when Shift-F1 is pressed from any module.
5. Press <do> **F10** to accept the changes and return to the Configuration Setup menu.

TO QUIT: To exit this module and return to the Configuration Setup menu later, select Options; the Main Options menu appears. You can exit OA or choose another module. If you exit, you must reload OA.

RESTART: Reload OA, Select "Utilities" from the Option menu; then select Configure.

After doing the previous exercises, you can use any character or combination of characters from the ASCII table in a Return String. The function-keys can then be used to perform such operations as drawing a box in a word-processor document.

Default-Files

The Default-Files command is used to enter default filenames for the files that OA uses to store internal information. For example, OA needs files to store data generated by several Desk Accessory commands such as the contents of the "Business Cards," the "Appointments." and values from the "Value Converter." In the following hands-on exercise, just look at how the current default filenames are set; you will not change any.

Hands On

1. Select "Default-Files" from the Configuration Setup menu. This displays the Default Filenames window (Figure 3-7). The entries are described in Table 3-3.
2. Press <do> **F10** to return to the Configuration Setup menu.

```
(c) Copyrig            Default Filenames                 nal, Inc.

                       Note Pad  C:NOTEPAD.TXT
                   Appointments  APPTSPI.DF
                 Business Cards  CARDSPI.DF
                Value Converter  DEFCONV.DIF
         AutoDial Default Modem  VHAYES12.MDM
            WP Default Document  DEFAULT.DOC
          Applications MNU File  A:APP.MNU

        <do> <undo> <menu> <up> <down> <search>

                   Configuration Setup
   Misc-Parameters   Time_Parameters   Function-Keys  Searching_Order
            Default-Files  Printer-Parameters  Options

                    <do> <undo> <arrows>
```

FIGURE 3-7

TABLE 3-3 Default Filenames

Program	*Default Filename*
Note Pad	Filename may be changed. File extension must be .TXT (DOS Text File).
Appointments	Filename may be changed. File extension must be .DF (DF = Database format).
Business Cards	Filename may be changed. File extension must be .DF (DF = Database format).
Value Converter	Filename may be changed. File extension must be .DIF (DIF = Data interchange format).
Autodial Default Modem	Filename and file extension name may be changed. Used by the Autodial function in Business Cards.
WP Default Document	Filename and file extension name may be changed. Used by word processor to determine default settings when creating a new document.

Printer-Parameters

The Printer-Parameters command allows you to configure a printer, then test the configuration or edit any of the current printer configurations. Any of the settings may be deleted or changed. In the following hands-on exercise, you will view the various parameters. Again, consult your instructor for the proper settings to be used if the printer is different from any of those already defined.

```
                    Printer Parameters      [    792 ]
      Printer Identification:              IBM QUIETWRITER
      Output Device:          CON:    File    LPT1:   COM1:   COM2:
(c)   Baud Rate:              110 150 300 600 1200 2400 4800 9600      c.
      Parity:                 None   Odd   Even
      Number of Stop Bits:    One   Two
      Number of Data Bits:    5   6   7   8
      Etx/Acknowledge:                       True   False
      Xon/Xoff:                              True   False
      Graphics Printer?                      True   False
      Plotter?                               True   False
      Using Single Sheets?                   True   False
      Pause for Color Change?                True   False
      Pause for Typeface Change?             True   False
      Print Class:                              1
      Height of Paper:                     11.0000     inches
      Width of Paper:                      8.0000      inches
      Indention Column:                    0.0000      inches
      Printable Length:                    11.0000     inches
                <do><undo><move_keys><line_ins><line_del>

                          <do> <undo> <arrows>
```

FIGURE 3-8

Hands On

1. Select "Printer-Parameters" from the Configuration Setup menu. This displays the Output Device Configurations window.
2. Use <arrows> to select the IBM Quietwriter printer. This is selected for demonstration only. If you have another printer that is listed, you may want to select it to view.
3. Press <do> **F10**. The Printer Parameters window appears (Figure 3-8).
4. Press <arrows> to scroll through all the possible parameters. View but do not change any of the parameters unless your instructor directs you to at this time.
5. Press <undo> **Esc** twice to return to the Configuration Setup menu.

The Printer Parameters window contains configuration details to set up a printer or plotter. These may be changed by pressing the <change> F6 key. Pressing <do> F10 will accept all the changes made and return to the Configuration Setup menu. If you set the "Graphics Printer?" option to "True," as in the IBM Quietwriter example, an additional Graphics Information window follows the basic Printer Parameters window for setting graphics parameters. Your instructor will provide instructions for the printer you are using if it is not already defined.

If you set "Plotter?" as "True," a Plotter Information window is displayed to set your plotter configurations.

Because not all printers can print all the characters that are possible to produce on your monitor, a Translatable Characters Table lists the Translatable Characters for the selected printer. This is necessary when the ASCII-Character Set for the computer and the ASCII-Character Set for the printer do not match. The Translatable Character Table lists the characters that can be translated; the printing sequence is altered to produce the same character. If the printer cannot print the character, you may define a substitute character.

If your printer is not listed in the Output Device Configurations window, you can create a new printer configuration set up. The following hands-on exercise demonstrates how to create a new printer configuration.

Hands On

1. Select "Printer-Parameters" from the Configuration Setup menu. The Output Device Configurations window appears.
2. Press <line_ins> **Ctrl-Return** to create a new printer configuration. A prompt appears on the screen. If you press <do> **F10**, it makes the configuration you highlighted the default choice; if you press <undo> **Esc**, a blank record appears in which to configure a new printer.
3. Press <undo>. The Printer Parameters window appears. As you can see, no printer name is entered in the Printer Identification field and no other values are entered. At this point you would need to define all the appropriate parameters for a designated printer. Consult your instructor for details.
4. Press <undo>. The Abandon Changes window is displayed.
5. Press <do> to abandon changes and proceed. This returns the Output Device Configurations window.
6. Press <undo> to return to the Configuration Setup menu.

To check the configurations of Printer Parameters, perform the test routine in the next hands-on exercise. This test routine will not work for plotters, and it will not check to see that the printer has been turned on. Make sure the printer is on before trying the test.

During the test, the left side of each line will describe what is to be printed, and the rest of the line will be text printed in that form. If you do not have a printer, skip the following hands-on exercise.

Hands On

1. Select "Printer-Parameters" from the Configuration Setup menu. The Output Device Configurations window appears.
2. Press <arrows> to highlight the printer you are using and wish to test.
3. Select <test> **F7**. The prompt "Press <do> to test selection" asks you if you want to continue with the test.
4. Press <do> **F10** to start the test.
5. Press <undo> **Esc** to return to the Configuration Setup menu when the test is finished.

Options

The Options command returns you to the Options menu. Practice with the following hands-on exercise.

Hands On

1. Select "Options" from the Configuration Setup menu to return to the Options menu.
2. Select "Utilities" from the Options menu to reenter the Utilities module. The Utilities menu appears on your screen.

Macro_Edit

A macro is a series of keystrokes that can be stored in a file and then "replayed" once or as often as necessary. With a macro, repetitive functions can be reduced to a single keystroke. In this way a series of often-repeated instructions can be executed easily.

In this section you will create, name, and execute a macro. You have already learned how to define a function key to execute a macro with only one keystroke in the discussion of the Function-Keys command. You will also learn about the Macro_Edit command, which allows a macro file to be converted into a text file for editing and then converted back to a macro file for execution.

Creating a Macro

Macros can be very helpful tools when used with modules such as the Database, Word Processor, and Spreadsheet. A macro must be executed from the same module where it was created; otherwise, the series of keystrokes may have different effects. This is because some keystrokes do not have the same meaning in all of the modules. Table 3-4 shows a list of the module-dependent keys and their generic names.

TABLE 3-4 Module Dependent Key Symbols

Module	*Function*	*Generic Key Name*
Spreadsheet	<window>	<key5>
	<justify>	<alt6>
	<graph1>	<key7>
	<graph2>	<alt7>
	<edit>	<key9>
	<query>	<alt9>
	<ss_macro>	<alt10>
Database	<rec_back>	<key5>
	<rec_fwd>	<key7>
	<select>	<key9>
	<eval>	<alt10>
Word Processor	<para_fwd>	<key5>
	<para_back>	<alt5>
	<format>	<alt6>
	<sent_fwd>	<key7>
	<sent_back>	<alt7>

TABLE 3-4 (continued)

Module	*Function*	*Generic Key Name*
	<word_fwd>	<key9>
	<word_back>	<alt9>
Communications	<format>	<alt6>
	<status>	<alt7>
	User Definable Function Keys	
	Programmable Function Key 1	<user1>
	Programmable Function Key 2	<user2>
	Programmable Function Key 3	<user3>
	Programmable Function Key 4	<user4>
	Programmable Function Key 5	<user5>
	Programmable Function Key 6	<user6>
	Programmable Function Key 7	<user7>
	Programmable Function Key 8	<user8>

The macro created in the next hands on exercise is relatively short and simple and intended only to illustrate how to use the commands for creating a macro. In particular, the macro you will create simply displays a help window and prints a message you inserted in the macro.

Hands On

1. Press <macro> **Alt-F8**. The Macro Commands window appears on the screen (Figure 3-9). The Macro Commands window can be accessed from almost anywhere in any of the modules.
2. Select "Learn" from the menu. This initiates the process where the macro is created.
3. Type [MYMACRO] for the name of the macro and press <do> **F10**. Any keystrokes entered from now until you exit the Learn mode will become part of the macro. Note there is no special window or menu at this point. Any keys that you use become part of the macro.
4. Press <help> **F1**. This enters the Help Screen menu into the macro. The Learn process can be interrupted to insert a message or a pause.
5. Press <macro> and the Macro Learn Mode Options window appears (Figure 3-10).
6. Select "Pause." This inserts a Pause during macro execution.
7. Press <macro> to exit from the Pause mode and re-enter the Learn mode.
8. Press <macro> again to display the Macro Learn Mode Options window.
9. Select "Message." With this command you can type a one line message of up to 55 characters, which will appear on the screen.
10. Type [This is my macro.].
11. Press <ret> **Return** to accept the message.
12. Press <macro> to continue in the Learn mode.

13. Select <macro> again to display the Macro Learn Mode Options window.
14. Select "Save" to save the contents of the macro into a macro (.MON) file.
15. Press <undo> **Esc** to clear the screen.
16. Select <macro> to access the Macro Commands window.
17. Select "Execute."

```
                                                                 Options

                                                           Spread_Sheet
                         Open Access II Limited Version    Communications
   (c) Copyright 1984,1985,1986,1987 Software P
                              All rights reserve      Utilities       er
                                                                      cessor
                                                                      s
                              Macro Commands                          g_System
                       Execute   Learn   Repeat              ivers
                                                                      > <do>
                         <search> <do> <undo>                          <undo>
                                                             do>
                                                  <search> <undo>
```

FIGURE 3-9

```
                              Function Key Setup
<do>          =    F10  |<jump_right>    = Ctrl-End    |<halt> = Ctrl-Break
<undo>        =    Esc  |<jump_left>     = Ctrl-Home   |
<help>        =    F1   |<home>          =      Home   |
<menu>        =    F2   |<end>           =      End    |
<print>       =    F3   |<line_ins>      = Ctrl-Ret    |
<search>      =    F4   |<line_del>      = Ctrl-BkSp   |
<change>      =    F6   |<word_fwd>      = Ctrl-Right  |
<des                                         -Left     |
<mac        Macro Learn Mode Options                   |
<asc   Save  Pause  Message  Abort  Call               |
<prt                                         t F1-F8   |
              <search> <do> <undo>

 This is an options menu.  Each option accesses a different
 program module.  Select an option by either using the arrow
 keys or by pressing the first letter(s) of the desired option.
 The Operating System selection will terminate the program and
 exit to the operating system.
 <search> can be pressed for operations to files which are
 utilized by the highlighted option.

         Help Window: <up><down> to scroll help text,  <undo> to quit
```

FIGURE 3-10

18. Type [MYMACRO] as the name of the macro to execute, or press <search> **F4** to select from a list of macros that are currently stored.
19. Press <do> and the macro will execute. Notice that since you inserted a Pause, you need to press <macro> as indicated at the top of the screen to continue.
20. Press <macro>. The macro continues to execute and the message "This is my macro." is displayed.
21. Press <macro> to continue. The macro completes its execution and the message "End of Macro Command" is displayed for a short time and then is removed.
22. Press <undo> to exit to the Utilities menu.

Other commands in the Macro Command menu include the REPEAT command to repeat a macro a specified number of times. The ABORT command and the CALL command are selections from the Macro Learn Mode Options window. The ABORT command "aborts" or stops creating the macro in the Learn mode and no file is saved. When this command is selected, you are prompted to confirm your decision by pressing <do> **F10**. The CALL command calls, or inserts, another macro within the present macro. You can also specify a repeat factor in a "Call." Macros can only be inserted or nested to three levels.

Macro and Text File Conversion Using Macro_Edit

The Macro_Edit utility converts a macro file (.MON) to a text (.TXT) file so it can be edited without recreating the entire macro through the Learn command. This editing can be done in the word processor module, in the Desk Accessories Note Pad, or with the DOS edit commands. The text file can then be converted back to a macro file so it can be executed. The following hands-on exercise demonstrates this.

Hands On

1. Select "Macro_Edit" from the Utilities menu. The Macro/Text File Conversion menu appears.
2. Select the "Macro_to_Text" command.
3. Type [MYMACRO]. (Press the <search> **F4** key if you want to search for a previously created or a different macro file.)
4. Press <do> **F10** to accept the entry.
5. Press <do> again to accept the default text file name MYMACRO.TXT and to view the contents of the macro file. The text file may now be edited using a word processor or text editor. In this example, you will not edit the macro but simply convert the text file back to a macro file.
6. Select "Text_to_Macro".
7. Type [MYMACRO] as the text file to be changed to a macro file.
8. Press <do> to accept the entry.
9. Press <do> again to accept the default name of the macro file. The prompt Remove Old "macro name"? appears. After a macro file is edited, you can change the name of the file now by entering a new name if you do not want to destroy the original macro file. Since the macro is unchanged, use the same filename.
10. Press <do> to save under the same filename. This returns you to the Macro/Text File Conversion menu.

Exiting Macro_Edit

The Options command returns you to the Options menu from Macro_Edit. Practice with this hands-on exercise.

Hands On

1. Select "Options" from the Macro/Text File Conversion window. The Options menu appears.
2. Select "Utilities" from the Options menu.

Graphics_Drivers

A graphics card is required to display graphics. Programs called graphics drivers are also necessary to enable these cards to display graphics. The Graphics_Drivers selection allows you to change, or define for the first time, the graphics driver that will be used. This must be done if you change graphics cards or install one for the first time. Skip the following hands on exercise if you do not have a graphics card installed.

Hands On

1. Select "Graphics_Drivers" from the Utilities menu. This displays the "Install program for Graphics Routines" instruction window (Figure 3-11).
2. Insert the OA_Install/Drivers diskette into the appropriate drive (drive B on a dual-diskette system, drive A on a hard-disk system). Dual-diskette system users must also insert the OA_Spreadsheet diskette in drive A as well.
3. Press <do> **F10**. A list of the available graphics drivers is displayed. If the search window is empty, press PgDn until the nickname defined for drive A is highlighted and the list of graphics drivers is displayed. To change graphics drivers, use <arrows> to highlight the appropriate drive and press <do>. For now, we will leave things as they are.
4. Press <undo> **Esc** to return to the Options menu.

```
              Install program for Graphics Routines
   Place DRIVERS Disk in Drive B and Spread_Sheet Disk in drive A
       If using hard disk, then place DRIVERS  Disk in drive A

              Type <do> to continue, <undo> to abort
```

FIGURE 3-11

Command Summary

Following is a brief summary of the commands grouped according to their menu.

Command	Description
Utilities Menu	
Configure	Sets or changes various hardware and program parameters.
Macro_Edit	Creates or edits a macro, and changes back and forth from text to macro files.
Graphics_Drivers	Changes or upgrades graphics driver, which supports graphics cards to display graphics.
Configuration Setup Menu	
Misc-Parameters	Sets the following system parameters: default printer, date field format, decimal character, screen identification, volume name for scratch files, default extensions for the spreadsheet and word-processor files.
Time_Parameters	Sets Desk Accessories time zones and appointment intervals.
Function-Keys	Used as programmable keys for entry of key sequences, text strings, or graphic characters.
Searching_Order	Enters the series of volumes and pathnames that the program will use when searching for files.
Default-Files	Enters default filenames for Note Pad, Appointments, Business Cards, Value Converter, Autodial Default Modem, and Word Processor Defa Document.
Printer-Parameters	Sets or changes printer configurations.
Options	Returns to the main Options menu.
Macro Commands Menu	
Execute	Executes a macro file already created.
Learn	Creates macro, all key strokes are recorded into a macro file.
Repeat	Enters the number of times the macro is to be repeated.
Macro/Text File Conversion Menu	
Macro_to_Text	Changes a macro file to a text file.
Text_to_Macro	Changes a text file to a macro file.
Options	Returns to the main Options menu.
Macro Learn Mode Options Menu	
Save	Saves macro and cancels learn mode.
Pause	Places a pause in the macro until the <macro> Alt-F8 key is presse
Message	Allows the placement of a short message on the screen.
Abort	Stops or aborts the macro being created and erases the file.
Call	Inserts the nesting of up to three levels of macros and asks for a number of repetitions.

Study Questions

1. What is the purpose of the Misc-Parameters command in the Configuration Setup menu?
2. Describe the devices CONSOLE, FILE, and PRINTER listed in the Output Devices Selection window.
3. Describe the purpose of the Time_Parameters command in the Configuration Setup menu.
4. Describe the purpose of the Functions-Keys command in the Configuration Setup menu.
5. Describe the purpose of the Searching_Order command in the Configuration Setup menu.
6. Describe the purpose of the nickname used in the searching order.
7. Describe the purpose of the Default-Files command in the Configuration Setup menu.
8. Describe the purpose of the Printer-Parameters command in the Configuration Setup menu.
9. Describe how to test a Printer Configuration.
10. Describe the purpose of the Options command in the Configuration Setup menu.
11. What is a macro?
12. Name and describe the purpose of the options in the Macro/Text File Conversion menu.
13. Why must a macro only be executed from the same module where it was created?
14. Define the purpose of the Graphics_Drivers command.
15. Access the Time Default Parameters. Choose two of the following cities that are not in your time zone: New York, Chicago, or Los Angeles. Enter as time zone 1 and time zone 2 with the appropriate offset times from your location. Use + for times ahead (e.g., if you're in Los Angeles the offset for New York City is +3) and - for times behind your present time (e.g., if you're in New York City the offset for Los Angeles is -3). Set the appointment interval to 15 minutes. Press <desk> F8 to display Desk Accessories and then print the screen to show the changes made.
16. Use the Function-Keys command and paste the character with ASCII value 160 in User F-Keys field. Print this window when completed.

Chapter 4
Desk Accessories

Introduction
Calculator
Time
Alarm
Date
Value Converter
Stopwatch
Business Cards
Appointment Scheduler
Note Pad
Command Summary
Study Questions

Introduction

The Desk Accessories module offers a convenient way to keep track of appointments and many other day-to-day activities. It also contains handy devices such as a calculator, note pad, and stopwatch, among others. The Desk Accessories may be accessed from almost anywhere within any one of the modules. Table 4-1 lists the function keys and their meanings as used in the Desk Accessories module.

TABLE 4-1 Function Keys for Desk Accessories

Name	*Key*	*Function*
<paste>	F7	Copies or returns current value.
Date		
<pg_down>	PgDn	Displays the next month.
<pg_up>	PgUp	Displays the previous month.
<search>	F4	Allows new date to be entered.
Alarm		
<change>	F6	Toggles ACTIVE/INACTIVE alarm state.
Calculator		
<statistics>	F5	Accesses statistics window.
<up_prec>	F9	Increases display precision.
<down_prec>	Alt-F9	Decreases display precision.
<grouping)	Alt-F7	Toggles the grouping on/off in the number display.
<change>	F6	Changes sign of number being input.
Value_Converter		
<add>	F5	Adds value to total line.
<subtract>	Alt-F5	Subtracts value from total line.

TABLE 4-1 (continued)

Name	Key	Function
Stop_Watch		
<on_off>	F5	Toggles on/off viewing of split times.
<line_del>	Ctrl-BackSpace	Clears/resets stopwatch.
<change>	F6	Starts and stops stopwatch.
Appointments		
<cut>	Alt-F5	Makes a copy and deletes it at the same time.
<select>	F9	Blocks out time periods.
<copy>	F5	Copies an appointment.
Business_Cards		
<dial>	F9	Allows user to connect to a modem.
Note_Pad		
<select>	F9	Selects area to be edited.
<deselect>	Alt-F9	Causes selected areas to be empty.
<ins>	Ins	Toggles between Insert and Exchange mode.
<place>	Alt-F7	Places value at cursor location.

Calculator

The Calculator performs the four basic mathematical functions (addition, subtraction, multiplication, and division) and also contains basic trigonometric and statistical functions. It has ten memories to store and retrieve numbers. The Calculator Main window contains the available operators of the calculator. The Functions window contains the commands necessary to perform basic trigonometric calculations. The Statistics window contains the commands for basic statistical analysis. The specific operators and commands for each window are listed in Table 4-2.

TABLE 4-2 Functions and Operators for the Calculator

Window	Key	Function
Main Window		
	0-9	Number Keys.
	+	Addition.
	-	Subtraction.
	*	Multiplication.
	/	Division.
	=	Equals (performs calculation).

TABLE 4-2 (continued)

Window	*Key*	*Function*
	C	Clears the display.
	P	Pi (3.1416).
	I	Gives inverse of current value.
	S	Stores value into one of ten registers (memory).
	R	Recalls value from the register (memory).
	H	Converts decimal display to hexadecimal, press [H] again to toggle back to decimal.
Functions Window		
	Sin	Calculates the sine of the display.
	Cos	Calculates the cosine of the display.
	Tan	Calculates the tangent of the display.
	Root	Calculates the square root of the display.
	ASin	Calculates the arcsine of the display.
	ACos	Calculates the arccosine of the display.
	ATan	Calculates the arctangent of the display.
	Sqr	Calculates the square of the display.
	Log	Calculates the common log of the display.
	Ln	Calculates the natural log of the display.
	Fac	Calculates the factorial of a positive integer.
	Stat	Accesses the Statistics window.
	Alog	Calculates the antilog of the display.
	Exp	Calculates the exponential function of the display.
	Y(X)	Calculates Y raised to the X power.
	X-Root	Calculates the Xth root of Y.
Statistics Window		
	+Sum	Adds the display to the value stored in the statistical register.
	-Sum	Subtracts the display from the value in the statistical register.
	Mean	Calculates the mean (average) of the result in the statistical register.
	Var	Calculates the variance of the sum.
	Dev	Calculates the standard deviation of the sum.
	Clr	Clears both the display and the statistical registers (registers 7, 8, and 9).

The following hands-on exercise accesses the calculator and examines some of its options. OA should be loaded and the Options menu should be on the display screen. In a two diskette drive system, the Utilities diskette should be inserted in Drive A.

Hands On

1. Press <desk> **F8** to access the Desk Accessories module. This displays the Desk Accessories menu along with a clock and calendar (Figure 4-1).
2. Select "Calculator" from the menu. This displays the main window of the Calculator (Figure 4-2).
3. Press <menu> **F2** to view the Functions window (Figure 4-3).
4. Select "Stat" from the Functions window to view the commands in the Statistics window (Figure 4-4). (The Statistics window can also be accessed by pressing <statistics> **F5** when in the Calculator Main window.)
5. Press <undo> **Esc** to return to the main Calculator window. You will add two numbers then take the cosine of the number.
6. Type [56]. Press the plus sign (+), then type [89], and press the equal sign (=). The current value, 145.00, is displayed in the upper right corner of the Calculator window.

```
                                                     Options

                                                   Spread_Sheet
              Open Access II Limited Version Configu  Communications
  (c) Copyright 1984,1985,1986,1987 Software Products In  Database
                         All rights reserved        Programmer
                                                   Word_Processor
                                                   Utilities
                                                              ystem
         Current Time          September                1987
          01:20:25 PM          Wk  Sun Mon Tue Wed Thu Fri, Sat  do>
                               36              1   2   3   4   5  ndo>
                               37   6   7   8   9  10  11  12
       Munich       LONDON     38  13  14  15  16  17  18  19
    10:20:25 PM   09:20:25 PM  39  20  21  22  23  24  25  26
                               40  27  28  29  30
                               41
   M                 Desk Accessories                       r
        Calculator   Time   Alarm   Date   Value_Converter
        Stop_Watch  Appointments  Business_Cards  Note_Pad
                     <search><page_keys><desk>
```

FIGURE 4-1

```
=:                                0.00
    (7) (8) (9)    (+) (C) (PI)
    (4) (5) (6)    (-) (() (STO)
    (1) (2) (3)    (*) ()) (RCL)
    (,) (0) (.)    (/) (=) (INV)
  <menu>,<paste>, <change> toggles
   sign, <statistics>, <grouping>
      <up_prec>    <down_prec>
```

FIGURE 4-2

```
=:                                0.00
      Sin    ASin   Log    ALog
      Cos    ACos   Ln     Exp
      Tan    ATan   Fac    Y^(X)
      Root   Sqr    Stat   X-Root


      <move_keys> <do> <undo>
```

FIGURE 4-3

```
  0                                         0.00
+Sum      -Sum        Clr
Mean                        0.00
Var                         0.00
Dev                         0.00

      <move_keys> <do> <undo>
```

FIGURE 4-4

7. Press <menu> to access the Functions window.
8. Select the "Cos" function. The cosine (radian measure) of the number appears in the upper right corner. The cosine of 145 is 0.88.
9. Press <up_prec> **F9** to increase the precision of the answer to 0.884.
10. Press <up_prec> again to increase the precision of the answer to 0.8839.
11. Press <undo> to return to the Options menu.

Time

The Time command is used to change the time in the Desk Accessories clock. It also updates the system time of your computer. The following hands-on exercise describes how to change the current time in the Desk Accessories clock.

Hands On

1. Press <desk> **F8** to access Desk Accessories.
2. Select "Time" from the Desk Accessories menu. The cursor jumps to the Current Time field.
3. Type [1200A] or the correct time for your area. If in the 12-hour default mode, be sure to indicate either AM or PM.
4. Press <do> **F10** to accept the new time. This also returns you to the part of the program from which you accessed Desk Accessories. In this case, it is the Options menu.

Alarm

The Alarm command lets you set an audible alarm with your computer. A message can be entered that will appear on the screen, e.g., a reminder that it's time to leave for a scheduled meeting. The following hands-on exercise sets both the audible alarm and the message display.

Hands On

1. Press <desk> **F8** to access Desk Accessories. Make note of the exact time displayed in the current time window.

```
                         Alarm
 Set Alarm Time:    12:00 AM          Status: INACTIVE
 Msg:

              <do><undo><up><down><change>
```

FIGURE 4-5

2. Select "Alarm" from the Desk Accessories menu. This displays the Alarm window (Figure 4-5). Now set the alarm.
3. Enter the time, for a minute or two past the time set on the Desk Accessories clock, so you can see and hear the alarm work now.
4. Press <ret> **Return** to accept the entry and move to the message prompt.
5. Type [Meeting at noon today.].
6. Press <change> **F6** to change the Alarm "Status" to "Active."
7. Press <do> **F10**. The alarm is now set. If you set it for a few minutes past the desk clock, wait for it to go off. When the alarm goes off, the message you typed also appears on the screen. Now proceed to step 8.
8. Press <desk> and select "Alarm" from the menu to turn off the alarm.
9. Press <do> because the alarm has been set to inactive.

Date

The Date command changes the date in the Desk Accessories and updates the system date for your computer. The following hands-on exercise changes the date.

Hands On

1. Press <desk> **F8**.
2. Select "Date" from the Desk Accessories menu. The Date window appears.
3. Type [04131988] (April 13, 1988) or use today's date.
4. Press <do> **F10** to enter the new date and return to the Options menu.

Value Converter

The Value Converter in the Desk Accessories module is a convenient table in which values can be converted from one unit of measurement to another. For example, you can set up the table to convert miles to feet and meters. The Value Converter Table is composed of three columns:

Quantity Column	Contains the quantity of each value and is located on the left side of the table.
Description Column	Provides a description of the value and is in the center of the table.
Ratio Column	Enters a ratio or comparison value and is located on the right side of the table.

```
 Conversion Window              Ratios
 ------Convert miles------
       1.00 miles                 1.00  Version         Options
   5,280.00 feet              5,280.00  Products In
   1,609.34 meters            1,609.34  ed              Spread_Sheet
                                                        Communications
                                        1988            Database
                                                        Programmer
                                                        Word_Processor
                                                        Utilities
                                                        Operating_System

                                                         <arrows> <do>
                                                        <search> <undo>

              Total : 0
 <tabs><up><down><print><menu><paste>
    <grouping><up_prec><down_prec>
     <add> adds value to total,
 <subtract> subtracts value from total
```

FIGURE 4-6

The first entry in the Value Converter Table is the default entry, and any other entries are compared or set to a ratio of this value. For example, if one mile is the first entry, then each succeeding entry would be given as a ratio to one mile. In Figure 4-6, one mile is the default entry in the Ratio column and succeeding entries in the ratio column indicate that there are 5,280 feet in one mile and 1,609.34 meters in one mile. When a number such as 10 is entered in the quantity column, the ratios in the ratio column are used to automatically calculate the number of feet (52,800.00) and the number of meters (16,093.40) in ten miles.

The Value Converter Table can be divided into separate areas for different value conversions, such as monetary units, length, area, or time. The following hands-on exercise sets up a value converter table that will convert miles into feet and meters.

Hands On

1. Press <desk> **F8** to access Desk Accessories.
2. Select "Value_Converter" from the Desk Accessories menu. This displays the Conversion window.
3. Press <line_ins> **Ctrl-Return**; then press <tab> **Tab** to move to the Description column where you can type a description of the quantity entries.
4. Type [Convert miles].
5. Press <change> **F6**. This sets up a heading title or divider between conversion sections.
6. Press the down <arrow> once and then press <line_ins> to set up the first entry. The default entry has a value of one. The cursor is now in the Description column.
7. Type [miles].
8. Press the down <arrow> once to position the cursor to the next line.
9. Press <line_ins>. The cursor is now in the Description column. The cursor should be flashing right under miles.
10. Type [feet].

11. Press <tab> to move to the Ratios column.
12. Type [5280], the number of feet in a mile.
13. Press the down <arrow> once to move to the next line. The Quantity column in the above line is automatically entered.
14. Press <line_ins> once; then press <tab> twice to move to where the next Description will be entered.
15. Type [meters].
16. Press <tab> to move to the Ratio column.
17. Type [1609.34], the number of meters in a mile.
18. Press the down <arrow> and the Quantity is automatically entered.

Now that the table is completed, it can be altered to change the values. The Quantity value may be changed at any time. For example, you may want to know how many feet and meters are in two and one-half miles, which you will do in the next hands-on exercise.

Hands On

1. Press the up <arrow> three times. This places the cursor on the first value in the Ratios column.
2. Press <tab> **Tab** once to place the cursor in the Quantity column on the left side.
3. Type [2.5].
4. Press <ret> **Return**. The other values in the Quantity column of the MILES table are updated to reflect their amounts in two and one-half miles. For example, in 2.5 miles there are 13,200 feet and 4,023.35 meters.
5. Type [1] and press <ret> to return to the original values.

Once the table has been created, you can save it for later reference. The table can be reentered into the Conversion window to be used or updated again. You can also clear the table and add or subtract values to the Total field located at the bottom of the Conversion window immediately above the available key listing. The following hands-on exercise will save and load a file; add to, subtract from, and zero the Total line; and clear the Conversion window.

Hands On

1. Press <menu> **F2** to display the Conversion window menu.
2. Select "Save" from the menu. The prompt "Filename:" is displayed.
3. Type [MILES] as the filename.
4. Press <do> **F10** to save the file. (Note: If you had chosen a name already in use, you would be prompted with "Remove Old 'Filename'". To remove, press <do>; to cancel the operation and return to the Conversion window menu, press <undo> **Esc**.) You will now practice loading the table.
5. Press <menu> to display the Conversion window menu.
6. Select "Load" from the menu. The prompt "Filename:" is displayed.
7. Type [MILES].

8. Press <do> twice to bypass the Abandon changes prompt and load the file into the Conversion window.
9. Press the down <arrow> once to position the cursor in the Quantity column for feet. The cursor is positioned on 5,280 in the Quantity column.
10. Press <add> **F5** and the value 5280 is added to the Total field. The Total appears directly above the function key list at the bottom of the Conversion window.
11. Press the down <arrow> once to position the cursor at 1609.34.
12. Press <subtract> **Alt-F5** to subtract this value from the Total field. The Total now reads 3,670.66.
13. Press <menu> to access the Conversion window menu.
14. Select "Zero_Total." This automatically sets the Total field to zero.
15. Press <menu>.
16. Select "Clear." The window is cleared, but since the file was saved, it can be reloaded.
17. Press <undo> to return to the Options menu. If the "Abandon Changes?" window appears, press <do>.

You can print the completed conversion table by pressing <print> F3 when the Conversion window is still displayed and then selecting the appropriate printer from the list in the Output Device Selection window. Make sure the printer is ready (turned on, paper in, online, and connected to your computer) before proceeding.

Stopwatch

The Stopwatch feature can time events and view split times; it operates like a pocket stopwatch. The following hands-on exercise explains how to set and use the stopwatch.

Hands On

1. Press <desk> **F8** to access Desk Accessories.
2. Select "Stop_Watch" from the Desk Accessories menu. The Stop Watch window appears (Figure 4-7).
3. Press <change> **F6** to start the stopwatch.
4. Press <on_off> **F5** to see the split time. While you view the split time, the stopwatch continues to run.
5. Press <on_off> to see the stopwatch running again.
6. Press <undo> **Esc**. This allows you to move on to other tasks, but the stopwatch continues to run. (Note: the Desk Accessories menu is not currently displayed on the screen.)
7. Press <desk> to access the Desk Accessories menu.
8. Select "Stop_Watch." Notice that the stopwatch is still running.
9. Press <change> to stop the stopwatch.
10. Press <line_del> **Ctrl-Back Space** to set the stopwatch back to zero.
11. Select <do> **F10** or <undo> to exit the stopwatch feature.

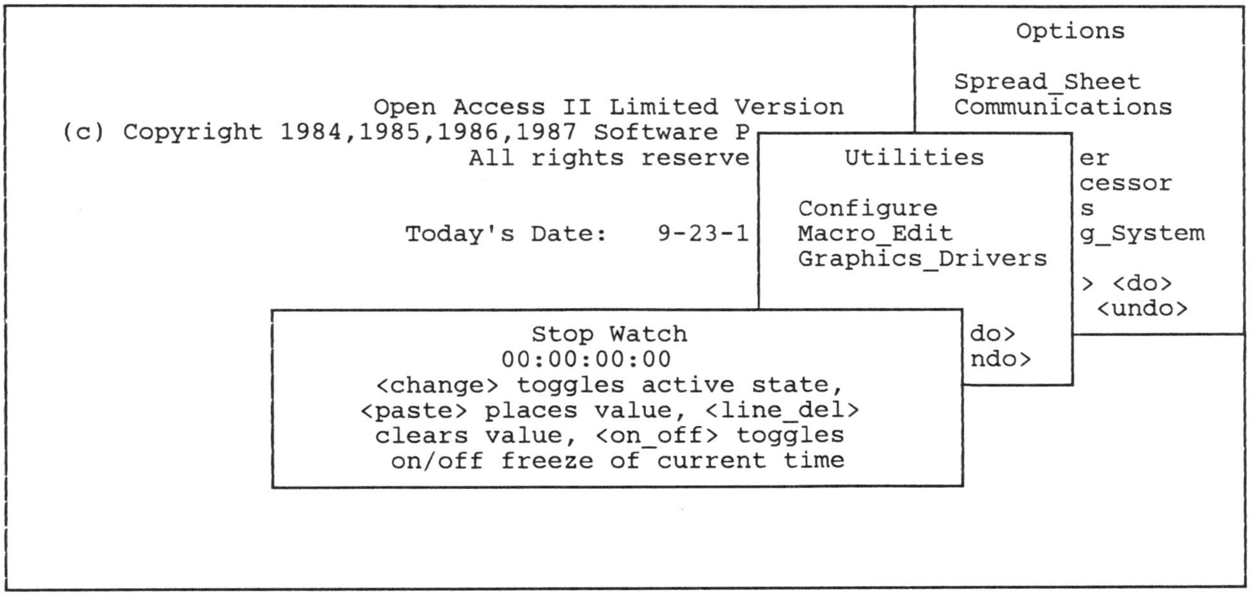

FIGURE 4-7

Business Cards

The Business Cards feature is a computerized address book with which you can easily search and sort business card files or add, delete, and print business cards. Included with Business_Cards is a feature that uses a modem to automatically dial a phone number stored in a business card. The following hands-on exercise enters two new business cards into the business card file.

Hands On

1. Press <desk> **F8**. Select "Business_Cards" from the Desk Accessories menu. If there is currently no business card file, the prompt "Couldn't find drive: CARDSPI.DF Create it? (<do>/<undo>)" appears. Press <do> **F10** if it appears. This displays the Business Card window (Figure 4-8). Now create some new business cards.
2. Press <ins> **Ctrl-Return** to access the Business Card insert window.
3. Type [Mr.] in the Pfx (prefix) field and press <ret> **Return**.
4. Type [John] as the first name and press <ret>.
5. Type [Q.] as the middle name and press <ret>.
6. Type [Smith] as the last name and press <ret>.
7. Type [Jr.] as the suffix and press <ret>.
8. Type [Smith Inc.] as the company name and press <ret>.
9. Type [John] as the attribute and press <ret>. An attribute is defined as any type of data that an application requires, e.g., an extra phone number, salutation, or personal note. The attribute in this example can be used as a salutation when a mail-merge letter is created in the Word Processor module.
10. Type [(555) 555-6789] as the home phone and press <ret>.

```
                                                          Options

                                                          Spread_Sheet
                 Open Access II Limited Version           Communications
   (c) Copyright 1984,1985,1986,1987 Software P
                         All rights reserve      Utilities       er
                                                                 cessor
                                              Configure          s
                    Today's Date:    9-23-1   Macro_Edit         g_System

 LASTNAME                                   Business Card

                          Empty card file.  Use <ins> to add records.




<change> <search> <paste>
<print><edit_keys><dial>
  <left> <right> change
active field <copy><cut>
```

FIGURE 4-8

11. Type [(555) 555-1234] as the business phone and press <ret>.
12. Type [1397 Maple St.] and press <ret>.
13. Type [Yuma, AZ 99999] and press <ret>.
14. Press <do>. Now the screen looks like Figure 4-9.
15. Repeat steps 2 through 14 to enter the next Business Card using the following data. If a field has no data (for example, the name below has no entry for the Sfx (suffix) field), simply press <ret> to bypass it.

    Mrs. June R. Cortez (press <ret> to leave Sfx field empty)
    June's Gift Shop
    June
    (555) 555-2222
    (555) 555-2223
    167 Abbey Lane
    Hartford, CT 06666

16. Repeat steps 2 through 14 to enter the following data in a business card.

    Ms. Tiffany A. Warren (press <ret> to leave Sfx field empty)
    Warren Piece Goods
    Ms. Warren
    (555) 555-5555
    (555) 555-0000
    1206 Battery Parkway
    Topeka, KS 66066

```
                                                                  Options

                                                               Spread_Sheet
                      Open Access II Limited Version           Communications
  (c) Copyright 1984,1985,1986,1987 Software P
                          All rights reserve       Utilities        er
                                                                    cessor
                                                 Configure          s
                       Today's Date:    9-23-1   Macro_Edit         g_System

 LASTNAME                                 Business Card
SMITH
                               Name Mr. John Q. Smith Jr.
                            Company Smith Inc.
                          Attribute John
                         Home Phone (555) 555-6789
                           Business (555) 555-1234
                            Address 1397 Maple St.
                            (cont.) Yuma, AZ 99999
<change> <search> <paste>   (cont.)
<print><edit_keys><dial>    (cont.)
  <left> <right> change
active field <copy><cut>
```

FIGURE 4-9

The cursor should now be positioned on the name Smith in the window on the left of the screen. This window displays the field on which the business card records are sorted and lists the values for that field in sorted order. The following hands-on exercise changes the Sort field and searches for a specific value. The left and right <arrows> can be used to change the field by which the records are sorted. The Default field is "LASTNAME."

Hands On

1. Press the right <arrows> four times until you highlight "LASTNAME" again. Notice the change in the Sort field name and the order of the values.
2. Press <search> **F4** to search for a specific value.
3. Type [Cortez] at the prompt "Search for what value?".
4. Press <do> **F10** and the business card for "Cortez" appears on the right side of the screen.

Business cards can become outdated. The next hands-on exercise shows you how to delete them.

Hands On

1. Use the <arrows> to position the cursor on "Warren" in the LASTNAME window.
2. Press <line_del> **Ctrl-Back Space**. You are prompted to verify this decision.

3. Press <do> **F10** to delete. (If you do not want to delete, press <undo> **Esc** to abort the delete process.)

Business card files can be output to a printer or to a DIF file where they can be merged with another file such as a form letter or report from another module. The following hands-on exercise describes this procedure.

Hands On

1. Press <print> **F3** to access the Output Options window.
2. Select "Print" to display the Output Device Selection window and use the <arrows> to highlight the device "Console."
3. Press <do> **F10** to print the business cards to the screen.
4. Press <do> again to return to the Business Card window.
5. Press <print>.
6. Select "MailMerge." This accesses the MailMerge Output (DIF) window (Figure 4-10).
7. Type the filename [CARDS] at the cursor and press <ret> **Return**.
8. Press <change> **F6** to highlight "Separate." When "Separate" is highlighted, each name field (Pfx, First, Middle, Last, and Sfx) in a business card is saved separately; that is, each name field saved will stay in a separate column. "Concat" would eliminate spaces between the name fields and store them as one column.
9. Press <ret>. To output a specific range of business cards to a DIF file, letters identifying the starting range would be entered in the Starting field and letters

```
                                                          Options
               Open Access II Limited Version
 (c) Copyright 1984,1985,1986,1987 Software Products In   Spread_Sheet
                    All rights reserved                   Communications
                                                          Database
                                                          Programmer
                                                          Word_Processor
                 Today's Date:  10- 7-1988                Utilities
                                                          Operating_System
 LASTNAME                           Business Card
CORTEZ
SMITH                          Name Mrs. June R. Cortez
                     MailMerge Output (DIF)

                  File Name
                 Name Parts  Concat  Separate
                   Starting
<change> <search> <  Ending ZZ
<print><edit_keys><  DIF Labels  Include  Exclude
  <left> <right> ch
active field <copy>      <search> <do> <undo>
```

FIGURE 4-10

identifying the ending range would be entered in the Ending field. However, here you will output all the business cards.

10. Press <ret> twice to bypass the Starting and Ending fields to indicate that all the records are to be included.
11. Press <change> to highlight "Include" if it is not already highlighted.
12. Press <ret> to Include DIF labels, which are necessary for the file to be used as part
13. of a mail merge operation with the Word Processor.
14. Press <do> and the records are entered to a DIF file.

With a modem it is possible to automatically dial the phone using one of the telephone numbers in a business card. If you are not using a modem, you may still want to run through this hands-on exercise to see how it would work.

Hands On

1. Use <arrows> to highlight "CORTEZ" from the FILENAME window.
2. Press <dial> **F9**, which accesses the Modem Configuration window (Figure 4-11). The window contains the name of the person you are calling, the modem configuration, and the home and business phone numbers of the person to be called.
3. Press <change> **F6**. At this point, the default modem designation could be changed to the modem you are actually using. For now, just leave it as it is.
4. Press <undo> **Esc** to return to the Modem Configuration menu.
5. Use <arrows> to highlight "Business" to select the business number rather than the home number.

```
                                                          Options

                                                          Spread_Sheet
                      Open Access II Limited Version      Communications
   (c) Copyright 1984,1985,1986,1987 Software P
                           All rights reserve    Utilities        er
                                                                  cessor
                                                 Configure        s
                      Today's Date:    9-23-1    Macro_Edit       g_System
 LASTNAME                                 Business Card
 Voice Dial of: Mrs. June R. Cortez                    rtez
        Modem Configuration [VHAYES12.MDM]             p

   Phone Selection:      Home  Business

   Home Phone:           (555) 555-2222                666
   Business Phone:       (555) 555-2223

         <do> <undo> <down> <up> <change>
```

FIGURE 4-11

6. Press the down <arrow> twice after making your selection of number. You can change or enter a number at this point, but it will not update the number in the business cards. (If you had a modem, you would press <do> **F10** to access the Voice Dialing window. The number would be dialed. When dialing is complete, the prompt "Dialing Complete - Pick up phone and press <do>" appears. When finished with your conversation, press <do> to proceed with the hang-up and restore response for the modem.)
7. Press <undo> to return to the Business Card window.
8. Press <undo> to return to the Options menu.

Appointment Scheduler

The Appointment Scheduler is an electronic appointment book in which each day is divided into time increments where you can enter appointments. These time increments are set in the Configuration Setup window using the Time_Parameter command discussed in Chapter 3, "Utilities."

Also included are a calendar, a clock, and a "To Do List" that provides space to write notes or reminders. The "To Do List" is a text file that can be loaded and used in the Word Processor module or in the Note_Pad section of the Desk Accessories module.

In the following hands-on exercise, you will enter an appointment, change the appointment, highlight the appointment in a different color, and set aside blocks of time for an appointment.

Hands On

1. Press <desk> **F8** and select "Appointment" from the Desk Accessories menu. The prompt "Couldn't find *drive*:.APPTSPI.DF. Create it? (<do>/<undo>)" appears.
2. Press <do> **F10** to create the default file and to display the calendar, the To Do List, and the appointment window (Figure 4-12).
3. Use <arrows> to position the cursor to 9:00a in the appointment window.
4. Type [staff meeting] and press <ret> **Return**.
5. Press <line_ins> **Ctrl-Return**. This accesses the New Appointment window (Figure 4-13) from which you can set a new date and time for the appointment.
6. Press <ret> to keep the date the same.
7. Type [0700A] to set a new time and press <ret>.
8. Type [new staff meeting] in the Note field and press <do>. The new appointment is entered at 7:00a in the appointment window.
9. Press <tab> **Tab** to change the color or attribute (e.g., underline, blinking, reverse video) of the appointment at 9:00a. You can choose any one of seven colors if you have a color monitor.
10. Use <arrows> and move to "7:00a new staff meeting." If the appointment is to be longer than one time increment, you can block out several increments of time.
11. Press <select> **F9**.
12. Press the down <arrow> three times.
13. Press <do> to accept the entry of blocked time.

Notice that when the new appointment was set for 7:00a, the old 9:00a time was not erased. The next hands-on exercise shows you how to move an appointment and delete the old one at the same time.

```
September     03:45:09 PM    1988 Friday         23.September 1988
Wk  Sun Mon Tue Wed Thu Fri Sat    7:00a
36                   1   2   3      :15
37   4   5   6   7   8   9  10      :30
38  11  12  13  14  15  16  17      :45
39  18  19  20  21  22  23  24    8:00a
40  25  26  27  28  29  30          :15
41                                  :30
                                    :45
 To Do List      [Inserting]      9:00a
                                    :15
 _____________________________      :30
                                    :45
                                  10:00a
                                    :15
                                    :30
                                    :45
                                  11:00a
                                    :15
                                    :30
                                       <edit_keys> <menu> <search> <print>
                                  <change> change windows, <desk> Business Cards
                                  <select> mark appointments, <tab> change color
```

FIGURE 4-12

```
October       07:34:31 PM    1988 Sunday         2.October 1988
Wk  Sun Mon Tue Wed Thu Fri Sat    7:00a
40                           1      :15
41   2   3   4   5   6   7   8      :30
42   9  10  11  12  13  14  15      :45
43  16  17  18  19  20  21  22    8:00a
44  23  24  25  26  27  28  29      :15
45  30  31                          :30
                                    :45
 To Do List      [Inserting]      9:00a staff meeting
           +-----------------------------------------------------+
 _________ |                    New Appointment                  |
           | Date 10- 2-1988                                     |
           | Time 09:00 AM                                       |
           | Note                                                |
           |       <search> on Date lets you use the calendar    |
           |    Note: Multiple entries per timeslot are allowed  |
           +-----------------------------------------------------+
                                    :15
                                    :30
                                       <edit_keys> <menu> <search> <print>
                                  <change> change windows, <desk> Business Cards
                                  <select> mark appointments, <tab> change color
```

FIGURE 4-13

Hands On

1. Use <arrows> to position the cursor back on 9:00a. Now let's change this meeting time to 10:00 AM.

2. Press <cut> **Alt-F5**.
3. Use <arrows> to move to 10:00a.
4. Press <paste> **F7**. This enters the cut appointment into the new time slot.

The Appointment menu contains commands to change the appointment window from a book format, (where all time increments appear), to a compressed format where only the time increments that have entries appear.

From the Appointment menu you can search through the appointment book, delete an appointment or a whole day's schedule. When scheduling appointments you can copy names from a business card file to the Appointment window. You can also create or load different Appointment windows so that more than one person can schedule their time. The next hands-on exercise looks at the commands in the Appointment menu.

Hands On

1. Press <menu> **F2** to display the Appointment menu (Figure 4-14).
2. Select "Change_Format." This changes to the compressed format and only those times where actual appointments are scheduled appear.
3. Press <menu> and select "Change_Format" again to return to the book format.

The <search> F4 key jumps to any date and time in the Appointment Scheduler. You can jump ahead to the appropriate date and time to enter a new appointment or locate an existing appointment. Now practice searching for an existing appointment.

```
September     05:24:42 PM    1988 | Friday          23.September 1988
Wk   Sun Mon Tue Wed Thu Fri  Sat |  7:00a
36                    1   2    3  |  7:00a new staff meeting
37    4   5   6   7   8   9   10  |    :15  ~~~
38   11  12  13  14  15  16   17  |    :30  ~~~
39   18  19  20  21  22  23   24  |    :45  ~~~
40   25  26  27  28  29  30   \   |  8:00a
41                                |    :15
                                  |    :30
 To Do List      [Inserting]      |    :45
      ____________________________________________________________
 ——  |                    Appointment Menu                        |
     |                                                            |
     | Batch_Delete  Change_Format  Search_Notes  Owner  Print    |
     |                                                            |
     |              <left> <right> <do> <undo>                    |
     |____________________________________________________________|
                                  |    :45
                                  | 11:00a
                                  |    :15
                                  |      <edit_keys> <menu> <search> <print>
                                  | <change> change windows, <desk> Business Cards
                                  | <select> mark appointments, <tab> change color
```

FIGURE 4-14

Hands On

1. Press <search> **F4** to access the Search by date and time window.
2. Type tomorrow's date and press <ret> **Return**.
3. Type [1000A] and press <do> **F10**. Notice that the appointment book is set for the next day's date. You can enter appointments in advance or view activities already scheduled for that day. The search function finds an appointment if you know the name of the meeting or person to meet but you can't remember the time or day.
4. Press <menu> **F2**.
5. Select "Search_Notes" from the menu. This displays a list of appointment notes.
6. Highlight "staff meeting" using <arrows> if it is not already highlighted and press <do>. This displays the appointment window and highlights the appointment. Now delete appointments by time and day.
7. Press <line_del> **Ctrl-Back Space** to erase the 10:00 appointment.

Delete a day or more at a time with the "Batch_Delete" command, shown in the following hands-on exercise.

Hands On

1. Press <menu> **F2**.
2. Select "Batch_Delete" to access the Batch Delete window. The first date and the last date to be included in the delete are entered.
3. Type the date shown at the top of the appointment window as both the first and the last date. This deletes the entire day's appointments. For example, if the date shown is 15.June 1988, type [06151988] for both entries.
4. Press <do> **F10** and all appointments between those dates are deleted.

More than one person can use the Appointment window. The "Owner" command is used to load an existing file or create a new appointment file for another person.

Hands On

1. Press <menu> **F2**.
2. Select "Owner." The Owner window appears (Figure 4-15). (If you were to continue in this window, you could (a) enter an existing file name and press <do> **F10** to load an existing appointment file, (b) enter a new filename and press <do> to create a new one, or (c) press <undo> **Esc** to return to the appointment window.)
3. Press <undo> to return to the Appointment window.

```
September     10:00:10 PM    1988 Friday         23.September 1988
Wk  Sun Mon Tue Wed Thu Fri Sat     :45
36                    1   2   3   8:00a
37   4   5   6   7    8   9  10     :15
38  11  12  13  14   15  16  17     :30
39  18  19  20  21   22  23  24     :45
40  25  26  27  28   29  30       9:00a
41                                  :15
                                    :30
 To Do List      [Inserting]        :45

 ———————      Owner - (Load a different Appointment File)

           New Appointment File :APPTSPI.DF

             This will create a new file or load an existing one.
               <search> shows the existing files.  You may only
           load files that were created by the appointment module.
                  <undo> returns you to the current file.

                                      <edit_keys> <menu> <search> <print>
                                 <change> change windows, <desk> Business Cards
                                 <select> mark appointments, <tab> change color
```

FIGURE 4-15

Data from a Business Card can be pasted directly into the Appointment window. The following hands-on exercise gives a demonstration.

Hands On

1. Press <desk> **F8**. This displays the Desk Accessories "Business_Cards." You can insert the name from a business card into the Appointment window.
2. Use the <arrows> to highlight "SMITH."
3. Press <paste> **F7** to remove the Business Card.
4. Use the <arrows> to position the cursor at the appropriate time interval for the appointment, in this case, 8:00a.
5. Press <paste> again to enter the name into the selected interval.

Along with the calendar, clock, and appointment window, this window also contains a "To Do List." This feature is an electronic scratch pad for making notes to yourself.

The "To Do List" is a text file that is automatically saved using the same filename as the appointments file. This text file can be used by the Word Processor or the Note_Pad. The next hands-on exercise inserts text into the "To Do List."

Hands On

1. Press <change> **F6** to enter the "To Do List" window. You can enter any text into the "To Do List."
2. Type [pull resume for John Q. Smith].
3. Press <change> again to return to the Appointment window.

The note stays in the "To Do List" providing a reminder until you erase it.

Any one of the features--calendar, appointments, or "To Do List"--may be output to a text file or to a device such as a printer. Table 4-3 lists the choices in the Output Options window.

TABLE 4-3 Output Options

Option	*Description*
Book_Format	Prints in the book format.
Compressed	Prints only the appointments and no empty time slots.
Calendar	Prints specified months.
To Do List	Prints the To Do List.

If the "To Do List" is selected, the Output Device Selection window would appear. You would then need to select the appropriate printer and press <do> F10. When any of the other options are selected, a window appears in which you specify the date or month for inclusion in the print. The following hands-on exercise shows how to select the Output Options window.

Hands On

1. Press <menu> **F2** to access the Appointment menu.
2. Select "Print." This displays the Output Options window (Figure 4-16).
3. Select "Compressed" to display the Compressed Output window.
4. Press <do> **F10** to accept the date entries and display the Output Device Selection window.
5. Select "Console" or the appropriate printer to print John Smith's appointment.
6. Press <do> to return to the Appointment window.
7. Press <undo> **Esc** to return to the Options menu.

```
September     10:06:14 PM    1988 Friday          23.September 1988
Wk  Sun Mon Tue Wed Thu Fri Sat     :45
36                   1   2   3    8:00a Mr. John Q. Smith Jr.
37   4   5   6   7   8   9  10     :15
38  11  12  13  14  15  16  17     :30
39  18  19  20  21  22  23  24     :45
40  25  26  27  28  29  30        9:00a
41                                  :15
                                    :30
 To Do List      [Inserting]        :45
pull resum
                              Output Options

           Book_Format  Compressed  Calendar  TO_DO_LIST

                       <left> <right> <do> <undo>

                                    :45
                                 12:00p
                                    :15
                                       <edit_keys> <menu> <search> <print>
                                 <change> change windows, <desk> Business Cards
                                 <select> mark appointments, <tab> change color
```

FIGURE 4-16

Note Pad

The Note Pad is a text editor that can be used to write memos or small reports. It can be accessed and used from any module. In "Note_Pad," you can edit, delete, copy, move, format, search, and replace the text material, as well as save and print a file.

In the following hands-on exercise, the text entries have been kept short so you can concentrate on the commands and the procedures for using them to create a new file, enter data, and save it. You will then reload the file back onto the screen.

Hands On

1. Press <desk> **F8** and select "Note_Pad" from the Desk Accessories menu. This displays the Note Pad window (Figure 4-17). You can enter text at this point, but instead look at the Note Pad Menu first to examine the commands New, Save, and Load.
2. Press <menu> **F2**. The Note Pad menu appears (Figure 4-18).
3. Select "New." This saves the current file and clears the edit window buffer so that you can start entering text into a new file.
4. Type the paragraph below just as you see it. Press <ret> **Return** after each line has been typed.

   [The Note Pad can be used to write memos or small reports. It
   can be accessed and used from any module. In "Note_Pad", you
   can edit, delete, copy, move, format, search, and replace the
   text material, as well as save and print a file.]

```
[-- New File --]                    Note Pad                    [Inserting ]
______________________________________________________________________________

      <menu> gets submenu, <format><search><change><print><edit_keys>
```

FIGURE 4-17

```
[-- New File --]                    Note Pad                    [Inserting ]
______________________________________________________________________________

                               Note Pad Menu

             New        Load       Save        Write     Merge
             Delete     Indent     Format      Quit

             <search><change><print><arrows><do><undo>

      <menu> gets submenu, <format><search><change><print><edit_keys>
```

FIGURE 4-18

5. Press <menu>.
6. Select "Save." This displays the Save File window.
7. Type [NOTE] as the filename and press <do> **F10** to accept. This saves the file and returns to the Note Pad window where you can enter more text. Now load a file.
8. Press <menu>.

9. Select "New" to clear the screen.
10. Press <menu>.
11. Select "Load," which displays the Load Existing File window.
12. Type [NOTE] as the filename to be loaded.
13. Press <do> to accept and reenter the file into "Note_Pad."

To use the Note_Pad features of copying, moving, indenting, and formatting, begin by first selecting an area of text. You can also copy a selected area of text created in the Note Pad to another .TXT file and bring a file into "Note_Pad." You will practice all these features in the hands-on exercises that follow.

Hands On

1. Use the <arrows> to position the cursor on the "T" in "The" in the first line of the paragraph if it is not already there.
2. Press <select> **F9** to begin selecting lines of text.
3. Press the down <arrow> three times to move to the last line of the paragraph to select the entire paragraph.
4. Press <select> again to end the selection of lines. If you make a mistake, press <deselect> **Alt-F9** to undo the selection.
5. Press <copy> **F5** to copy the selected area into the edit buffer.
6. Press the down <arrow> three times.
7. Press <paste> **F7** to enter the copied text at this point. This makes a new copy of the text but does not erase the old text. Let's copy the text but this time erase the old text.
8. Use <arrows> to move the cursor to the beginning of the original paragraph. Note that the area is still selected.
9. Press <cut> **Alt-F5**. This removes the text from the window but keeps it in a buffer waiting for you to indicate where you want it moved.
10. Press the down <arrow> ten times.
11. Press <paste> to enter the text at this point.

Now format the paragraph by setting the amount of space you would like to indent the entire paragraph from the left margin.

Hands On

1. Press <menu> **F2** to access the Note Pad menu.
2. Select "Indent."
3. Press <do> **F10** in answer to the prompt "Indent Entire Buffer?". This displays the Indent Selected Area window (Figure 4-19) at the bottom of the screen.
4. Press the right <arrow> five times. This indents each of the selected lines five spaces.
5. Press <do> to accept the changes.

```
                           Note Pad                         [Indenting ]

The Note Pad can be used to write memos or small reports.  It
can be accessed and used from any module.  In "Note_Pad", you
can edit, delete, copy, move, format, search, and replace the
text material, as well as save and print a file.



The Note Pad can be used to write memos or small reports.  It
can be accessed and used from any module.  In "Note_Pad", you
can edit, delete, copy, move, format, search, and replace the
text material, as well as save and print a file.

 ____________________________________________________________________



                     Indent Selected Area
 Use <left><right><tab><jump_left> to adjust, <undo> reverts, <do> accepts
```

FIGURE 4-19

The next hands-on exercise with Note_Pad gives you practice with basic text editing, such as correcting a typographical error. But first, delete the second paragraph. The Note Pad is in the Inserting mode, as indicated at the top right of the screen. As new text is entered in the Inserting mode, it pushes existing text to the right. There is also an Exchanging mode; as new text is entered in this mode, it replaces, or exchanges, the existing text.

Hands On

1. Use <arrows> to position the cursor to the "T" in "The" of the second paragraph.
2. Press <line_del> **Ctrl-Back Space** and the entire first line is deleted.
3. Repeat step 2 three more times.
4. Type [Thiss execise was performed bye <u>yourname</u>.] exactly as is, including the mistakes. Remember to type your own name in place of <u>yourname</u>. There are different ways in which you may edit text.
5. Use <arrows> to position the cursor to the right of the second "s" in "Thiss."
6. Press <backspace> **Back Space**. This removes the character to the immediate left of the cursor.
7. Use <arrows> to position the cursor on the "e" in "bye."
8. Press <del> **Del** and the character under the cursor is deleted.
9. Use <arrows> to move the cursor to the "c" in "execise." You will insert the letter "r."
10. Type [r]. Notice how the letter is inserted, pushing the letters in front to the right. This is the called the Inserting mode.
11. Use <arrows> to place the cursor on the "p" in "performed".
12. Press <ins> **Ins** and the Edit window changes to an Exchanging mode from the Inserting mode. This status is displayed in the upper right corner of the window.

13. Type [completed]. As new text is entered in the Exchanging mode, it replaces, or exchanges, the existing text.
14. Press <ins> again to switch back to the Inserting mode. The <ins> key toggles between the two modes.

In Note_Pad, you can format the area selected by setting the left margin, right margin, and paragraph indentations. The following hands-on exercise sets these three format settings.

Hands On

1. Use the <arrows> to position the cursor on the "T" in "The" in the top first paragraph.
2. Press <select> **F9** to begin selecting lines of text.
3. Press the down <arrow> three times to select the paragraph.
4. Press <select> again to end the selection of lines. If you make a mistake, press <deselect> **Alt-F9** to undo the selection.
5. Press <menu> **F2** to display the Note Pad menu.
6. Select "Format." This displays the Format Selected Area window (Figure 4-20) so that you can format the area selected. Each selected area is treated as a separate paragraph.
7. Type [5] for the "Left" margin and press <ret> **Return**.
8. Type [66] for the number of spaces to the right of the left margin and press <ret>.
9. Type [10] to indent the first line of a paragraph from the left side of the screen and press <ret>.

```
 [C:NOTE.TXT]                          Note Pad                       [Inserting ]

The Note Pad can be used to write memos or small reports.  It
can be a
can edit                      Format Selected Area
text mat
                 Left:   0
                Right:  78
            Paragraph:   5

This exe                       <do><undo><arrows>


      <menu> gets submenu, <format><search><change><print><edit_keys>
```

FIGURE 4-20

10. Press <do> **F10** to accept the formatting changes. Any blank lines in the area would be deleted.

You can copy text to another file and insert another text file into the current one. To illustrate this, you will place the sentence with yourname into a file under another name, and then enter it back into the NOTE file by retrieving it under that name. Do the following hands-on exercise.

Hands On

1. Use the <arrows> and move to the "T" in "This" of the sentence containing yourname.
2. Press <select> **F9** to begin selecting lines of text.
3. Press <select> again to end the selection of lines. If you make a mistake, you press <deselect> **Alt-F9** to undo the selection.
4. Press <menu> **F2** to access the Note Pad menu.
5. Select "Write" from the menu. This displays the Write Selected Area to a File window so you can copy the selected text into another file.
6. Type [WRITE] as the file name.
7. Press <do> **F10** to enter the text to the new file. You can also enter text from another file to the Note Pad.
8. Use the <arrows> and move to the very first line on the screen.
9. Press <menu>.
10. Select "Merge" to display the Merge (Inserting an Existing File) window.
11. Type [WRITE] as the file to be input.
12. Press <do>. This inserts the text from the WRITE file to the NOTE file at the cursor position.

You can also perform search and replace operations within Note_Pad. Both search and replace start from the cursor position; so in order to search or replace text in the entire document, position the cursor at the beginning of the document. The following hands-on exercise searches for a fragment pattern and a word pattern. A fragment search locates any occurrence of the pattern, whether it is a complete word, phrase, or part of a word. A word search finds the pattern only if it exists as a complete word or phrase. For example, if you selected "Fragment" and the search pattern is "act," it will find the pattern in the word "act" and in the word "action". If you select "Word," the pattern "act" would be found only in the word "act."

Hands On

1. Press <search> **F4**. This displays the Search window (Figure 4-21).
2. Type [mo] as a simple pattern to search for and press <ret> **Return**. Words or phrases can be entered as the pattern.
3. Press <ret> to select "Fragment" to search for all occurrences of words that contain the pattern "mo."

```
 [C:NOTE.TXT]                      Note Pad                     [Inserting ]
This exercise was completed by Donna.


     rep ┌──────────────────────────────────────────────────────┐
     "No │                        Search                        │
     sea │  Pattern:                                            │
     pri │     Type:  Fragment  Word                            │
         │                                                      │
         │                   <do><undo><arrows>                 │
         └──────────────────────────────────────────────────────┘

This exercise was completed by Donna.
 ____________________________________________________________________________




      <menu> gets submenu, <format><search><change><print><edit_keys>
```

FIGURE 4-21

4. Press <do> **F10** to start the search. The cursor will flash after the first occurrence of the pattern.
5. Press <search>; then press <do> again to position the cursor after the next occurrence of the pattern.
6. Press <search>; then press <do> again to position the cursor after the next occurrence of the pattern.
7. Press <search>; then press <do> again. When the pattern is not found, a message "Pattern Not Found. Press <do>" will flash in the Search window.
8. Press <do>; then press <undo> **Esc** to exit the Search window.
9. Use <arrows> to position the cursor at the top left corner of the screen. (Press <home> **Home** to move quickly to the top line of the current screen.)
10. Press <search> to display the Search window.
11. Type [move] as the pattern to search for and press <ret>.
12. Press <change> **F6** to select "Word."
13. Press <do> to accept the change and begin searching. The cursor flashes after the occurrence of the word "move."
14. Press <search> and then <do> to enter the Search window and find that there is no other occurrence of the word.
15. Press <do>, then <undo> to exit the Search window.
16. Use the <arrows> to position the cursor at the beginning of the document.
17. Press <change> to access the Change window (Figure 4-22). From the Change window, you can replace present text with new text. The Type choices--"Fragments" and "Word"--work the same as in the Search window.
18. Type [can] and press <ret>.
19. Type [may] and press <ret>.
20. Press <ret> to select "Word."
21. Press <ret> to select the count as 1. This is the number of times to search and replace.

```
                                   Note Pad                        [Replacing ]
This exercise was completed by Donna.


     rep                         Change
     "No
     sea       Pattern: move
     pri  Replace with: move
                  Type:  Fragment  Word
                 Count:     1
               Replace:  Count  All
                Verify:  Yes  No
This exe
                        <do><undo><arrows>





      <menu> gets submenu, <format><search><change><print><edit_keys>
```

FIGURE 4-22

22. Press <change> to highlight "All" and press <ret>. The search and replace occurs throughout the entire file. Selecting "All" supersedes the count number selected above.
23. Highlight "Yes" using <arrows> to verify the replacing of text. (If you select "No," all instances of the pattern are automatically changed without prompting a verification.)
24. Press <do> to start the search and replace. Notice at the bottom of the screen that you are asked to verify the change. This happens at each occurrence because you selected "Yes." You have the option of pressing <do> to replace the text or <search> to skip over to the next pattern found.
25. Press <do> to replace the text.
26. Press <do> twice more to complete the search and replace.

As with most files, you can print the text to an output device. You can also save the file with the Quit command. The following hands-on exercise prints the file and "quits" the Note Pad.

Hands On

1. Press <print> **F3** to access the Output Device Selection menu. You can print the entire file, or you can print only selected parts of the file if you select an area before pressing <print>.
2. Use <arrows> to select the output device (select "Console" if you do not have a printer); press <do> to print. The contents of the file are printed. If you selected "Console," press <do> in response to the prompts at the bottom of the display screen.
3. Press <menu> **F2** to access the Note Pad menu.

```
 [C:NOTE.TXT]                      Note Pad                      [Inserting ]
This exe
        The current file has changed.  What do you want to do?

                     Save  Cancel  Abandon_Changes
     rep
     "No       "Save" prompts to save the file and continues.
     sea       "Cancel" or <undo> cancels the command.
     pri       "Abandon_Changes" discards changes and continues.


This exercise was completed by Donna.
 ____________________________________________________________________________




       <menu> gets submenu, <format><search><change><print><edit_keys>
```

FIGURE 4-23

4. Select "Quit." The Quit window appears (Figure 4-23). (You can choose to "Save" the file, "Cancel" the Quit command and return to the previous screen where the cursor was, or "Abandon_Changes," which totally disregards any changes made and returns you to the location before accessing Desk Accessories.)
5. Select "Save." The Save File window appears. The current filename is automatically inserted. Since this is the correct name, we proceed to the next step.
6. Press <do> **F10** to save the file and exit Desk Accessories.

Command Summary

Following is a brief summary of the commands in the major menus of the Desk Accessories module.

Desk Accessories Menu

Calculator	Performs full functions, including statistics and scientific calculator, with ten memories.
Time	Changes the time in the desk accessories and updates the system time of the computer.
Alarm	Gives audible alarm; a clock that displays a message.
Date	Changes the date in the desk accessories and updates the system date of the computer.
Value_Converter	Helps construct a table from which you may perform various conversions of measurements, currency, etc.
Stop_Watch	Operates as conventional stopwatch with split times.
Appointments	Serves as electronic appointment book with days blocked in time increments you set.

Business_Cards	Creates electronic card file for names, addresses, phone numbers, etc.
Note_Pad	Permits the creation of note files, includes a text editor.
Appointment Menu	
Batch_Delete	Allows deletion of multiple appointments or days.
Change_Format	Toggles between book and compressed format for Appointments window.
Search_Notes	Allows a search of appointment notes without time or date.
Owner	Allows multiple users of Appointments.
Print	Used to output to various options.
Output Options (appointments) Menu	
Book_Format	Prints the appointment book, all time periods are printed.
Compressed	Prints the appointment book, only actual appointment periods are printed.
Calendar	Prints calendar of specified months.
TO_DO_LIST	Prints any entries in the To Do List.
Output Options (business cards) Menu	
Print	Offers selection of print devices from Output Device Selection menu.
MailMerge	Outputs business card file to .DIF to allow inclusion in a mail merge.
Note Pad Menu	
New	Saves the current file and clears the Edit window buffer.
Load	Saves the current file and loads a file into the Edit window.
Save	Saves the file by writing it to disk.
Write	Copies an area of the current file to another file.
Merge	Copies existing text file into the Edit window buffer at cursor.
Delete	Deletes a selected area from the Edit window.
Indent	Allows insertion or deletion of spaces for the left margin in a selected area.
Format	Allows specification of paragraph parameters and reformats a selected area.
Quit	Accesses Quit window.
Quit Window	
Save	Enters filename and saves file.
Cancel	Aborts the Quit command and returns to previous position.
Abandon_Changes	Returns to point of entry to Desk Accessories and disregards any changes made to the file.
Conversion Window Menu	
Load	Enters a DIF file.
Save	Saves the current values to a DIF file.
Zero_Total	Sets the Total line to a value of 0.
Clear	Clears the current conversion window.

Study Questions

1. How is the Desk Accessories module accessed? Can it be accessed from within another module?
2. List and briefly describe the nine features of the Desk Accessories module.
3. Describe the three windows of the calculator function.
4. Describe the three columns in the Value Converter window.
5. Describe the purpose of the attribute fields in a Business Card.

6. How can the appointment time periods in the Appointments Scheduler be changed?
7. What is the difference between book and compressed formats in Appointments?
8. Describe the purpose of the Owner command in the Appointment menu.
9. When performing a search in Note Pad, what is the difference in searching for a fragment as compared to searching for a word?
10. When editing in Note Pad, you may be in the Inserting or Exchanging mode. What is the difference between the two modes?
11. Access the stopwatch feature of Desk Accessories and start the time running. Freeze the stopwatch at a split time of between 15 seconds and 30 seconds. Start the stopwatch running again. Stop the stopwatch and reset the value to zero.
12. Use the Calculator to perform the following mathematical calculations. What are the results of these calculations?
    (a) 2*5+6
    (b) calculate the square root (Root) of 256
13. Set the Alarm to go off one minute from the current time and display the message "Time to get up!".
14. Create a new business card using the following data.

Name	Dr. John W. Post Jr.
Company	St. Mary's Hospital
Attribute	Dr. Post
Home Phone	(555) 555-4567
Business Phone	(555) 555-8894
Address	1353 Broadway
(cont.)	Miami, FL 33333

    Remember to press <do> F10 to add the card to the file after entering the above data. Now print the business card file to the CONSOLE to verify the addition of the new business card.
15. Schedule an appointment for noon one week from this Friday. Block off two hours of time and insert Dr. Post's name from the Business Card file. Use the compressed output option to print the appointments to the CONSOLE.
16. Change the appointment in Exercise 15 to 1:30 that same day. Print the appointments to the CONSOLE in compressed output format.
17. Enter the following meeting notes in the Note Pad:

    1. Approved minutes
    2. All present
    3. Proceeded with Dr. Jones--guest speaker
    4. Adjourned for lunch
    5. Resumed speech by Dr. Jones
    6. Motion to adjourn
    7. Meeting adjourned at 1:50

    Save the file using the name MEETING.
18. Reload the file MEETING from Exercise 17 if it is not currently on your display screen. Change the name of the doctor from Jones to Smith using the Change window method to search and replace. Print the corrected version of the meeting notes to the CONSOLE.

19. Use the Calculator to perform the following mathematical calculations. What are the results of these calculations?

(a) 2*3 - 10/5
(b) calculate the common log (Log) of 100.

20. Use the Value Converter command to create the following two tables in the Conversion window. Label the first table Table 1. It converts yards to feet (1 yard = 3 feet), to inches (1 yard = 36 inches), and to centimeters (1 yard = 91.44 centimeters). Label the second table Table 2. It converts miles to feet (1 mile = 5280 feet), to yards (1 mile = 1760 yards), and to meters (1 mile = 1609 meters). Now change the Quantity value for yards in Table 1 to 25 and the Quantity value for miles in Table 2 to 25. Print the final Conversion Table to the CONSOLE. What are the quantities?

Chapter 5

Word Processor

Introduction

This chapter will demonstrate Open Access II Publisher's Version Word Processor module. A word processor is a program that simplifies the process of writing and editing documents.

Remember to use <help> F1 any time you need a Help window. The function keys available at that point are shown as well as other valuable information. Table 5-1 lists the keys that are used in this program that are not used with every Open Access module. As with the other modules, all the position and move keys are available.

TABLE 5-1 Word Processor Function Keys

Name	*Key*	*Function*
<sent_fwd>	F7	Moves the cursor one sentence forward.
<sent_back>	Alt-F7	Moves the cursor one sentence backward.
<word_fwd>	Ctrl -->	Moves the cursor one word forward.
<word_back>	Ctrl <--	Moves the cursor one word backward.
<para_fwd>	F5	Moves the cursor one paragraph forward.
<para_back>	Alt-F5	Moves the cursor one paragraph backward.
<jump_right>	Ctrl-End	Moves the cursor to the end of the line.
<jump_left>	Ctrl-Home	Moves the cursor to the start of a line.
<home>	Home	Moves the cursor to top of the screen.
<home> <home>	Home-Home	Moves the cursor to the top of the file.
<end>	End	Moves the cursor to bottom of the screen.
<end> <end>	End-End	Moves the cursor to bottom of the file.
<tab>	Tab	Moves the cursor one tab stop forward.
<back_tab>	Shift-Tab	Moves the cursor one tab stop back.
<format>	Alt-F6	Accesses the Format menu.

Also remember that <undo> Esc can be used if you select an incorrect menu or command. It returns you to the previous menu or command from which you can start again.

Four permanent files have been created on the data diskette for you to use in the hands-on exercises in this chapter. They are

1. A short letter. There are hands-on exercises for you to practice editing text, styling text, reformatting paragraphs, saving a file, and printing a file.
2. Two pages of minutes of a meeting. You will learn to center text, move or delete blocks of text, and search and replace.
3. A mail-merge letter.
4. Addresses for the mail-merge letter. Hands-on exercises demonstrate setting up a letter that can be addressed to several people.

Selecting the Word Processor Module

Select the Word Processor module the same way you select any of the other programs from OA. The Word Processor is accessed from the Options menu as described in Chapter 2, "Getting Started on Open Access II Publisher's Version."

Hands On

1. When the Options menu appears on the screen, use the <arrows> to highlight your selection, "Word_Processor."
2. Press <do> **F10**. The File Selection menu now appears on the screen (Figure 5-1).

```
              Open Access II Limited Version Word_Processor
   (c) Copyright 1984,1985,1986,1987 Software Products International, Inc.
                          All rights reserved

                 Word Processor  -  File Selection Menu
        Read_Old  Create_New  Form_Change  Type_Change  Options

Default Form File: DEFAULT.DOC               File Type Mode: Document
                   <arrows>  <do>  <undo>  <change>
```

FIGURE 5-1

Optional method to select Word_Processor: Enter [w] when the Options menu appears. Do not press <do>.

Selecting an Existing File

First, look at a file that already exists. With the File Selection menu on the screen, you are ready to select, or retrieve, an existing document from those that have been created and stored on the data disk.

In this case, the document to be selected is a letter that you can change and print. Use the following hands-on exercise to select the file.

Hands On

1. Select "Read_Old" from the File Selection menu. A blinking cursor and a space is provided to type the name of the file you want to read or edit.
2. Type [LETTER] on the blank line--the name of the document when it was created. You may type lowercase letters; the program automatically displays them as uppercase letters.
3. Press <do> **F10**. The LETTER file is now displayed on the screen. If you incorrectly enter the name of a file already stored, for example LETER, a PROBLEM message appears at the top of the screen explaining that that file cannot be found. Then press <do> **F10**. The cursor returns to the File Name line. Now correctly type the name of the file and press <do> again.

```
+-----+1L----P+--2-----+-----3--+--------4+--------+5------+--6-----+-----R--+
          Mr. Fred Mayer
          Science Magazine
          239 Third Avenue West
          Chicago, Illinois 33333

          Dear Mr. Mayer:

          On October 2, I subscribed to Science Magazine and
     maild you a check for $39.50 for a one-year subscriptioon.
     My bank tells me that the check has cleared my account.▪
     But it is now December 12, and the first issue has not yet
     arrived.

          Please look into this matter as soon as possible and
     informa me when I can expect the subscription to start. ▪I
     am looking forward to getting Science Magazine.

[A:LETTER.DOC]                     Insert                          98%
INSERT: All characters are entered into text at the cursor position.

        <del><menu><search><print><format><change><line_del><line_ins>
```

FIGURE 5-2

Figure 5-2 shows the contents of the LETTER file--a letter to *Science Magazine*--before any editing changes.

Word Processor Menus

Menus in the word processor are special windows that provide choices of options or commands. The main Options menu is displayed at the beginning of the program and others are accessed by various means. For example, the Command Selection menu is accessed by pressing the <menu> F2 key. Some menus are automatically displayed with commands by typing a letter or a number. Some menu entries lead to submenus.

The two main menus that you will use in this chapter are the File Selection menu and the Command Selection menu.

- *File Selection Menu.* From this menu the document, or file, that you want to work with is selected. The four selections are as follows:

Read_Old	Used to select an existing file.
Create_New	Used to create a new file.
Form_Change	Used to change the filename of the Default Form File, a file that can be used as a template when creating new files.
Type_Change	Used to change the type of a file. A .DOC file is the file type used to create the document using the word-processor formatting capabilities. A .TXT file is the basic DOS text file that the word processor uses to communicate with other programs when sending or receiving files.

Figure 5-1 shows the File Selection menu that appears at the bottom of the display screen.

- *Command Selection Menu.* When you are working in the Edit window (the main work area on the screen), you can access this menu. Table 5-2 contains a brief description of the commands you may choose from the Command Selection menu.

TABLE 5-2 Command Selection Menu Commands

Command	*Description*
Insert	Inserts text into the Edit window.
Exchange	Exchanges or retypes text during editing.
Copy	Copies parts of text from one place in the file to another.
Move	Moves a part of the file without copying.
Delete	Erases a part of the file.
Alter	Sets new style for a block of text.
Reform	Reformats each paragraph of the file as specified.
Set_Marks	Places a mark in the file to later facilitate cursor movement to that particular placemark.
Background	Allows paragraph formats to be viewed and changed or to enter abbreviations--a glossary function.
View_Breaks	Displays page breaks.
Format	Sets or changes paragraph parameters.
Print	Accesses the Print window.
Search	Searches for a marker or text pattern.
?Directory	Shows accessible word-processor files.
Update	Saves the current file and returns to the Edit window.
New_File	Saves the current file and returns to the File Selection menu.
Options	Returns to the main Options menu.

Figure 5-3 shows the Command Selection menu at the bottom of the screen. To see the Command Selection menu on the display screen, practice with the following hands-on exercise.

```
[A:LETTER.DOC]              Command Selection Menu                      98%
  Insert Exchange Copy Move Delete Alter Reform Write Set_Marks  Background
  View_Breaks  Format  Print  Search  ?Directory  Update  New_File  Options
       <move_keys> <do> <ins> <del> <format> <print> <search> <change>
```

FIGURE 5-3

Hands On

1. Press <menu> **F2**. This displays the Command Selection menu.
2. Press <undo> **Esc**. This removes the Command Selection menu and returns the display screen to the same place in the document LETTER where you accessed the menu.

Edit Window--Your Work Area

The Edit window is the work area on the display screen where you enter (type) and edit text. In the Edit window, you now see the top part of the text of the letter. The <arrow> or cursor-movement keys are used to scroll the text up or down to view the entire file. When a new letter or document is created, which you will do later, the window is empty.

Also on the screen above the work area is a ruler line that contains formatting information including left and right margins and tab settings. Below the work area is the status area--information about the system and the document.

The ruler line at the top of the window displays the following information:

- Left and right margins for the current paragraph
- Paragraph indent for the current paragraph
- Tab stops
- Marks showing column numbers

The bottom of the screen provides the following information:

- The mode the system is in; here it is "Insert"
- Commands that can be used with the current mode
- Column number where cursor is currently positioned
- Nickname (Volume/Pathway designator. This setting was defined using the Searching Order command in the Utilities module).
- Filename
- File type
- Percentage of file left to be filled

Also the area at the bottom of the screen displays prompts or questions from the program.

Figure 5-2 showed the Edit window in the Insert mode. The Edit window automatically remains in the Insert mode unless you change it. Notice the ruler line above and status area below the window.

In the Insert mode, text is entered without writing over existing text. In the Exchange mode, newly entered text writes over old text. The Insert mode is used, for example, to correct "ener" to "enter" by placing the cursor over the second "e" and pressing "t." In the Exchange mode "enfer" is changed to "enter" by placing the cursor over the "f" and pressing the "t" key.

Inserting Text

Some word-processing changes are needed before the LETTER letter is ready to print. First, let's insert new text. This can be done without destroying any existing text because the Edit window is in the Insert mode. It can be changed from the Command Selection menu. With the LETTER file still on the screen, the following hands-on exercise will demonstrate how to insert a paragraph in the middle of the letter.

Hands On

1. Use <arrows> to position the blinking cursor on the "P" in "Please."
2. Type [Your advertisement stated that it would be no more than five weeks for the first issue to arrive .]. Use lowercase and uppercase letters appropriately. Don't worry about your typing errors now. You can correct them later after you learn how.
3. Press <ret> **Return** twice. The new paragraph is inserted and the cursor should once again be on the "P" in "Please." Notice that a "hard space" (the solid box) was automatically inserted at the end of the sentence after typing the two spaces. This keeps the extra space from being removed if the text is reformatted. The symbol will not print.

In the next hands-on exercise, enter your name and address and the date at the top of the letter. The <home> Home key moves the cursor to the beginning of the letter. The <tab> Tab key places the cursor for the return address.

Hands On

1. Press <home> **Home** to move the cursor to the line above the inside address of the letter. It is a blank line.
2. Press <tab> **Tab** four times to move the cursor in position to type your name.
3. Type [your name] (using no more than thirty characters) and press <ret> **Return**. Because the default setting for the word processor specifies the "Autoindent" option as "on," the left margin moved when you pressed <tab>. So when you press <ret>, the cursor returns right under the first letter in your name. Autoindent is one of several ways you may format, or set defaults for the structure of the paragraph. This will be covered in more detail in the section on Reformatting Paragraphs.
4. Type [your street address] and press <ret>.
5. Type [your city, state, zip code] and press <ret> twice. Again, use no more than thirty characters.
6. Type [December 12, 1987] and press <ret> twice. Your name, address, date, and a blank are entered above the inside address.

The letter needs a closing and a signature at the bottom. The <end> End command jumps to the bottom of the letter. With the following hands-on exercise, insert the closing.

Hands On

1. Press <end> **End** twice to place the cursor at the end of the last paragraph of the letter.

2. Press <ret> **Return** two times and <tab> **Tab** four times to move the cursor to column 41.
3. Type [Sincerely,].
4. Press <ret> four times. This leaves enough space for your signature.
5. Type [your´name].
6. Press <ret>.

Editing Text

This section demonstrates some editing techniques that change text that has already been entered. Using the same letter, practice making changes and corrections in the next exercises by entering and deleting characters.

Inserting Characters

A letter or character can be inserted by placing the cursor on the spot you want to make the insertion. The letter under the cursor will not be deleted; it will simply be moved to the right. This occurs because the OA program remains in the Insert mode unless you change it.

Now, correct the spelling of "maild" with the following hands-on exercise.

Hands On

1. Move the cursor to the "m" in "maild" in the first paragraph.
2. Use <arrows> to place the cursor on the "d" in "maild."
3. Type [e] to correct the spelling. When the letter "e" is inserted, all the characters to the right of the cursor move one space to the right making room for the added letter.

Deleting Characters

Notice that there is an extra "o" in "subscriptioon." Characters can be removed one at a time using the <del> Del key. When a character is deleted, all text to the right moves left to fill in the space created by the deletion. Practice deleting a character now.

Hands On

1. Press <jump_right> **Ctrl-End**. Option: You could have used <arrows>.
2. Use <arrows> to place the cursor on the second "o" in the word "subscriptioon."
3. Press <del> **Del**. The extra "o" is deleted and the letters to the right shift one space left.

Also, let's remove the unwanted "a" in "informa" with this hands-on exercise.

Hands On

1. Press <jump_left> **Ctrl-Home** and use <arrows) to place the cursor on the "a" in "informa" found in the last paragraph.
2. Press <del> **Del** to remove the "a."

Sometimes when an insertion or deletion is made, there will be extra space at the end of the line. The program adjusts this space when you move on to the next action or move the cursor to the line above or below the deletion.

Exchanging Characters

To exchange, or substitute, one character for another, the Edit window must be in the Exchange mode. With the LETTER file still on the screen, practice with the following hands-on exercise.

Hands On

1. Use <arrows> to place the cursor on the "g" in "getting" in the last line at the bottom of the letter.
2. Press <menu> **F2** and select "Exchange." Instead of inserting new letters, you will type over the old ones.
3. Type [read] right over the letters "gett," replacing "getting" with "reading."
4. Now go back and correct any typing errors that you made when you entered new text.

Styling Text

There are times when you might want certain words or phrases to print in italics, boldface, underlined, or in a combination of these styles. With the LETTER file still on the screen, you will alter text style after it has already been typed. In this hands-on exercise, underline the name of the magazine.

Hands On

1. Press <menu> **F2**. The Command Selection menu appears.
2. Select "Alter" to change the type style. The prompt "Move cursor to start of block and press <do>." appears.
3. Use <arrows> to place the cursor on the "S" in "Science" in the first paragraph.
4. Press <do> **F10**. The prompt "Move cursor to end of block and press <do> again." appears.
5. Use <arrows> to place the cursor on the space after the "e" in "Magazine." The text to be altered, or underlined, is now highlighted.
6. Press <do>. The prompt "Alter marked area to which Type Style?" appears (Figure 5-4).

```
+1L----P+--2-----+-----3--+---------4+--------+5--------+--6-----+-----R--+
mailed you a check for $39.50 for a one-year subscription.
My bank tells me that the check has cleared my account.▪
But it is now December 12, and the first issue has not yet
arrived.

     Your advertisement stated that it would be no more than
five weeks for the first issue to arrive.▪

     Please look into this matter as soon as possible and
inform me when I can expect the subscription to start. ▪I
am looking forward to reading Science Magazine.


     Sincerely,



     Donna Pulschen

[A:LETTER.DOC]                    Alter Type Styles                    97%
Alter marked area to which Type Style?:
   1-Normal   2-Bold   3-Underline   4-BU   5-Italics   6-BI   7-UI   8-BUI
```

FIGURE 5-4

7. Type [3] to underline the marked words, "Science "Magazine." The program then automatically returns to the Insert Mode showing Science Magazine underlined. (With a graphics monitor, this may show up as reversed video.)
8. Repeat steps 1 through 7 to underline the other occurrence of Science Magazine in the last paragraph.

Reformatting Paragraphs

This section shows how to reformat paragraphs, that is, to change the way they look. Format refers to margins and tabstops, wordwrap, automatic indention, and left, right, and center justification. Eight different paragraph type formats can be specified, stored, and recalled to be used later. Each type is given a different letter, A through H.

When the paragraph parameters (called the background) are set, they may be stored and used later. To store, you must specify a paragraph type by one letter, [A] through [H]. By selecting the Background command from the Command Selection menu, these parameters may be viewed in the Background window.

At the top of the Edit window notice the letters "L," "R," and "P." These indicate the left (L) and right (R) margins and the paragraph indentation (P). The tabs are indicated by vertical lines. You can change these parameters by selecting "Margins & Tabstops" from the Paragraph Format menu (Figure 5-5).

Wordwrap is shown as "on." This means that words wrap around automatically to the next line after text reaches the right margin. This option can be changed by selecting "Wordwrap" as "On" or "Off."

```
[A:LETTER.DOC]                    Paragraph Format                         97%
FORMAT:       Recall  Margins_&_Tabstops  Wordwrap  Autoindent  Justify  Store
                                             On         On        Left
                        <left> <right> <do> <menu>
```

FIGURE 5-5

Autoindent can be selected and set as "On" or "Off" depending whether or not you want the paragraph indentions to automatically occur. Here, autoindent is shown as "on." This selection caused the newly entered text to be automatically indented. A line indention occurs each time <ret> Return is pressed.

Justify lets you set the justification of the paragraph as "Left," "Right," "Both," or "Center."

Use the Format commands in the next hands-on exercise to set the paragraph parameters so you can reformat all the items except your address and the date in your letter to be blocked.

You should still have LETTER on your screen.

Hands On

1. Use <arrows> to position the cursor on "M" in "Mr." in the inside address.
2. Press <menu> **F2** to access the Command Selection menu.
3. Select "Format." (Option: Press <format> **Alt-F6**). The Paragraph Format menu appears (Figure 5-5).
4. Select "Margins_&_Tabstops." The cursor moves to the Ruler Line at the top of the screen.
5. Press right <arrow> until the cursor is on column 11. The column location of the cursor is indicated in the lower left portion of the screen.
6. Press [l] (lowercase "L") and then [p] to specify that you want both the left margin of the letter and the paragraph indention to be at column 11. Notice that the line beginning with "Mr." has now moved to the left margin.
7. Press <do> **F10**. The Paragraph Format menu reappears.
8. Select "Store." The prompt "Store as paragraph type:" appears (Figure 5-6).
9. Type [a] to store this margin and paragraph indention setting. You could have specified any letter A through H.

The paragraph format is stored and can be viewed using the Background command. You can also edit these parameters from the Background window (Figure 5-7).

The following hands-on exercise shows you the Background window.

Hands On

1. Press <menu> **F2** to access the Command Selection menu.
2. Select "Background." The Background window appears.
3. Press <undo> **Esc** to return to the letter.

```
+--------+1L------+--2------+------3--+---------4+---------+5-------+---6-----+-----R--+----
                                                  Donna Pulschen
                                                  12345 Main Street
                                                  Downtown, KS▪ 55555

                                                  December 12, 1987


          Mr. Fred Mayer
               Science Magazine
               239 Third Avenue West
               Chicago, Illinois 333333

               Dear Mr. Mayer:

               On October 2, I subscribed to Science Magazine and
          mailed you a check for $39.50 for a one-year subscription.
          My bank tells me that the check has cleared my account.▪
          But it is now December 12, and the first issue has not yet
          arrived.

[A:LETTER.DOC]                  Paragraph Format                          97%
STORE FORMAT:
Store as paragraph type:
                                [A]..[H] <undo>
```

FIGURE 5-6

```
+--------+1L------+--2------+------3--+---------4+---------+5-------+---6-----+-----R--+----
       Left_Margin  Par_Indent  Right_Margin  Word-wrap  Auto-indent  Justify
A        11             11          70          On          On         Left
B            11         16          70          On          On         Left
C            11         16          70          On          On         Left
D            11         16          70          On          On         Left
E            11         16          70          On          On         Left
F            11         16          70          On          On         Left
G            11         16          70          On          On         Left
H            11         16          70          On          On         Left

 Abbreviations:  Short text           Full text

          1

[A:LETTER.DOC]                      Background                            97%
BACKGROUND:   Type new setting, or press <change> to switch on/off.
            Paragraph types
                       <arrows> <change> <help> <menu>
```

FIGURE 5-7

Notice that the bottom portion of the Background window contains the heading "Abbreviations:." This is a glossary function in which up to ten short texts may be entered in the left column. Their corresponding long texts are entered on the right. When one of the short texts is typed in Insert mode as a whole word (separated from other words by space or punctuation), the long text will automatically be substituted.

Donna Pulschen
12345 Main Street
Downtown, KS 55555

December 12, 1987

Mr. Fred Mayer
Science Magazine
239 Third Avenue West
Chicago, Illinois 33333

Dear Mr. Mayer:

On October 2, I subscribed to Science Magazine and mailed you a check for $39.50 for a one-year subscription. My bank tells me that the check has cleared my account. But it is now December 12, and the first issue has not yet arrived.

Your advertisement stated that it would be no more than five weeks for the first issue to arrive.

Please look into this matter as soon as possible and inform me when I can expect the subscription to start. I am looking forward to reading Science Magazine.

Sincerely,

Donna Pulschen

FIGURE 5-8

You have just specified and viewed the parameters for paragraph type "A." Now in the next hands-on exercise apply those parameters to all paragraphs in your letter except the return address and the date to create a "blocked" letter style.

Hands On

1. Press <menu> **F2**. The Command Selection menu appears.
2. Select "Reform." The prompt "Move cursor to start of block and press <do>." appears on the screen.
3. Use <arrows> to place the cursor on the "M" in "Mr." in the inside address (it may already be there).
4. Press <do> **F10**. The prompt "Move cursor to end of block and press <do> again." appears.
5. Press <end> **End** twice to position the cursor on the line after your typed name. The area that you have marked to be reformatted is now highlighted.
6. Press <do>. The prompt "Reform marked area to which Paragraph Type:" appears.
7. Type [a]. The area you marked is now reformatted to the parameters you stored as Paragraph Type A.
8. The LETTER should look like Figure 5-8.

Updating and Saving a File

Whether you create a file or work with an existing one, you should from time to time save (or store) the work from the computer to a disk. A power interruption or computer failure will mean any part of your file that has not been saved will be lost. Frequent saving of files is a good habit to develop. Save the files before you leave your computer to recall them later.

Before you print the LETTER letter, save the version you just edited. The following hands-on exercise describes the steps to update and save your work.

Hands On

1. Press <menu> **F2**. The Command Selection menu appears.
2. Select "Update." The prompt "Update changed current file "nickname:LETTER.DOC"?" appears.
3. Press <do> **F10**. The file with your changes (updates) is now saved on your disk. But it also remains on your display screen.

Printing a File

When you use the Print command, the Print Configuration window is displayed on the screen. It presents options regarding how a document will look after it is printed--spacing, page numbering, headers and footers, margins, printers, and merging capabilities (Figure 5-9).

```
 ┼────────┼1L─────┼──2────┼────3──┼──────4┼────────┼5─────┼──6───┼─────R──┼──────
  Header:         Line number:       1          Special: None


  Subheader:      Line number:       2          Special: None


     Footer:      Line number:       2          Special: None
 |-#-|


      Paper width:       80        Top margin:        3    First page:        1
     Paper length:       60     Bottom margin:        4    Start page:        1
  Alternate headings: Off     Paragraph block:        4     Stop page:    32767
          Spacing:        1       Left offset:        0

  Print device: IBM QUIETWRITER
  Merging: Off                 Merge Data File:
  Single Merge: Off            Merge Record:

  [A:LETTER.DOC]               Print Configuration                            97%
[ PRINT:  Use arrows to move, press <print> to print, <menu> to return to edit
I         Type new settings or press <change> to switch on/off
           <arrows> <ret> <change> <print> <do> <undo> <menu> <search>
```

FIGURE 5-9

TABLE 5-3 Printer Configuration Parameters

Parameter	*Description*
Header	Text that will appear at the top of a page.
Subheader	Additional text that will appear beneath the Header.
Footer	Text that will appear at the bottom of the page. *Note:* The Header, Subheader, and Footer may be justified as right, left, center, or a combination of the three. A line number is also specified as to where the Header and Subheader will be from the top of the page, and where the Footer will be from the bottom of the page. The Special print parameters the Header, Subheader, and Footer to be printed as None — Nothing is printed. Skip First — Prints on all pages after the first. Skip Odd — Prints on only even-numbered pages. Skip Even — Prints on only odd-numbered pages.
Paper Width	Sets paper width for the printer as defined in the Print Configuration window.
Paper Length	Specifies length of page as defined in the Print Configuration window.
Alternate Heading	When printing with double-sided pages, setting this to "On" will switch or alternate the right and left parts of the Header or Subheader on odd-numbered pages.
Spacing	Sets the number of spaces between each line, up to 13 spaces.
Margins	Sets the number of blank lines at the top or bottom of the page.
Paragraph Block	Determines whether to break a paragraph at the bottom or to move the whole paragraph to the next page.
Left Offset	You may set the number of spaces from the left margin for the printer to start printing.
First Page	Number of the first text page.
Start Page	Number of the first page to be printed.
Stop Page	Number of the last page to be printed.
Print Device	Input the device in which to print.
Merging	Used with Mail Merge. Set to "On."
Single Merge	Set to "On" to merge to a single record.
Merge Data File	Name of DIF file.
Merge Record	Name of single DIF file record.

The Print Configuration window contains the parameters shown in Table 5-3. You may need to consult your printer manual for some of the settings.

Use the next hands-on exercise to print the letter you have just edited. The LETTER file should still be on the screen.

Hands On

1. Press <menu> **F2** to access the Command Selection menu.
2. Make sure the printer is prepared for printing: the paper is inserted, the printer is turned on, and it is connected properly to your computer.
3. Select "Print," or alternatively, press <print> **F3**. The Output Device Selection menu appears. Select the appropriate printer and press <do> **F10**. The Print Configuration window appears.
4. Use <arrows> to place the cursor on |-#-| under the heading "Footer:". This format will print a page number surrounded by hyphens at the center of the bottom of the page. The vertical bars on each side of the footer indicate that the footer information is to be centered. To place the footer on the right side of the page, only the right vertical bar would be used, for example, -#-|. To place the footer on the left side of the page, only one vertical bar would be used on the left of the footer. The use of vertical bars also applies to headers. Since this letter is only one page long, a printed page number is unnecessary.
5. Press <space> **Space Bar** and <ret> **Return**. The prompt "Throw away old footer?" appears.
6. Press <do> **F10** to indicate that you do want the footer removed.
7. Use <arrows> to position the cursor after "Print device:". Enter the appropriate printer. If you are not sure, ask the class instructor or press <search> **F4** for the Output Device Selection menu and make the appropriate selection.
8. Press <print>. The letter starts to print. The Print window remains on the screen even after printing is completed.

Exiting the Word Processor Program

When you want to stop working on a file or if you have printed a document and are finished, prepare to exit the word processor. You might want to access another program or shut down the computer.

The following hands-on exercise shows how to do this. The Print Configuration window from LETTER is still on the screen.

Hands On

1. Press <menu> **F2** to exit the Print Configuration window from the last exercise. The Edit window of the LETTER returns to the screen.
2. Press <menu> again to display the Command Selection menu.
3. Select "Options." If no changes have been made since the last time the document was saved, the Options menu appears; however, if changes have been made, you are prompted to update the letter.

4. Press <undo> **Esc** to exit the letter if the prompt appears. The Options menu appears. From here you may proceed to other Open Access programs or select "Operating System" to return to DOS.

So far you have learned how to select the word processor program, how to select a file to edit, how to insert text in the file, how to delete text using <del>, how to change the type style of words using the Alter command, how to format paragraphs using <format> and the Reform command, how to save a file, how to print a one-page document, and how to exit the program.

In the next sections you will learn how to create a new file, edit blocks of text, search and replace text, and how to perform a mail merge.

Creating a New File

Now you are ready to create, save, and print your own document, one of the most common applications of a word processor.

Create a short document, following the steps in the hands-on exercise and refer to the previous sections if you need to refresh your memory.

Hands On

1. Select "Word_Processor" from the Options menu. The File Selection menu appears on the screen.
2. Select "Create_New." A blinking cursor appears with a blank line for you to type the new file name.
3. Type [FRIEND] as the title of your new document.
4. Press <do> **F10**. In a few seconds you will see a message at the top of the screen saying "File DEFAULT.DOC not found." The default file, if present, would contain the paragraph parameters and any stored abbreviations. These parameters would be transferred to the new file.
5. Press <do> to remove the error message. A blank Edit window (your new work area) appears.
6. Type [A friend in greed is a friend indeed.]
7. Edit the document changing "greed" to "need."
8. Print the document to the console or to a printer if one is available. If you print to the console, press <do> to return to the Print Configuration window.

Retrieving an Existing File Using <search>

The section "Selecting an Existing File" showed you how to retrieve a file by typing the file's name on the blank line. However, if you forget the name of the file you want, pressing <search> F4 displays a list of all files on your disk. From that list, a selection can be made.

In the hands-on exercise, practice using <search> by retrieving the file with minutes from a meeting to edit.

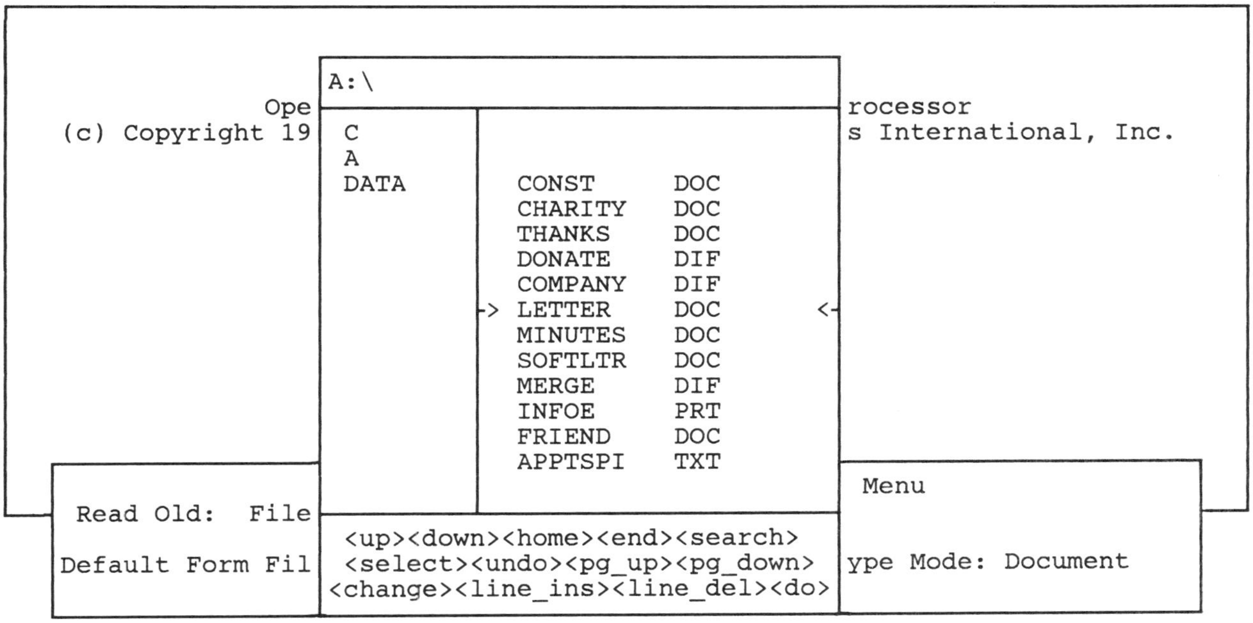

FIGURE 5-10

Hands On

1. Press <menu> **F2** twice to exit the Print menu from the FRIEND document. The Command Selection menu appears.
2. Select "New_File" indicating you want to access another file. The prompt "Update changed current file drive: FRIEND?" appears on the screen if the file was not saved or changes were made since the file was last saved.
3. Press <do> **F10** if the prompt appeared. This saves the FRIEND letter. The File Selection menu appears on the screen.
4. Select "Read_Old" to access an existing file. The blinking cursor appears at the blank line where you enter the name of the file you would like to retrieve.
5. Press <search> **F4**. A window appears with the list of all the files on your disk usable by the word processor module (Figure 5-10).
6. Use <arrows> to scroll the list until the name of the file MINUTES appears highlighted, if it is not already highlighted.
7. Press <do>. The name of the file MINUTES is transferred to the blank line; you do not have to type it.
8. Press <do> again. The contents of the file MINUTES is displayed.

Centering Text

Part of the minutes of the meeting of the Writers' League should appear on the screen. The entire minutes are shown in Figure 5-11. Enter and center the title and subheadings in the minutes with the following hands-on exercise.

The October 15 meeting of the Writers' League was called to order at 7:30 p.m. by acting president, Averill Stoakes. Mr. Stoakes explained to the group that League president Marian Vandiver was absent because of a sudden writing assignment from Midtown magazine.

Secretary Katharine Newbold read the minutes from the September 21 meeting. The minutes were approved as read.

Old Business

Members present were Lydia Swift, Lester Noble, John Gaspari, Edward Cline, Katharine Newbold, Rachel Simpson, Donald Croft, and Fletcher Knowles. Absent were Marian Vandiver, Jacqueline Moore, Leon Rivers, and Seth Goldman.

Reporting for the fundraising committee, Mr. Noble said that the committee had settled on three possible projects to earn money for the League's scholarship fund: (1) publication and sale of a writer-oriented cookbook, tentatively entitled "Literary Luncheons"; (2) a "roast" of Professor Alton Cameron, director of creative writing at Tremont College and author of the bestselling novel, Outrage and Olives; and (3) creation of a Writers' League Speakers Bureau, all proceeds from which, except for actual speakers' expenses, would be given for scholarships.

Mr. Noble moved and Ms. Simpson seconded that the League members consider these three proposals until the November meeting, at which time a vote would be taken to choose the preferred proposal to follow. The motion was approved.

Mr. Gaspari reported that the insurance committee was still investigating group plans to present to the League. He said he hoped to have all the pertinent information ready by the next meeting.

New Business

Mr. Stoakes appointed Mr. Cline, Ms. Simpson, and Mr. Knowles to suggest alternate places for subsequent monthly meetings, owing to a dispute with the management of the Bailes Hotel, the site of League meetings the past year.

Mr. Croft moved and Mr. Knowles seconded that the League hold a Christmas party and poetry reading some time during the week of December 11-18. The motion was approved. Mr. Stoakes appointed Mr. Croft and Mr. Knowles to work out details for the party and to report back to the group at the November meeting.

-1-

FIGURE 5-11

Announcements

Mr. Knowles said that his book on the life of Gerald Ford was progressing nicely but that he would appreciate any help he could get from the group on methods of marketing the finished product. Mr. Stoakes announced that the next meeting will be held November 22 at a place yet to be determined. Members will be notified by telephone, he said, of the new location.

Ms. Simpson announced that she had just had an article accepted by *Crosswinds* magazine on the subject of shopping for used clothing.

Ms. Simpson announced that she had just had an article accepted by *Crosswinds* magazine on the subject of shopping for used clothing.

There being no further business to conduct, the meeting was adjourned at 9 p.m.

Respectfully submitted,

Lydia Swift, Secretary

-2-

FIGURE 5-11 (continued)

Hands On

1. Type [MINUTES OF THE WRITERS' LEAGUE] (using uppercase letters) at the blinking cursor, which is on a blank line at the top of the screen.
2. Press <menu> **F2**. The Command Selection menu appears.
3. Select "Format." The Paragraph Format menu appears. (Alternate method to access the Paragraph Format menu: Press <format> **Alt-F6**.
4. Select "Justify" and press <do> **F10** until the word "Center" is specified under "Justify." Notice how the heading moves across the screen corresponding to the Justify setting.
5. Press <menu>. The Paragraph Format menu disappears; the text remains centered.
6. Use <arrows> to place the cursor anywhere on the subhead "Old Business." Follow Steps 2-5 to center that subhead.
7. Use <arrows> to place the cursor anywhere on the subhead "New Business." Follow steps 2-5 to center it.
8. Use <arrows> to place the cursor on the subhead "Announcements." Follow steps 2-5 to center it.

Moving a Block of Text

In the section "Old Business," the paragraph beginning with "Members present" is out of place and should appear earlier. The Move command from the Command Selection menu moves a block of text from one place to another.

The following hands-on exercise demonstrates moving a block of text.

Hands On

1. Press <menu> **F2**. The Command Selection menu appears.
2. Select "Move." The prompt "Move cursor to start of block and press <do>." appears.
3. Use the <arrows> to move the cursor to the "M" in "Members" under Old Business and press <do> **F10**. The prompt "Move cursor to end of block and press <do> again." appears.
4. Use <arrows> to move the cursor to the "R" in "Reporting" at the start of the next paragraph to include all of this paragraph and the blank line following it and press <do>. The block to be moved is highlighted in reverse video. The work area is now divided into two windows. The top window displays the selected (highlighted) block of text to be moved; the lower window displays the current file so you can indicate where to move the block (Figure 5-12). The prompt "Move cursor to destination and press <do> again." appears.
5. Use <arrows> to place the cursor on the "S" in "Secretary" in the paragraph above Old Business.
6. Press <do>. The text is now moved to its new location (Figure 5-13).

```
|-------|1L----P|--2----|-----3--|-------4|--------|5------|--6----|----R--|
        Gaspari, Edward Cline, Katharine Newbold, Rachel Simpson,
        Donald Croft, and Fletcher Knowles.▪ Absent were Marian
        Vandiver, Jacqueline Moore, Leon Rivers, and Seth Goldman.

             Reporting for the fundraising committee, Mr. Noble
        said that the committee had settled on three possible
        projects to earn money for the League's scholarship fund:
        (1) publication and sale of a writer-oriented cookbook,
|-------|1L----P|--2----|-----3--|-------4|--------|5------|--6----|----R--|
        during the week of December 11-18.▪ The motion was
        approved.▪ Mr. Stoakes appointed Mr. Croft and Mr. Knowles
        to work out details for the party and to report back to the
        group at the November meeting.

                              Announcements

             Mr. Knowles said that his book on the life of Gerald
        Ford was progressing nicely but that he would appreciate
        any help he could get from the group on methods of
        marketing the finished product.▪ Mr. Stoakes announced that
MOVE:
        Move cursor to destination and press <do> again.
                      <move_keys> <do> <undo> <search>
```

FIGURE 5-12

```
|-------|1L----P|--2----|-----3--|-------4|--------|5------|--6----|----R--|
                      MINUTES OF THE WRITERS' LEAGUE
             The October 15 meeting of the Writers' League was
        called to order at 7:30 p.m. by acting president, Averill
        Stoakes.▪ Mr. Stoakes explained to the group that League
        president Marian Vandiver was absent because of a sudden
        writing assignment from Midtown magazine.

             Members present were Lydia Swift, Lester Noble, John
        Gaspari, Edward Cline, Katharine Newbold, Rachel Simpson,
        Donald Croft, and Fletcher Knowles.▪ Absent were Marian
        Vandiver, Jacqueline Moore, Leon Rivers, and Seth Goldman.

             Secretary Katharine Newbold read the minutes from the
        September 21 meeting.▪ The minutes were approved as read.

                               Old Business

             Reporting for the fundraising committee, Mr. Noble
        said that the committee had settled on three possible
[A:MINUTES.DOC]                    Insert                            89%
INSERT: All characters are entered into text at the cursor position.

      <del><menu><search><print><format><change><line_del><line_ins>
```

FIGURE 5-13

Deleting a Block of Text

The Delete command will remove the block of text from the minutes. The text following the deleted material automatically moves up to fill the space.

The paragraph next to the last one under the heading "Announcements" in the report has been repeated. Follow the steps in the following hands-on exercise to delete this redundant block of text.

Hands On

1. Press <menu> **F2**. The Command Selection menu appears.
2. Select "Delete." The prompt "Move cursor to start of block and press <do>." appears.
3. Press <PgDn> **PgDn** three times to quickly move the cursor to the "Announcements." You will see two paragraphs that are the same. Now with <arrows> move the cursor to the "M" in the first occurrence of "Ms." Press <do> **F10**. The prompt "Move cursor to end of block and press <do> again." appears.
4. Use <arrows> to move the cursor to the next paragraph and place it on the second occurrence of "M" in "Ms." The block to be deleted is now highlighted in reverse video (Figure 5-14).
5. Press <do>. The paragraph is removed and the remaining text moves up (Figure 5-15).

```
+--------+1L----P+--2------+------3---+-------4+-------+5-------+---6----+----R---+
                                     Announcements

          Mr. Knowles said that his book on the life of Gerald
     Ford was progressing nicely but that he would appreciate
     any help he could get from the group on methods of
     marketing the finished product.• Mr. Stoakes announced that
     the next meeting will be held November 22 at a place yet to
     be determined. Members will be notified by telephone, he
     said, of the new location.

          Ms. Simpson announced that she had just had an article
     accepted by Crosswinds magazine on the subject of shopping
     for used clothing.

          Ms. Simpson announced that she had just had an article
     accepted by Crosswinds magazine on the subject of shopping
     for used clothing.

          There being no further business to conduct, the
[A:MINUTES.DOC]                    Delete Block                                89%
DELETE:  Move cursor to end of block and press <do> again.

                    <move_keys> <do> <undo> <search>
```

FIGURE 5-14

```
+--------+1L----P+--2-----+-----3---+---------4+---------+5--------+---6-----+----R--+
          Mr. Knowles said that his book on the life of Gerald
     Ford was progressing nicely but that he would appreciate
     any help he could get from the group on methods of
     marketing the finished product.▪ Mr. Stoakes announced that
     the next meeting will be held November 22 at a place yet to
     be determined. Members will be notified by telephone, he
     said, of the new location.

          Ms. Simpson announced that she had just had an article
     accepted by Crosswinds magazine on the subject of shopping
     for used clothing.

          There being no further business to conduct, the
     meeting was adjourned at 9 p.m.

                                  Respectfully submitted,

[A:MINUTES.DOC]                       Insert                              90%
INSERT: All characters are entered into text at the cursor position.

       <del><menu><search><print><format><change><line_del><line_ins>
```

FIGURE 5-15

Searching and Replacing

OA can search for a pattern or string of text. The pattern may be either an entire word or merely a fragment of a word. For example, if you search for the word "on," OA will find only that word; however, a fragment search finds "action" and "information."

In the minutes, Mr. Stokes's name has been incorrectly spelled as "Stoakes." The Search and Replace command menu finds all occurrences of that name and changes it to the specified correct spelling.

When the program searches a file, it begins searching from the current position of the cursor, downward. So placing the cursor at the beginning of a file allows the entire file to be searched.

The following hands-on exercise searches for "Stoakes" and replaces all occurrences with "Stokes."

Hands On

1. Press <home> **Home** twice to move the cursor to the beginning of the file.
2. Press <search> **F4** to access the Search/Replace menu (Figure 5-16).
3. Select "Replace." The prompt "How many times (press <search> to replace "all")" appears.
4. Press <search> again. This indicates that you want all occurrences of the target word to be replaced. The prompt "Enter pattern:" appears.

```
+1L----P+--2----+----3--+------4+--------+5------+--6----+----R--+
                    MINUTES OF THE WRITERS' LEAGUE

        The October 15 meeting of the Writers' League was
   called to order at 7:30 p.m. by acting president, Averill
   Stoakes.▪ Mr. Stoakes explained to the group that League
   president Marian Vandiver was absent because of a sudden
   writing assignment from Midtown magazine.

        Members present were Lydia Swift, Lester Noble, John
   Gaspari, Edward Cline, Katharine Newbold, Rachel Simpson,
   Donald Croft, and Fletcher Knowles.▪ Absent were Marian
   Vandiver, Jacqueline Moore, Leon Rivers, and Seth Goldman.

        Secretary Katharine Newbold read the minutes from the
   September 21 meeting.▪ The minutes were approved as read.

                         Old Business

        Reporting for the fundraising committee, Mr. Noble
[A:MINUTES.DOC]                 Search / Replace                  90%
SEARCH:  Press <undo> to exit, <search> to find again
           Find  Marker  Replace  Line_Number
                       <arrows> <do> <undo> <search>
```

FIGURE 5-16

5. Type [Stoakes] in response to the prompt and press <do> **F10**. The target word (the incorrectly spelled word) is now specified. The prompt "(Verify On) Replace "Stoakes" with what:" appears.
6. Type [Stokes] and press <do>. The system begins to search for the target word "Stoakes."
7. Press <do> each time the target word is encountered to indicate that it is to be replaced. The system replaces the incorrect word each time you press <do>. The system stops searching after the last occurrence of "Stoakes" is found and corrected.

The two-page MINUTES is ready to print. You can print the MINUTES report by following the next hands-on exercise. Again, you need to know the type of printer available. If you don't know, ask the class instructor.

Before printing, you may wish to see where the page breaks occur for the current output device selected. This can be done by selecting the View_Breaks command from the Command Selection menu. When in "View_Breaks," use the <arrow> keys to scroll through the file for the page breaks. Try this with the following exercise.

Hands On

1. Press <home> **Home** twice to place the cursor at the beginning of MINUTES.
2. Press <menu> **F2** for the Command Selection menu.
3. Select "View_Breaks." Use <arrows> to scroll through MINUTES to see the page breaks.
4. Press <undo> **Esc** to exit "View_Breaks."

Now print the MINUTES document by completing the following hands-on exercise. Make sure the printer is prepared for printing: the paper is inserted, the printer is turned on, and it is connected properly to the computer.

Hands On

1. Press <print> **F3** to access the Print Configuration window.
2. Use <arrows> to place the pointer on "Print Device." Use <search> **F10** to select the printer--unless the appropriate default value is already there.
3. Press <print> again. The MINUTES document is printed with page numbers at the bottom of each page. (If you print to the CONSOLE, press <do> to "print" all the pages.)
4. Press <menu> **F2** twice. The Command Selection menu appears.
5. Select "New File." The prompt "Update changed current file '<u>nickname</u>:MINUTES.DOC'?" appears.
6. Press <do> **F10** to save the MINUTES file. The File Selection menu appears.

TO QUIT: To exit this module and return to the File Selection menu later, select "Options" and the main Options menu appears. From here you may exit OA or use another module. If you exit to the Operating System, you must reload OA.

RESTART: Reload OA. Select "Word_Processor" from the Options menu. The File Selection menu appears and you can continue with the next section.

Mail Merge

Combining a form document and a data file into a single document is called a mail-merge operation. For example, a data file of names and addresses can be combined with a form document to personalize each letter. In OA, data that have been stored in a Data Interchange Format file (a DIF file) can be merged into a DOC or TXT file at designated places. This section describes how to accomplish a mail-merge operation.

Follow the instructions in the following hands-on exercise to access a letter that has already been created for this purpose.

Hands On

1. Select "Read_Old" from the File Selection menu. A blinking cursor and a blank line appear for you to enter the name of the existing file you want to see.
2. Type [SOFTLTR]. Press <do> **F10** and the file called SOFTLTR is now displayed on your screen.

This letter requests information you need from software companies for a term paper. The same letter, each an original, can be merged with names and addresses from a DIF file (which has already been created for you) to be mailed to several companies (Figure 5-17).

[Your Name]
[Your Street]
[Your City]
[Date]

^@prefix^ ^@firstname^ ^@lastname^
(Name of Company)
(Address)
(City, State Zip)

Dear (Salutation Name):

I am a student at [Name of Your School] and my assignment for the class, Computers in Elementary Education, is to write a report describing various types of educational software for elementary school children.

Information from (Name of Company) about this subject and your software products would be helpful in writing this report. Please send me brochures and other product information on some of the educational software offered by your company.

My instructor has suggested that I also preview a tutorial for fifth grade students. If you will send me a math tutorial to preview, it will be returned to you within two weeks.

Thank you, (Salutation Name), for assisting me in this college paper assignment.

Sincerely,

[Your Name]

FIGURE 5-17

Substitution Fields

The caret (^) symbol indicates the beginning and end of each substitution field. The (@) symbol indicates the remainder of the command is either a field expression or a field format. A field expression is a DIF field name, or a conditional statement, using an IF|Then|Else expression. For example: ^@firstname= 'Stacy'|'Hello Stacy'|firstname^ means that if "Stacy" is in the DIF field--firstname, then substitute Hello Stacy; if the name "Stacy" is not in the DIF field, then simply print the name contained in the DIF field firstname.

A field format is used to define an integer precision or a date format; for example, ^@price@2^ would print the value of price with two decimal places, and ^@sysdate^ would substitute the date according to the current default date format.

The items in parentheses in the letter indicate what the actual data should be. These are where you will later enter the Mail Merge substitution fields. Data from a DIF file must be entered, or substituted, for the inside address name, company name and address, and the salutation name. The appropriate data is substituted each place where there are substitution fields. When the letter is printed, the names and addresses from the DIF files will be substituted for these fields.

A file of fictitious company names and addresses has already been prepared on the data disk for this Mail Merge demonstration.

The file called MERGE.DIF, which has been created, contains two records with the names, addresses, company names, and attribute names used in the salutation. The field names for each record and what they contain are shown in Table 5-4. (You may want to refer to Desk Accessories in Chapter 4 for a review on creating Business Cards. The DIF Business Card files may be used for applications such as this.)

TABLE 5-4 Substitution Fields for Merge Letter

Field Name	*Contents*
^@prefix^	title (for example, Mr. or Ms.)
^@firstname^	first name of company representative
^@lastname^	last name of company representative
^@company^	name of the software company
^@add1^	company's street address
^@add2^	city, state, and zip code
^@attribute^	salutation name (for example, Ms. Achter)

You need to insert the current date, your own name and address as the return address, the name of your school, and your name at the bottom of the letter. These elements will remain constant in each letter you send. Do the following hands-on exercise to enter these items in the letter.

Hands On

1. Press <line_ins> **Ctrl-Return.** The Edit window toggles to "Exchange" mode.
2. Use <arrows> to place the cursor on the "[" in "[Your Name]."

3. Type [your name] and press <ret> **Return**, [your street] and press <ret>, [your city, state abbreviation, and zip code] and press <ret>. Use <del> **Del** to remove any extra characters.
4. Type the current [date].
5. Press <line ins> again to return the Edit window to "Insert" mode.
6. Use <arrows> to move to [name of your school] in the body of the letter and enter your school name. Use <del> **Del** to remove the extra characters.
7. Use <arrows> to move to "[Your Name]" at the bottom of the letter and enter your name. Use <del> to remove any extra characters.

Preparing the Letter for Merging

Now you are ready to prepare the letter for merging with the fields in MERGE.DIF.

First, the appropriate substitution fields for the words in parentheses are entered into the letter using the field names from Table 5-4. You should remove the parentheses and everything inside them. They were placed in the letter only to show you the position of the field substitutions. For example, you will replace "(Name of Company)" with [^@company^], and "(Address)" with [^@add1^].

The first three substitutions in SOFTLTR (^@prefix^, ^@firstname^, and ^@lastname^) have already been done for you so you can see how they should look. The following hands-on exercise will walk you through the next two substitutions and then you can do the remaining ones.

Hands On

1. Position the cursor on the beginning parenthesis on the line titled (Name of Company) in the inside address. Press <del> **Del** until "(Name of Company)" is deleted, but do not remove the return marker. The return character is hidden under the blinking cursor. Or you may enter the "Exchange" mode to write over the text and use <del> to remove extra characters. Do not remove the return characters.
2. Type [^@company^].
3. Use <arrows> to position the cursor on the beginning parenthesis on the line titled (Address). Press <del> until "(Address)" is deleted, or you may enter the "Exchange" mode to write over the text.
4. Type [^@add1^].
5. Repeat the process of the first two steps for the remaining substitution fields that are enclosed in parentheses throughout the letter--there are four more. Refer to the list in Table 5-4 for the field names to be substituted. (If you are in the "exchange" mode, press <menu> **F2** and select "Insert" when you are finished entering the substitution fields.)

Preparing the Print Configuration Window

Now that you have entered the substitution fields, prepare the Print Configuration window for mail-merge printing. Using the instructions in the following hands-on exercise, "print" the letters to the screen to preview what they will look like before they are actually printed on paper.

Hands On

1. Press <print> **F3**. The Print Configuration window appears.
2. Use <arrows> to position the cursor on the "Merging:" parameter.
3. Press <change> **F6** to toggle "Merging" from "Off" to "On" and press <ret> **Return**. The cursor moves to "Merge Data File:".
4. Press <search> **F4** to prepare "Merge Data File" to receive the name of the DIF file, select "MERGE.DIF," and press <ret>. The Print Configuration window is still on the screen.

Viewing the Merged Letters

The display screen will show how the merged letters look when they are printed. Use the following hands-on exercise to display the letters.

Hands On

1. Use <arrows> to position the pointer on "Print Device:". Select "Console" in order to preview rather than print on paper.
2. Press <print> **F3**. The display screen should appear like the one in Figure 5-18. Only the return address shows.
3. Press <do> **F10** in response to the prompt at the bottom of the display screen to view the two letters in their entirety. When you have finished, the Print Configuration window will reappear. Press <undo> **Esc** to return to the Print Configuration window if you do not want to continue viewing the Merge letters in their entirety.

```
                                         Donna Pulschen
                                         12345 Main Street
                                         Middleburg, NV 77777
                                         December 25, 1987

------------------------------------------------------------------------

               Pause to change page, press <do> to continue.
```

FIGURE 5-18

Printing the Mail Merge Letter

Now you are ready to print the letters. Follow the steps in this exercise.

Hands On

1. Use <arrows> to move the pointer to "Print device." Use <change> **F4** and select your printer (not "Console") as the "Print device."
2. Make sure the printer has been prepared with paper, is plugged in, and is properly connected to the computer.
3. Press <print> **F3**. The letters now begin to print.

To exit the word processor, perform the following hands-on exercise.

Hands On

1. Press <menu> **F2** twice. The Command Selection menu appears.
2. Select "Options" and the main Options menu appears. If you've made changes that were not saved, the prompt "Update current file "A:SOFTLTR.DOC"?" will appear first. If the prompt appears press <do> **F10** and the Options menu will appear. From here you may exit OA.

Command Summary

The following is a brief summary of the commands listed in the main menus of the Word Processor module.

File Selection Menu

Read_Old	Used to access an existing file.
Create_New	Used when creating a new word-processing file.
Form_Change	Used to change the default form filename. The default form file contains paragraph formats and abbreviations for new files.
Type_Change	Used to toggle the file type from DOC to TXT and back.

Command Selection Menu

Insert	Used to insert text into the Edit window.
Exchange	Places you into the Exchange text mode.
Copy	Used when copying text from within the document or from an external document to the current file.
Move	Used to move text from one location in a file to another.
Delete	Erases text in the current file.
Alter	Allows you to style text for printing.

Reform	Reformats paragraphs in a block of text.
Set_Marks	A mark can be placed at a location to which the cursor can be moved directly.
Background	Used to change paragraph formats.
View_Breaks	Used to view page breaks.
Format	Used to change current paragraph parameters.
Print	Accesses the Print window.
Search	Used to search and/or replace a marker or text.
?Directory	Displays disk files which can be used by the Word Processor.
Update	Used to save the current file and return to the Edit window.
New_File	Used to save the current file and return to the File Selection menu.
Options	Saves current file and returns to the Main Options Menu.

Paragraph Format Menu

Recall	Used to set current paragraph parameters by recalling paragraph parameters from the Background window.
Margins_&_Tabstops	Used to set margins, tabs, and paragraph indentions.
Wordwrap	Used to toggle wordwrap between on and off.
Autoindent	Used to toggle autoindent between on and off.
Justify	Sets the paragraph justification to right, left, both, or center.
Store	Saves current paragraph parameters in the Background window.

Study Questions

1. What is the difference between the INSERT mode and the EXCHANGE mode?
2. Describe the choices available to change the style of text.
3. What do the letters L, P, and R signify at the top of the Edit Window?
4. Explain what occurs when the Autoindent format selection is set at "on."
5. Explain the purpose of the Background command.
6. Which command is used to relocate text within the same file?
7. In a search and replace operation, what is the difference in specifying a word or a fragment?
8. Which key is used to view the files on your diskette.
9. Describe a mail-merge operation.
10. Describe the symbols used in substitution fields. Give an example.

The file CONST.DOC is used to perform the following exercises.

11. Load the file CONST.DOC into the word processor.
12. Insert the following text at line 6 column 47 after the word "Union": [establish Justice, insure domestic Tranquility,]. Remember to include a space after the comma.
13. Type over the word "provide" in the phrase "provide the general Welfare," located at line 8, column 20, and replace it with the word "promote."
14. Delete the phrase "of America" in the phrase "We the People of the United States of America" in the first paragraph. Remember to delete the space before the word "of" but *not* the comma after the word "America."
15. Correct the spelling and capitalize all letters of "constatuton" in the heading to correctly read "CONSTITUTION."

16. Boldface both lines of the heading "Constitution of the United States of America."
17. Center both lines of the heading.
18. Insert the following new paragraph at the end of the document: [What follows is the text to the preamble to the Constitution of the United States of America.]
19. Move the third paragraph (the one just inserted in Exercise 18) that begins with "What follows. . ." to the line above the heading.
20. Delete the headings "Article I" and "Section 1" and the paragraph that begins with "All legislative Powers. . . ."
21. Search the entire document for the character string "hour" and replace all occurrences, whether a word or part of a word with the character string "our."
22. Print a hard copy of the file, without a footer, to a printer or to the console (display screen) if a printer is not available. When you print to the CONSOLE, what is the bottom line on the first screen?

The following exercises use the file MEMO.DOC, which you will create next.

23. Create a new document called MEMO.DOC.
24. Set the left margin to 10, the paragraph indent to 10, and the right margin to 57.
25. Enter the following text starting at line 1, column 10:

    [MEMORANDUM
    FROM THE DESK OF:

    TO: All Accounting Personnel
    FROM: Accounting Manager
    RE: Spreadsheet Design Articles

    It is recommended that all accounting personnel read the articles on spreadsheet design in the following magazines:

    1. Spreadsheet Today, June issue
    3. Computers and Accounting, June issue
    4. The Electronic Accountant, June issue

    Monday, May 1]

26. Insert the following text on the line above the date: [The magazines can be found in the department library.] Leave a blank line between the magazine list and the newly inserted text.
27. Search the entire document for the word "June" and replace each occurrence of the word with the word [May] to correct a mistake in the issue in which the articles are found.
28. Delete the second line: "FROM THE DESK OF:".
29. Move the date from the bottom of the memo and insert it on the line below the title "MEMORANDUM."
30. Center the first two lines of text that contain the heading "MEMORANDUM" and the date.
31. Bold the headings [TO:], [FROM:], and [RE:] in the memo.
32. Type over the numbers "3" and "4" in the magazines list, replacing them with the numbers [2] and [3].
33. Underline the names of the three magazines in the magazine list.
34. Print a hard copy of the file to a printer or print the file to the console if a printer is not available.

The finished MEMO document should appear as shown.

MEMORANDUM
Monday, May 1
TO: All Accounting Personnel
FROM: Accounting Manager
RE: Spreadsheet Design Articles

It is recommended that all accounting personnel read the articles on spreadsheet design in the following magazines:

1. Spreadsheet Today, May issue
2. Computers and Accounting, May issue
3. The Electronic Accountant, May issue

The magazines can be found in the department library.

The following exercises use the files CHARITY.DOC and DONATE.DIF located on the data diskette. CHARITY.DOC is a form letter. The file DONATE.DIF is a data file that was created for you in the Business Card file option of the Desk Accessories module.

35. Load the file CHARITY.DOC into the word processor.
36. The variable items in the form letter have been indicated by enclosing them in parentheses. Replace each item (parentheses and word) with an appropriate mail-merge substitution field. The field name for each variable item is as follows:

Variable Item	*Field Name*
(Prefix)	prefix
(First Name)	firstname
(Last Name)	lastname
(Address 1)	add1
(Address 2)	add2
(Contribution amount)	attribute

    What are the substitutions that must be made on the first line of the inside address?
37. Prepare the Print Configuration window to allow the form letter CHARITY.DOC and the data file DONATE.DIF to be merged.
38. Print the merged letters to the console so they can be previewed. To whom are the letters addressed?
39. Print a hard copy of the merged letters if a printer is available.

The following exercises use the files THANKS.DOC and COMPANY.DIF located on the data diskette. THANKS.DOC is a form letter. The data file COMPANY.DIF was created in the Business Card file option of the Desk Accessories module.

40. Load the file THANKS.DOC into the word processor.
41. The variable items in the form letter have been indicated by enclosing them in parentheses.

Replace each item (parentheses and word) with an appropriate mail-merge substitution field. The field name for each variable item is as follows:

Variable Item	*Field Name*
(Prefix)	prefix
(First Name)	firstname
(Last Name)	lastname
(Company)	company
(Address 1)	add1
(Address 2)	add2
(Salutation)	attribute

What substitution field is replaced in the body of the letter?

42. Prepare the Print Configuration window to allow the form letter THANKS.DOC and the data file COMPANY.DIF to be merged.
43. Print the merged letters to the console so they can be previewed. What is printed on the first screen? How many letters are printed?
44. Print a hard copy of the merged letters if a printer is available.

Chapter 6
Database

Introduction

A database is a collection of related files, and a file is a collection of related records. A record contains data in fields that are particular to that record. This chapter will teach you how to create a small database and then manipulate the data stored there.

OA incorporates a relational database. Many of the database operations rely on the use of key fields. Key fields have special indexes associated with them that allow those key fields to be used to retrieve information faster than nonkey fields. Some commands can be performed only on key fields. Any field may be designated as a key field by the user and can be changed as necessary.

Several database files have been created to illustrate how they are set up. These files are small, but they illustrate the basic features of the database module. This OA program allows you to create a database file of up to 50 records. Naturally, the commercial version of Open Access II software allows much larger databases to be created.

Selecting the Database Module

In the OA Database module, a command is selected by using <arrow> keys to highlight the command and pressing <do> F10 to accept that command. Most commands in the database menus start with a different letter; therefore, commands can also be selected by pressing the key for the first letter of the command. For example, to select the Design command from the Database Main menu, simply press [D]. However, where there is more than one command that starts with the same letter, you must type the first two letters to select the appropriate command (or as many as needed to fully identify the command). When you are instructed to select a command in the hands-on exercises, use either method. At the bottom of each window, the key options from which you select are listed. These function keys are summarized in Table 6-1.

TABLE 6-1 Database Function Keys

Name	*Key*	*Function*
<do>	F10	Accepts command or last entry.
<undo>	Esc	Cancels entry or returns to Main menu.
<help>	F1	Displays function key setup.
<menu>	F2	Displays submenus.
<print>	F3	Prints a record.
<search>	F4	Displays window of available files or forms.
<prt_scr>	Alt-F3	Prints content of screen.
<line_ins>	Ctrl-Ret	Inserts line in query.
<line_del>	Ctrl-BkSp	Removes record or query line.
<change>	F6	Selects data to be changed and returns when done.
<eval>	Alt-F10	Performs calculations.
<ret>	Return	Accepts entry or moves cursor to next query line.
<arrows>	Arrows	Moves cursor and highlights.
<page_keys>	PgUp PgDn	Moves through screens or records.

Now, start by selecting the Database module from the Options menu.

Hands On

Select "Database" from the Options menu. You can highlight the word "Database" and press <do> **F10**, or simply press [D]. The Database Main menu appears on the screen (Figure 6-1).

Browsing a File

The Browse command allows you to scan the records in a file and to see the file's contents. All the records in a file are retrieved for viewing when you use the Browse command. The following hands-on exercise shows how the records of a company's customers look when they are retrieved by "browsing."

```
                    Open Access II Limited Version Database
   (c) Copyright 1984,1985,1986,1987 Software Products International, Inc.
                             All rights reserved



                              Database Main Menu
                    Retrieve    Browse    Enter_Data    Print
                    Design      Macros    Options
                                   <do> <undo>
```

FIGURE 6-1

Hands On

1. Select "Browse" from the Database Main menu. The Browse File Specification menu appears (Figure 6-2). The blinking cursor indicates a space provided to enter the name of the file you want to browse.
2. Type [CUSTOMER], the name of the file. Press <do> **F10**. The CUSTOMER.NAME Browse window appears on the screen (Figure 6-3). CUSTOMER is the name of the file and NAME is the key field, which is displayed on the left side of the screen. (If a flashing PROBLEM message appears at the top of the screen, you may have incorrectly entered the word "CUSTOMER." Check spelling and punctuation.)

The Browse window is a split window. The left side shows the key field. The right side of the screen shows the entire record for the highlighted field on the left. The key field is also highlighted in the record at this point. The name of the file and the key field being displayed appear beneath the window just above the options line. You can see at a glance which file is being browsed and the current key field being displayed in the left window. For example, CUSTOMER.NAME tells you that from the CUSTOMER file, the key field NAME is being displayed.

The <arrows> are used to browse through all the records by each key field. Up and down <arrows> control the key field highlighted on the left side of the window. The right and left <arrows> browse through the key fields of the record. By combining the various <arrows>, you can browse through all the records by each key field. Notice that the key fields in this example are NAME, RATING, ZIPCODE, PURCHASES, and BALANCE. Other selections at the bottom of the Browse window pertain to changing data and are discussed later.

```
                Open Access II Limited Version Database
(c) Copyright 1984,1985,1986,1987 Software Products International, Inc.
                          All rights reserved

                        Browse File Specification
Database file:
                           <search> <do> <undo>
```

FIGURE 6-2

```
BUCK, NIEL            NAME        BUCK, NIEL
DAVIS, JOHN           RATING      04
HAYES, WALTER         ADDRESS     909 WESTERN
JAMES, RALPH          CITY        NORMAN
LONG, M. DAVID        STATE       OKLAHOMA
SCHULTZ, JAN          ZIPCODE     73071
SCOTT, RUBY           PURCHASES   45.00
SMITH, DON            PAYMENTS    25.00
TEAGARDEN, WILLIAM    BALANCE     20.00
THOMAS, BOB C.        PHONE       (405) 555-0834
TOLLE, IVAN

                         A:CUSTOMER.NAME
      <arrows> <change> <line_ins> <line_del> <search> <undo>
```

FIGURE 6-3

In the following hands-on exercise, locate data with the Browse command using <search> F4. With this method you can find data using approximate values, i.e., a word or number close to the one you actually want to access. With the CUSTOMER.NAME Browse window still on the screen, search for data in the NAME and ZIPCODE fields.

Hands On

1. Press the down <arrow>. Notice as the cursor moves down through the key fields in the left column, the corresponding record is displayed on the right. The key field, NAME, remains highlighted in each record.
2. Press the right <arrow> twice to browse through the records by the ZIPCODE field as shown in Figure 6-4. A different key field is highlighted and the associated record is displayed each time the <arrow> is pressed. Continue to browse through the records by trying all the <arrow> keys.
3. Press the <arrow> keys to again display the NAME key field on the left.
4. Press <search> **F4** to search for approximate values from the NAME key field currently displayed on the left.
5. Type ['LANGE'] after the prompt "Expression:". (When entering text, date, or true/false values, enclose them with single quotation marks.)
6. Press <do> **F10**. This searches the "NAME" field for the closest value alphabetically to "Lange" (in this case, Long, M. David) and displays the corresponding record on the right.
7. Press <search> and now browse a record by the ZIPCODE key field. After the prompt "Expression:", enter the key field, followed by a comma, followed by the data you are looking for. If the data is a string, it must be enclosed in quotes. If the data was defined as a numerical value, it does not need quotes.
8. Type [ZIPCODE, 60000]. No quotes are entered around ZIPCODE because this is the field name--not a field value. You do not need quotes around 60000 because the field type was designated as a number when the database was created. Press <do> to display the record with the zip code closest in numerical order to 60000; in this case it is 73071.
9. Press <undo> **Esc** to return to the Database Main menu.

```
27713 | NAME        DAVIS, JOHN
33166 | RATING      01
43219 | ADDRESS     85494 MAIN
43652 | CITY        PHOENIX
45428 | STATE       ARIZONA
48502 | ZIPCODE     85008
55124 | PURCHASES   23.56
73071 | PAYMENTS    0.00
78704 | BALANCE     23.56
85008 | PHONE       (602) 555-9546
97222 |

                 A:CUSTOMER.ZIPCODE
<arrows> <change> <line_ins> <line_del> <search> <undo>
```

FIGURE 6-4

```
NAME                                        CREDIT RATING

ADDRESS                                     PHONE

CITY

STATE                             ZIPCODE 0

                           PURCHASES        0.00

                           PAYMENTS         0.00
                          ---------------------------
                           BALANCE          0.00


   <select> form mode, <eval> evaluate, <do> saves, <help> for other keys
```

FIGURE 6-5

Entering a New Record

In this section, you will practice adding new records to a database file using its screen form file. A screen form is a file created by the user. It provides a place to enter new records or change and delete old records. The screen form itself has already been created for this exercise; you will learn to create one later.

When the name of an existing file is entered, a screen form appears containing all the blank fields that are in each record of the file (Figure 6-5). There is no special significance to the field placement in this screen form. Individual screen forms are designed to meet the user's needs. More than one screen form can be created for a file.

With the following hands-on exercise, add a new record to the CUSTOMER file. Use right and left <arrow> keys to backspace to correct typographical errors when entering data in the fields.

Hands On

1. Select "Enter_Data" from the Database Main menu.
2. Type [CUSTOMER] when prompted for the name of a screen form. Press <do> **F10**. The screen form appears.
3. Type the name [SMITH, JACK] at the blinking cursor and press <ret> **Return**.
4. Type [01] as the credit rating; press <ret>.
5. Type [543 NORTHWAY] as the address; press <ret>.
6. Type [(212) 555-1234] as the phone number; press <ret>.
7. Type [NEW YORK] as the city; press <ret>.
8. Type [NY] as the state; press <ret>.
9. Type [10022] as the zip code; press <ret>.

10. Type [319.76] as the purchase amount; press <ret>.
11. Type [150.00] as the payment amount; press <ret>. Notice that the cursor returned to the NAME field and did not move to the BALANCE field. When a screen form is created, a field can be set so that data will be automatically calculated and filled in. In this case, the BALANCE field must be evaluated; it is equal to PURCHASES minus PAYMENTS.
12. Press <eval> **Alt-F10** to fill in the BALANCE field. The balance, 169.76, appears.
13. Press <do> to save this record. Another blank screen form appears so you can enter another record.
14. Press <menu> **F2** to return to the Database Main menu.

The Structured Query Language

Because there are just a few records and the files in this database are very small, it is possible to "Browse" through an entire file quickly and easily. But the files in some databases are many times larger, and browsing through the records could be a very slow and inefficient way to locate data. A more convenient way would be to retrieve *only* the specific files or records you want to see rather than browse through all of them.

The Structured Query Language (SQL) is a way for a user to easily retrieve the pertinent records from a file. With simple English-like words the user queries the database about the data that is desired. The query is composed of four clauses--FROM, SELECT, WHERE, and ORDER--that are used to specify search parameters. The clauses are described as follows:

- FROM Identifies from which file(s) to retrieve the records
- SELECT Identifies the field(s) to be retrieved
- WHERE Sets specific conditions that the field(s) data must meet to be retrieved
- ORDER Sorts records by a key field(s) in alphabetic or numeric sequence

The FROM clause is mandatory--it names the file to be searched; the other clauses are optional, and their use depends on the data being requested. All the clauses do not have to be used, but they must follow the sequence FROM, SELECT, WHERE, and ORDER when they are used. Both relational operators and logical operators can be used in the query. Relational operators are listed in Table 6-2.

TABLE 6-2 Relational Operators

Operator	*Meaning*
>	greater than
<	less than
>=	greater than or equal to
<=	less than or equal to
=	equal to
<>	not equal to

The logical operators are AND, OR, and NOT. An AND operation demands that all the stated conditions must be met for the records to be retrieved. In an OR operation any one, but not necessarily all, of the conditions may be met for the records to be retrieved. In a NOT operation, records are retrieved when the stated conditions are not met.

The following example illustrates the use of the SQL to retrieve a record.

```
FROM      CUSTOMER
SELECT    NAME, RATING, BALANCE
WHERE     BALANCE > 20 OR RATING = 01
ORDER     NAME
```

This query retrieves records from the CUSTOMER file. The fields chosen are NAME, RATING, and BALANCE. But records are selected only if the balance is greater than $20 or the credit rating is equal to one. When those records are selected they are put in alphabetical order by customer name.

The SQL is used to specify and display the exact data desired, making it much more efficient for the user than browsing through the entire file.

Retrieving Records

Records can be retrieved from a file once specific conditions are established. You can retrieve records by choosing one of three methods from the Data Retrieval Methods menu: Form_Query, Compose, and Pre_Defined. The Form_Query does not use the SQL; the Compose method does, however, and allows you to retrieve the specific fields and records needed using SQL.

Form_Query Method

The Form_Query method is an easy way to retrieve data for those who are unfamiliar with query languages or have little or no database experience. The Form_Query method specifies conditions for retrieval, but it has a few limitations. First, any conditions set for retrieval are automatically ANDed (taken as one set) together. Second, all fields in the record are retrieved; you cannot select specific ones. The following hands-on exercise retrieves all records from the CUSTOMER file that meet certain conditions: i.e., the CREDIT RATING is equal to 01, the STATE first initial is from L to Z, and BALANCE due is more than 20.

Hands On

1. Select "Retrieve" from the Database Main menu. The Data Retrieval Methods menu appears.
2. Select "Form_Query." The prompt asks for a screen form file.
3. Type [CUSTOMER] and press <do> **F10**. A blank screen form appears for you to specify the conditions for record retrieval. The cursor appears at the NAME field.
4. Press <ret> **Return**. This means no conditions are being set for the NAME field. The cursor appears at the CREDIT RATING field.
5. Type [01] in the RATING field to retrieve only those records where the rating is equal to 1. Press <ret>.
6. Press <ret> three more times to bypass the ADDRESS, PHONE, and CITY fields.
7. Type [>K] in the STATE field to retrieve records for those people who live in states starting with letters L through Z. Press <ret>.
8. Press <ret> three times to bypass the ZIPCODE, PURCHASE, and PAYMENT fields.

```
 NAME                         RATING     ADDRESS
>TOLLE, IVAN                  01         8549 DECATUR
>SMITH, DON                   01         2094 VALLEY
>HAYES, WALTER                01         78554 N. DIXIE
>SMITH, JACK                  01         543 NORTHWAY






                     record #1 of 4 records.
         (repeat factor)  <arrows> <change> <menu> <print>
```

FIGURE 6-6

9. Type [>20] and press <ret> to set the condition for the BALANCE field.
10. Press <do> for the program to accept the conditions and to retrieve and display all records that meet these conditions. A list screen appears showing the records retrieved (Figure 6-6). The message at the bottom "record #1 of 4 records." means there are four records that meet all the conditions. The cursor is now flashing in front of the first record.
11. Press right and left <arrow> keys to view all the fields for those records. Notice that the data fields scroll across the screen and wrap around to start over, showing all the data fields in the records.
12. Press <menu> **F2** to return to the Database Operations menu.
13. Select "Quit." Press <do> in response to the prompt "Quit Retrieval?" to clear the active workfile and return to the Database Main menu.

Compose Method

The Compose method of retrieval uses the SQL. You can more specifically define the records and fields to be retrieved by using the mandatory clause FROM and the optional clauses SELECT, WHERE, and ORDER. In the next hands-on exercise, you are to retrieve all the records from a file using the Compose method.

Hands On

1. Select "Retrieve." The Data Retrieval Methods menu appears.
2. Select "Compose." The cursor is blinking after the prompt "FROM." Remember, the FROM clause is mandatory and you must answer this to proceed.

3. Type [ORDERNO]. This file contains all the order numbers. Press <do> **F10** and all the records from the ORDERNO file are retrieved and displayed.

If at this point you want to retrieve only those records where the total cost of an order exceeds $25, you must use more than just the FROM clause. The FROM clause alone retrieves *all* the records. Each query clause must be separated from the condition statement (the specific retrieval statement) by a space. Although each clause does not have to be written on a separate line, it is done that way in this workbook for clarity.

In the next hands-on exercise, revise your query by adding a WHERE and a SELECT clause. This will cause only certain records to be retrieved.

Hands On

1. Press <menu> **F2** to return to the Database Operations menu.
2. Select "Revise." This returns the Query Composition window so you can edit or change the query. ORDERNO was already entered, and the cursor appears after it.
3. Press <ret> **Return** and type [WHERE TOTALCOST >25]. Press <do> **F10**. This retrieves only the records in which the total order is more than $25. However, notice that all the fields are still retrieved with each record.
4. Press left <arrow> twice to bring the total cost column into view.
5. Press <menu> and select "Revise."
6. Use left <arrow> or press <jump_left> **Ctrl-Home** to move the cursor to the left margin of the same line--the cursor is on the W of WHERE.

```
 NAME                                     TOTALCOST
>SCOTT, RUBY                                        29.61
>TOLLE, IVAN                                        46.08
>HAYES, WALTER                                      69.12















                          record #1 of 3 records.
              (repeat factor)  <arrows> <change> <menu> <print>
```

FIGURE 6-7

7. Press the <line ins> **Ctrl-Ret** to insert a line for the SELECT clause. (Remember that the SELECT clause must come before a WHERE clause if both are used.)
8. Type [SELECT NAME, TOTALCOST] and press <do>. This finds only the NAME and TOTALCOST fields for each record retrieved (Figure 6-7).
9. Press <menu> to return to the Database Operations menu.
10. Select "Quit."
11. Press <do> in response to the prompt to return to the Database Main menu.

In the previous exercise, you inserted a line with <line_ins>. A <line_del> Ctrl-BkSp option deletes an entire line to restructure a query.

The WHERE clause is powerful because of the variety of its uses. Following are examples showing how the WHERE clause can set specific retrieval conditions.

Range Criteria. It is possible to select records in which the value of a field falls within a given range. The format for this WHERE clause is

WHERE field name IN range

A parenthesis indicates the range boundary is included, an angle bracket indicates that it is not. A colon separates the beginning and the ending range values.

WHERE BALANCE IN (20:30>

This query retrieves all records where the balance is from $20 through $29.

WHERE PURCHASES IN (20:30)

This query retrieves all records where purchases were either $20, $30, or any value in between.

Text Matching. Text matching can be applied only to a text field. Two symbols called wildcards are used; they are '?' and '*'. The '?' represents any one character, and '*' represents any number of text characters. The format for this query is

WHERE field name MATCHES condition

For example,

WHERE NAME MATCHES 'S*'

This query selects all records where the data in the NAME field starts with the letter "S" and ends with any combination of letters.

Text Similarity. Like text matching, this query can be used only on text fields. This is a version of the WHERE clause and can be used if you are not sure of the name of the field. The format is

WHERE field name LIKE 'text value'

For example,

WHERE NAME LIKE 'SMYTHE'

This query finds records with the field NAME that are close to "SMYTHE", for example, SMITH.

Intra-Record Field Comparison. In the same file, fields of like type can be compared to each other by relational operators. For example, two decimal fields could be compared in the CUSTOMER file.

WHERE BALANCE > PAYMENTS

This query retrieves all records where the balance is larger than the customer's payments.

Multiple search conditions can be set to retrieve records with a WHERE clause, using the logical operators AND, OR, and NOT. They can be combined with the wildcards '?' and '*' and the relational operators <, >, =, < =, > =, and < >. Here is an example.

WHERE BALANCE < >0 AND RATING >'01'

This WHERE query retrieves records where two conditions are met: i.e., the BALANCE field is not equal to zero and the RATING field is greater than one.

Parentheses may also be used with the WHERE clause.

WHERE BALANCE < >0 AND (NAME MATCHES 'D*' OR NAME MATCHES 'B*')

This query first evaluates the condition set forth in the parentheses: retrieve a name beginning with "D" or "B" and containing any number of characters thereafter. If the data in a field matches any of those conditions, the record would be retrieved only if the value in the BALANCE field is not equal to zero.

The search conditions for retrieving records are virtually unlimited. You can specify exactly what you want to retrieve with the SQL.

You will use each of the WHERE clauses from the previous examples in the following hands-on exercises. Use only one WHERE clause at a time. If you get a flashing PROBLEM message at the top of the screen, you probably have mistyped the entry. Check spelling and punctuation.

Hands On

1. Select "Retrieve" from the Main menu. The Data Retrieval Methods menu appears.
2. Select "Compose."
3. Type [CUSTOMER] as the name of the file. Press <ret> **Return**.
4. Type [WHERE PURCHASES IN (20:30>]. Press <do> **F10**. This retrieves records where the balance is from $20 through $29. The records for Smith, Davis, Thomas, and Scott are shown.
5. Press <menu> **F2** and then select "Revise" from the Database Options menu. This brings up the Query Composition window.
6. Press **Back Space** once to delete the angle bracket.
7. Type [)]. Press <do>. This retrieves all the above records plus James where purchases were from $20 to $30. Press left <arrow> four times to verify the amounts in the PURCHASES column.

8. Press <menu> and select "Revise" from the Database Options menu.
9. Press <line_del> **Ctrl-BkSp** to delete the WHERE clause and press <ret> **Return**. Now substitute each of the following WHERE clauses a through d.

   a. [WHERE NAME MATCHES 'S*'] (Records of Jan Schultz, Ruby Scott, Don Smith, and Jack Smith are found.)
   b. [WHERE NAME LIKE 'SMYTHE'] (Records of Don Smith and Jack Smith are found.)
   c. [WHERE BALANCE > PAYMENTS] (Records of James; Davis; Thomas; Tolle; Smith, Don; Schultz; Hayes; Long; Scott; and Smith, Jack are found.)
   d. [WHERE BALANCE < >0 AND RATING >'01'] (Records of Thomas, Buck, and Scott are found.)

10. Type [WHERE BALANCE < >0 AND (NAME MATCHES 'D*' OR NAME MATCHES 'B*')]; press <do>. (Records of Davis and Buck are found.)

After you have practiced with these WHERE clauses, practice exiting the database module and returning to the main Options window. From there you can quit or restart and continue with more database exercises.

TO QUIT: Press <menu> to return to the Operations menu; select "Quit"; press <do> in response to the prompt. This returns you to the Database Main menu. Select "Options" and return to the main Options window. Select another module or exit to the operating system. If you exit to the Operating System, you must reload OA.
RESTART: Reload OA. Select "Database" from the Options menu and return to the Main menu.

Pre_Defined Method

The Pre_Defined query method retrieves records based on a previously stored SQL retrieval condition. This method is useful when the same records need to be retrieved often. The queries are composed as part of a screen, print, or table form, which is discussed later. The query can be changed and saved in another file for later use. The original query will not be lost.

Sorting Records

Records may be placed in alphabetical or numerical sequence using either the SQL ORDER clause or the "Order" command found in the Database Operations menu.

The ORDER clause is placed after all other clauses in a query. Only key fields can be sorted, but you can sort up to 15 key fields. The default setting sorts records in ascending order, that is, starting from letter A to Z and numbers from 1 upward. To sort in descending order, place a minus (-) sign in front of any field to be sorted.

Remember that records are sorted by the first entry in a field. If the first name was entered first in the field called NAME when the record was created, it will be sorted by the first name. If you want to alphabetize by last name, enter the last name first, as done in these examples. Another way to sort by the last name is to create two fields: FIRSTNAME and LASTNAME, instead of just one field for both names. Then, choose to sort by the field LASTNAME.

In the next hands-on exercise, perform a sort operation using the ORDER clause from the SQL.

Hands On

1. Select "Retrieve" from the Database Main menu. The Data Retrieval Methods menu appears.
2. Select "Compose" to use the SQL.
3. Type [CUSTOMER ORDER BALANCE] to complete the query. This query sorts all the records in the CUSTOMER file numerically by the BALANCE field. Remember, it is not necessary to enter the SQL clauses on separate lines.
4. Press <do> **F10**.
5. Press the left <arrow> key twice to verify that the list was sorted by the BALANCE field.

Sorting can also be done from the Database Operations menu. In the next hands-on exercise, perform a sort using the Order command rather than using the ORDER clause.

Hands On

1. Press <menu> **F2** and select "Order" from the Database Operations menu.
2. Press the <search> **F4** key to display a list of these fields. Press <undo> **Esc** to remove the search window. Type [-NAME] in response to the prompt.
3. Press <do> **F10**. This sorts the records in descending order by name (Figure 6-8).
4. Press <menu>; then select "Quit."
5. Press <do> in response to the prompt to return to the Database Main menu.

```
    BALANCE        PHONE                     NAME
>          26.08   (919) 555-8363            TOLLE, IVAN
>          14.00   (513) 555-8582            THOMAS, BOB C.
>           0.00   (313) 555-8362            TEAGARDEN, WILLIAM
>         169.76   (212) 555-1234            SMITH, JACK
>          20.82   (512) 555-8333            SMITH, DON
>          19.61   (612) 555-3743            SCOTT, RUBY
>          12.42   (419) 555-1423            SCHULTZ, JAN
>          13.52   (305) 555-2121            LONG, M. DAVID
>          20.00   (313) 555-5986            JAMES, RALPH
>          52.16   (503) 555-0390            HAYES, WALTER
>          23.56   (602) 555-9546            DAVIS, JOHN
>          20.00   (405) 555-0834            BUCK, NIEL

                         record #1 of 12 records.
              (repeat factor)  <arrows> <change> <menu> <print>
```

FIGURE 6-8

Changing and Updating Records

It is possible to change the contents of an entire record or of a single field in a record after it has already been created. Changes (updates) to one record at a time are made using Browse command and the <change> F6 key; changes to multiple fields are made with the Update command.

Change one record's address in the CUSTOMER file in the following hands-on exercise.

Hands On

1. Select "Browse" from the Main menu.
2. Type [CUSTOMER] to specify which file contains the record that needs to be changed. Press <ret> **Return**.
3. Press <arrows>, if needed, until the Buck, Niel record is highlighted.
4. Press <change> **F6** and then <do> **F10** to select the default screen form. This displays the record for Buck in the default screen form.
5. Press <ret> twice to position the cursor at the ADDRESS field and enter the new address [614 CENTRAL AVE.]. Press <do> to save the change in the record.
6. Press <change> again to display the changed record in the Browse screen.
7. Press <undo> **Esc** to return to the Database Main menu.

Let's say that a big shipment arrived at your office supply store and you restock all items that are out of stock. To reflect this arrival and update all the out-of-stock records at one time, you could use the Update command. The SQL could specify all the items, and further query could list all items not in stock.

In the next hands-on exercise, update all entries in one field using the Update command.

Hands On

1. Select "Retrieve" from the Main menu. The Data Retrieval Methods menu appears.
2. Select "Compose" so you can use the SQL.
3. Type the filename [ITEMS] and press <ret> **Return**.
4. Type [SELECT ITEMNUMBER, DESCRIBE, INSTOCK] to complete the query. Press <ret>; now type [WHERE INSTOCK = FALSE]. Press <do> **F10** to enter the query. This displays those records where the item is not in stock--file cabinet, felt-tip pen, organizer, printer ribbon, and bookbag.
5. Press <menu> **F2** to access the Database Operations menu.
6. Select "Update." The Update Field Values window appears with the prompt "Set:" asking for the name of the field to update.
7. Type [INSTOCK]; press <ret>. The prompt "Set Instock to:" appears.
8. Type the new value ['TRUE'].
9. Press <do> to save the changes. The updated list shows these items are now in stock (Figure 6-9).
10. Press <menu> to return to the Database Operations menu.

```
 ITEMNUMBER  DESCRIBE              INSTOCK
>      4909  FILE CABINET          TRUE
>      1922  FELT-TIP PEN          TRUE
>      7445  ORGANIZER             TRUE
>      9874  PRINTER RIBBON        TRUE
>      1773  BOOKBAG               TRUE



                          record #1 of 5 records.
             (repeat factor)  <arrows> <change> <menu> <print>
```

FIGURE 6-9

11. Select "Quit."
12. Press <do> in response to the prompt to return to the Database Main menu.

Deleting Records

To delete a record from the file means to remove it. Records can be deleted one at a time in the Browse window, or multiple files can be deleted by incorporating a query with the Delete command.

In the next hands-on exercise, delete only one record from the Browse window.

Hands On

1. Select "Browse" from the Main menu.
2. Type [CUSTOMER]. Press <do> **F10**. (If the default file name CUSTOMER is already next to the prompt, just press <do>.) The Browse window listing the records appears.
3. Press <arrows> to move down the list until the record for SMITH, DON is highlighted.
4. Press <line_del> **Ctrl-BkSp**. The prompt "Delete Record?" appears.
5. Press <do> to verify that this is the record to be deleted. The Browse window reappears with the SMITH, DON record removed.
6. Press <undo> **Esc** to return to the Database Main menu.

Remember the prompt that asked you to verify the deletion of the record? This prompt occurs before any record is deleted as a precaution against accidental deletions. However, you should make backup copies of all files to protect data against accidental deletions.

Multiple records can be deleted at the same time with the Delete command. Practice deleting multiple records. In this hands-on exercise, customers from Michigan were assigned to a new territory, and those records can now be deleted from this file.

Hands On

1. Select "Retrieve" from the Main menu.
2. Select "Compose" from the Data Retrieval Methods menu.
3. Type the file name [CUSTOMER] in response to the FROM prompt and press <ret> **Return**.
4. Type [WHERE STATE='MICHIGAN'] to set the condition for record retrieval.
5. Press <do> **F10** to accept the query. The records of both Michigan customers (James and Teagarden) are displayed in the List screen.
6. Press <menu> **F2** to access the Database Operations menu.
7. Select "Delete." A prompt asks "Destroy all records found?"
8. Press <do> to verify that the records retrieved are to be deleted. These records are deleted from the file, although they still appear on the screen. The Database Main menu is also on the screen.

Creating a File

In this section, you will learn to create two files: a data file, where the data are stored; and a screen form file to show how data are organized on the screen and provide a way to enter data into the file. A filename must start with a letter and can contain as many as eight characters. The other characters in a name can be letters, numbers, the number sign (#), or an underscore (_). Blank spaces are not allowed. The file to be created is first given a name. Practice with the following hands-on exercise.

Hands On

1. Select "Design" from the Main menu. The File Design and Maintenance menu appears.
2. Select "Create_File."
3. Type [BILLING] at the prompt as the name of your new file.
4. Press <do> **F10** for the program to accept that entry. At this point you see a blank screen--the Screen Definition window. The options shown at the bottom of the window include <edit_keys>, <change>, <select>, <menu>, and <search>.

Now you must set up the data field positions (determine where the data will be placed) and define their attributes (define the data with descriptors from the Field Attribute window). Table 6-3 provides an explanation of the attributes that are to be set.

TABLE 6-3 Field Attribute Window Options

Attribute	*Description*
Name	Descriptor for the field.
Kind	Unique-key and key fields are used for sorting and faster retrieval. Nonkey fields are used for normal retrieving. External fields are used with a Must Match field to display data from another file.
Type	These specify the type of data to be entered into the data field as text, date, number (no decimal points), True/False (yes/no), decimal (fixed point), and scientific (floating point).
Justify	The data is placed at the right or left field boundary, centered, or repeated across the field.
Evaluated	How the data value is entered. ■ Normal Data is manually entered. ■ Autodate The system date is automatically entered. ■ Form A field is quickly accessed if designated as a Form field to make changes and recalculate any dependent fields. ■ Skip This field may not be changed or deleted through a screen form. ■ Dependent This field is automatically calculated by an expression, which is dependent on values from other fields. ■ Autoincrement The value entered in this field is incremented by 1 (one) from the value entered in the same field for the last record. ■ Range The data entered in this field must be in a certain range of values.
Video mode	On a color monitor, the color can be changed; on a monochrome monitor, the video state may be changed to blinking, inverse mode, etc.
Must fill	There must be a value entered in this field.
Disp. width	The display width of the field can be set here.
Duplicate	Until you enter a new value in this field, it takes the value of the previous record's field.
Must match	To enter a value in this field it must match one from a designated field in another file.

The field name, like the filename, cannot contain spaces, must start with a letter, and be followed with any combination of letters, numbers, "_", or "#." The field name can be ten characters long. The system recognizes the word directly in front of the field location as the name of the field. For example, "Social Security" would be read as only the word "Security" as the field name. You might structure compound-word names, to use abbreviations of both words, for example, Soc_Sec. The underline character joins the two names.

```
ACCOUNT

DATE
                                             INSURED
CODE

DESCRIBE

DRNUM





                                                  CHARGES

                                                 PAYMENTS

                                                          _______

                                                  BALANCE

                 <edit_keys> <change> <select> <menu> <search>
```

FIGURE 6-10

Use Figure 6-10 as a guideline for the placement of the fields as you set up the BILLING file. In the next hands-on exercise, set the attributes for the ACCOUNT field. Table 6-4 contains the data needed to enter the attributes for all the remaining fields. You will also learn to create a new screen form for the billing file.

Hands On

1. Use <arrow> keys to position and type the field names as shown in Figure 6-10. The following list will help you:

Field	*Position*
ACCOUNT	Line 1, col. 1
DATE	Line 3, col. 1
CODE	Line 5, col. 1
DESCRIBE	Line 7, col. 1
DRNUM	Line 9, col. 1
INSURED	Line 4, col. 38
CHARGES	Line 14, col. 43
PAYMENTS	Line 16, col. 42
BALANCE	Line 20, col. 43

2. Enter an underscore line 7 characters long at line 18, col. 51.
3. After you have typed all the field names, move the cursor two places to the right of the field name, ACCOUNT.
4. Press <select> **F9** to begin to set the field width.

TABLE 6-4 BILLING File Attribute Data

Field Width	*Name*	*Kind*	*Type*	*Justify*	*Evaluated*
10	DATE	Key	Date	Left	Autodate
5	CODE	Key	Number	Left	Normal
15	DESCRIBE	Non-key	Text	Left	Normal
5	INSURED	Key	True/False	Left	Normal
3	DRNUM	Non-key	Number	Left	Normal
7	CHARGES	Key	Decimal	Right	Normal
7	PAYMENTS	Key	Decimal	Right	Normal
7	BALANCE	Key	Decimal	Right	Dependent*

*Enter the following formula when prompted for Expression:

[CHARGES - PAYMENTS]

5. Use <arrows> to move the cursor ten spaces to the right to set the field width, or length of the entry, to 11. The field width is indicated at the bottom of the screen.
6. Press <do> **F10** to reveal the Entry Attributes window (Figure 6-11). (Table 6-3 describes each attribute listed in the window.)
7. Press <ret> **Return** to move the cursor to the Kind attribute. (Use left and right <arrows> to highlight the attributes.)
8. Highlight "Unique-Key" after the Kind attribute. This means the account # is unique; no one else can have the same account number. Press <ret> **Return** to move to the Type attribute. The Text option is highlighted.
9. Press <change> **F6** to display the Text Entry Attributes window. These choices are available only for Text fields, and since ACCOUNT is a number field, press <undo> **Esc.** Highlight "Number" because the ACCOUNT field will contain a number. Press <ret>. This places the cursor in the Justify attribute.
10. Press the <ret> to accept the defaults till you reach the Must Fill attribute.
11. Use <arrows> to highlight "True" to set the Must Fill attribute to True. This means that an entry must be made in this field or the record will not be accepted.
12. Press <ret> three times until you reach the Must Match attribute; then press <do> to tell the program to accept all the default values. The Screen Form Definition window is again displayed. Now there is an underscore the length of the field; it may be blocked in a different color on a graphics monitor.
13. Repeat steps 3 through 11 to set attributes for the remaining fields. Use the file attribute data settings in Table 6-4.
14. Press <menu> **F2** when you have finished. The Screen Layout and File Definition menu appears.
15. Select "Save." This saves the screen form and returns to the Database Main menu.

TO QUIT: To exit this module and return to the Database Main menu later, select "Options" and return to the main Options window. Select another module or exit to the operating

Video Mode	Must Fill	Disp. Width	Duplicate	Must Match
Normal	False	10	False	False
Normal	True	5	False	False
Normal	False	15	False	False
Mode-1	False	5	False	False
Normal	True	3	False	False
Normal	True	7	False	False
Normal	False	7	False	False
Normal	False	7	False	False

system. If you exit to the Operating System, you must reload OA.

RESTART: Reload OA. Select "Database" from the Options menu. The Database Main menu appears. Continue with the next section.

```
ACCOUNT

DATE
                          Entry Attributes
CODE
DESC          Name:  ACCOUNT
              Kind:  Unique-Key  Key  Non-key  External
DRNU          Type:  Text  Date  Number  True/False  Decimal  Scientific
           Justify:  Left  Right  Center  Repeat
         Evaluated:  Normal  AutoDate  Form  Skip
                     Dependent  AutoIncrement  Range
        Video mode:  Normal  Mode-1  Mode-2  Mode-3              *
         Must fill:  True  False
       Disp. width:  11
         Duplicate:  True  False
        Must match:  True  False

                          <do> <undo> <up> <down>

Field width: 11
            <edit_keys> <change> <select> <menu> <search>
```

FIGURE 6-11

You have just created a screen form for the file BILLING. Each field was set to accept only certain types of data when you set the attribute values. Now there is a place to enter data into the new file BILLING.

Changing a Screen Form

Each file that is created can have more than one screen form file. Another screen form file might contain only some of the fields so that all of the information is not available to everyone. The original screen form field attributes can be changed, and the position of the fields can be realigned. The screen form can be up to fifteen pages long, so there is plenty of room for the data fields.

To alter an existing screen form or create a new screen form, you can use the Screen_Form command. You can alter an existing screen form with this command by (1) modifying or adding explanatory text or notes, (2) adjusting the location of the fields displayed, and (3) modifying any of the field attributes except name, type, and kind.

To add additional fields, change the Name, Type, or Kind of any of the already created fields, the Modify_File command must be used. In the next hands-on exercise, change the attribute of the CODE field by going back into the screen form.

Hands On

1. Select "Design" from the Database Main menu.
2. Select "Screen_Form." The File Identification window appears.
3. Type the name [BILLING] at the prompt "Template Mask File:" as the name of the screen form that you want to modify. Press <ret> **Return.**
4. Type [BILLING] at the prompt "Output Mask File:" as the name of the modified screen form and press <do> **F10.** This displays the Screen Definition window.
5. Use <arrow> keys to move the cursor to the first position in the CODE field. Information about the CODE field is displayed at the bottom of the Screen Definition window.
6. Press <change> **F6** to display the Entry Attributes window.
7. Use <ret> or <arrows> and highlight the Evaluated option. Then use left or right <arrows> to move to the Range option to set a range in which the data must fall to be accepted.
8. Press <change> and at the prompt "Lo range:" enter the lowest value that can be entered as ["100"]; then press <ret>.
9. Type the highest value ["999"]; then press <ret>.
10. Use <arrows> to move to the Disp. width option.
11. Type [3] to reset the field width.
12. Press <do> to accept the change.
13. Press <menu> **F2** to redisplay the Screen Layout and File Definition menu.
14. Select "Save" to save the changes and return to the Database Main menu.

Now practice entering data into your file using the data from Table 6-5. This will help familiarize you with fields that have specific attributes and show you how this affects data entry. Follow the hands-on exercise and enter the data exactly as shown in Table 6-5.

TABLE 6-5 BILLING File Data

Field	*Record 1*	*Record 2*	*Record 3*
ACCOUNT	6132	6133	6133
DATE	(This field is automatically filled in when AUTODATE was selected as an attribute.)		
INSURED	True	True	False
CODE	140	147	10
DESCRIBE	Office Call	Check Up	Injection
DRNUM	14	14	34
CHARGES	45.00	37.00	8.00
PAYMENTS	0.00	0.00	0.00
BALANCE	<eval> Alt-F10	<eval>	<eval>

Hands On

1. Select "Enter_Data" from the Database Main menu.
2. Type [BILLING] as the screen form filename and press <do> **F10**.
3. Type records 1 and 2 using the data in Table 6-5. Press <do> after each record has been entered. Follow the remaining steps for record 3.
4. Enter data for record number 3. When "10" is entered in the field CODE, a range window appears saying that you have entered a value that was out of range. Press <do> and enter [218] as the correct value in the CODE field. Continue entering the rest of the data in Table 6-5 for record number 3.
5. Press <do> after the data is entered. The error message "Duplicate Value in Unique Key" appears at the top of the screen because ACCOUNT was set as a unique key field. The same account number was assigned to two accounts.
6. Press <do> and enter [6134] as the correct account number. Press <do> to accept the change.
7. Press <menu> **F2** to return to the Database Main menu.

Passwords

Passwords are character strings of numbers, letters, or both that permit access to all or part of the file if the user correctly enters the string. There are three types of passwords: Database, Use_Form, and Change_Form.

The Database password restricts entry to those who try to access a file without using a screen form file, such as from the Compose window.

The Use_Form password restricts entry to the file from a screen form. The Change_Form password prevents unauthorized persons from making changes in the screen form.

A person can gain partial access to the screen form if the Use_Form password includes an ALLOW clause. This query comes after the FROM clause and before any other clause. The ALLOW clause is followed by a space and any one or more of the following letters, G (get or view), C (change), D (delete), or I (insert). A person who has the Use_Form password may be allowed limited access if the query includes an ALLOW clause.

A database password can be created or changed with the "Modify File" command. You will enter a database password for the BILLING file in the following hands-on exercise. The password may be up to 20 characters long.

Hands On

1. Select "Design" from the Database Main menu. This displays the File Design and Maintenance menu.
2. Select "Modify_File." This displays the Modify File window.
3. Type [BILLING] as the file that you plan to modify; press <do> **F10**. This displays the Modify File menu.
4. Select "Database_Password" to display the Set New Password window.
5. Type [abc]. The entry appears as dashed lines to prevent others from viewing the password. Press <do>.
6. Type [abc] again to verify that this is the correct password and press <do>. The password is now set.
7. Press <undo> **Esc** to return to the Database Main menu.
8. Select "Options" to display the Options menu. This removes the BILLING file from the computer's memory so that when it is reloaded you will be asked for the new password.
9. Select "Database."

Now try to access the BILLING file from a Compose window in the next hands-on exercise.

Hands On

1. Select "Retrieve" from the Database Main menu.
2. Select "Compose."
3. Type [BILLING] as the filename and press <do> **F10**. The Required Password Assignment window appears. You must enter the exact password to access the file.
4. Type [abc] as the password and press <do> to gain access to the file. The file appears on the screen.
5. Press <menu> **F2**. The Database Operations menu appears.
6. Select "Quit" and press <do> to return to the Main menu.

TO QUIT: To exit this module and return to the Database Main menu later, select "Options" and return to the main Options menu. Select a module or exit to the operating system. If you exit to the Operating System, you must reload OA.

RESTART: Reload OA. Select "Database" from the Options menu. The Database Main menu appears and you can continue with the next section.

Printing a Record or Report

Information can be printed either as a single record or as part of a report. You can print a record from the screen when it is with its screen form by pressing <print> F3 and then choosing the correct printer from the Output Device Selection window. This printing can be done from the Entry and Display screens, but not from the Browse window.

You can also print the contents of the screen at any time by pressing the <prt_scr> Alt-F3 key. This key combination prints a record, a menu window, or anything else that happens to be on the screen at the time.

Usually, though, data are printed in the form of a report. First, a print form file must be created for the report, and then the report is sent to a printer with the Print command. In the following hands-on exercise, create a print form for the BILLING file and set the number of columns that your printer can print.

Hands On

1. Select "Design" from the Database Main menu. The File Design and Maintenance menu appears.
2. Select "Print_Form." Press <ret> **Return** in answer to the prompt, "Print Form template file:". No print forms are stored for your BILLING file. The prompt, "Print Form output file:" appears.
3. Type [BILLING]. Press <do> **F10**. At this point, you must answer the FROM prompt on the Query Composition menu.
4. Type [BILLING] as the name of the Print_Form. While in the Query Composition window, you can add clauses to the query to SELECT any of the fields you would like in the report. You can also include WHERE and ORDER clauses. In this example, all the fields are included since no other clauses are entered.
5. Press <do> to retrieve all the records. If you exited the database module, you will be prompted to enter the password; type [abc]; press <do>; and continue.
6. Type [80] as the number of columns that your printer will print in one line. (If this is not correct for your printer or if you do not know this number, press <search> **F4**. From the list of printers, select the printer that closely matches yours. When the printer is selected, the display width is filled in automatically.)
7. Press <do>. The Header window is displayed (Figure 6-12).

The print form can contain up to six different sections. Each section is labelled at the top of the screen so there is no confusion about where you are. These sections are the

- Header Located at the top of the report; it contains the title of the report, page numbers, dates, etc.
- Group Header Headings for the subtotals at the levelbreaks
- Record Contains the layout of the report
- Subtotal When fields are sorted, levelbreaks occur when there is a change of value in a sorted field. A subtotal may be calculated and entered at these levelbreaks

```
                                  Header                ( 0,  0)

Page·PAG······················Database fields······················SYSDATE

Current entry: 'Page'
               <move_keys> <change> <select> <menu>
```

FIGURE 6-12

- Footer — Similar to the Header, but located at the bottom of the report
- Totals — A grand total can be calculated and entered at the end of the report.

You can control the appearance of an entry by using the Field Attributes Option window. The options in this window are listed in Table 6-6. The next hands-on exercise shows how to change the header and footer sections of the report.

TABLE 6-6 Field Attributes Options

Option	*Description*
Entry	Makes an entry or changes an entry; a text entry is enclosed in single quotes, while field names and mathematical expressions are enclosed in parentheses.
Width	Sets the width of the entry.
Justification	Places text to the left, right, centered, or repeated across the display.
Precision	Sets the number of decimal places.
Thousands	Places commas in numbers larger than 999 or smaller than -999.
Negative	Shows negative numbers in parentheses () or with a minus sign (-).
Auto currency	Places a dollar sign ($) in the field.

```
                                    Header                  ( 32,   0)

Page·PAG······················Database fields······················SYSDATE
·                                                                      ···
·                                                                      ···
·Entry           : 'Database fields'                                   ···
·Width           :  15                                                 ···
·Justification :    Left   Right   Center   Repeat                     ···
·Precision       :  0                                                  ···
·Thousands       :  Off   On                                           ···
·Negative by ():    Off   On                                           ···
·Auto currency :    Off   On                                           ···
·Bold            :  Off   On                                           ···
·Underline       :  Off   On                                           ···
·Italics         :  Off   On                                           ···
·High Quality    :  Off   On                                           ···
·Superscript     :  Off   On                                           ···
·Subscript       :  Off   On                                           ···
 Color           :  None   Color1   Color2   Color3   Color4
 Size            :  None   Size1    Size2    Size3

C                        <arrows> <do> <undo>
```

FIGURE 6-13

Hands On

1. Use <arrows> to move the cursor to the "D" in the text "Database fields." Press <change> **F6**. This displays the Field Attributes window (Figure 6-13).
2. Type ['BILLING REPORT'] as the text heading for the report. The other option defaults are appropriate as set. Press <do> **F10** to enter the title. The Page header automatically numbers the pages and SYSDATE prints the system date when the report is printed. These defaults are also appropriate as set, so continue to the Footer section.
3. Press <pg_down> **PgDn** four times to reach the Footer section.
4. Press the <arrow> keys to place the cursor on the "D" in the text "Database fields."
5. Press <change> to access the Field Attributes window.
6. Type the new text ['Report by Billing Department'].
7. Use <arrows> to move to the width attribute. It automatically changes to 28 to meet the width of the text entry.
8. Press <do> to enter the change.
9. Press <select> **F9** and use the left <arrow> to position the entry at coordinates (10,1). The current coordinates are shown at the upper right corner of the screen.
10. Press <do> to set the new text position.

The Header and Footer sections of the print form are complete. You may leave the fields where they are or move them to accommodate the report set up. You'll move one in the next hands-on exercise to show how it's done. Notice in Figure 6-14 that there are two field names. One is the text label, the other is the data field.

```
                                        Record                  ( 10,   1)

ACCOUNT·····ACCOUNT ··················································
DATE········DATE    ··················································
INSURED·····INSURED···················································
CODE········CODE    ··················································
DESCRIBE····DESCRIBE        ··········································
DRNUM·······DRNUM   ··················································
CHARGES·····CHARGES      ·············································
PAYMENTS····PAYMENTS     ·············································
BALANCE·····BALANCE      ·············································
······································································
······································································
······································································
······································································
······································································
······································································
······································································



                    <move_keys> <change> <select> <menu>
```

FIGURE 6-14

Hands On

1. Press <pg up> **PgUp** twice to access the Record section.
2. Use <arrows> to position the cursor on the "A" in the first ACCOUNT (not highlighted).
3. Press <select> **F9**.
4. Use <arrows> to move the text ACCOUNT to coordinate (45,3). Press <do> **F10**.
5. Use <arrows> to position the cursor on the "A" in the field ACCOUNT (highlighted).
6. Press <select>.
7. Move the field ACCOUNT to coordinate (45,5). Press <do>. You can rearrange the rest of the fields by repeating steps 2 through 7, using the appropriate field name.

In the Record section, you can create a "virtual field." A virtual field is one that is created in the Record section of the Print Form, but it is not saved to the actual database when the file is saved. A virtual field exists only in the Record section of a print form.

In the next hands-on exercise, you will add a virtual field that says if a customer pays at the time that services are rendered, the customer will receive a 10 percent discount on the bill; the amount the customer pays is entered here. Since this entry is in dollars and cents, you must set decimal places. This charge is the amount the customer pays if payment is made on the same day as services rendered. The Record section is still on the screen.

```
                                    Record                  (  0,   0)

·······························································································
DATE·······DATE       ········································································
INSURED····INSURED·······························································
CODE·······CODE      ························ACCOUNT·····················
DESCRIBE···DESCRIBE        ···································································
DRNUM······DRNUM     ························ACCOUNT ····················
CHARGES····CHARGES       ·····································································
PAYMENTS···PAYMENTS      ·····································································
BALANCE····BALANCE       ·····································································
·······························································································
·······························································································
·······························································································
·······························································································
·········SAME DAY PAY··"DISCOUNT":.9*CH························································
·······························································································
·······························································································



                     <move_keys> <change> <select> <menu>
```

FIGURE 6-15

Hands On

1. Use <arrows> to move the cursor to (23,13).
2. Press <select> **F9** to display the Field Attributes window.
3. Type ["DISCOUNT":.9*CHARGES] as the virtual field description. The format for a virtual field is ["expression NAME":expression]; the expression may be a mathematical formula. After creating the virtual field, you may want to also insert a descriptive name next to the virtual field to identify the contents of the field.
4. Use <arrows> to move down to the Precision option.
5. Type [2] and press <do> **F10** to display the Record screen. This sets two decimal places.
6. Use <arrows> to move the cursor to (9,13).
7. Press <select> and type the text entry ['SAME DAY PAY'] as the virtual field name that will appear on the report. (Single quotes are needed since this is a text field.)
8. Press <do> to enter and redisplay the Record Screen (Figure 6-15).

You can enter some statistical information in the report that will calculate the average charge for all the records. In the next hands-on exercise, you will access the Total screen to enter this information.

Hands On

1. Press <pg_dn> **PgDn** three times to view the Totals screen.
2. Place cursor on S in "SUM(ACCOUNT)."
3. Press <line_del> **Ctrl-BkSp**; prompt says "Entries will be lost."; press <do> **F10**.
4. Put cursor on S in "SUM(CODE)."
5. Press <line_del>; prompt says "Entries will be lost."; press <do>.
6. Put the cursor on SUM(DRNUM).
7. Press <change> **F6** to display the Field Attributes window.
8. Type the new entry [mean(charges)]. This takes the average, or mean, value of the field CHARGES.
9. Use <arrows> to highlight the width attribute and enter [9].
10. Press <do> to accept the entry.
11. Press <select> **F9**; use the right <arrow> to move the field over ten places to (23,1).
12. Press <do> to accept the new location.
13. Use <arrows> to move the cursor on the field name 'DRNUM' and press <change> to display the Field Attributes window.
14. Type ['Average Charges'] as the new text entry.
15. Press <do> to accept the entry.
16. Press <menu> **F2** to display the Print_Format menu (Figure 6-16).
17. Select "Save" to save the print form. The Database Main menu now appears.

To print this report, you first must have entered records the in Table 6-5 in the BILLING file. The following hands-on exercise will "print" the report to the screen to preview it.

```
                                   Totals                   (  0,   0)

Totals:·····························································
Average Charges·······mean(char·····································
CHARGES····SUM(CHARGES)     ········································
PAYMENTS···SUM(PAYMENTS)    ········································
BALANCE····SUM(BALANCE)     ········································
····································································
····································································
····································································
····································································
····································································
····································································
····································································
····································································
····································································
····································································
·                                                                  ·
                            Print Format Menu
    Save   Misc   Header   Group_header   Record   Sub-totals   Footer   Totals
                      Level_breaks   Query   New   Abandon
C                                <do> <undo>
```

FIGURE 6-16

Hands On

1. Select "Print" from the Database Main menu to print the report.
2. Type [BILLING] as the filename you wish to print.
3. Press <do> **F10**. The Output Device Selection list appears.
4. Highlight "Console" and press <do>. Your report is now printed to the screen. (If you choose to print hard copy, select the appropriate printer from the Output Device Selection list.)
5. Press <do> to scroll through the report. Notice how today's date is automatically entered in the SYSDATE field, the page number is entered, and the virtual field has calculated a 10% discount. The last page shows totals with Average Charges calculated at 30.00; Charges at 90.00; Payments at 0.00; and Balance at 90.00.
6. Press <do> until you return to the Database Main menu.

Joining Files

To join files means to combine two or more files into one. The new file created by joining is a temporary one, but it can be made to be a permanent file. Joined files must have at least one key field in common, and they must be of the same kind, e.g., text, decimal, etc.

When joining files, you must use a query composition containing a WHERE clause. The WHERE clause must follow a certain format. This format is the filename, then a period (.), then the field name common to the joined files, then an equal sign (=), and the name of the other file to be joined, followed by another period (.), and the common field name.

Files are joined in pairs and connected with the logical operator AND. In the following hands-on exercise, the CUSTOMER and ORDERNO files each contain a field called NAME that is the same, and the CUSTOMER and ITEMS files each contain a field called ITEMNUMBER that is the same. Common fields must connect the records for them to be joined into a new temporary file. This exercise creates the query necessary to join data from three separate files into one file.

Hands On

1. Select "Retrieve" from the Database Main menu.
2. Select "Compose." Press the <del> **Del** key to erase any words that follow the FROM clause.
3. Type [CUSTOMER, ORDERNO, ITEMS] after the FROM clause as the names of the files to be joined. (The names should be separated by commas.) Press <ret> **Return**.
4. Type [SELECT NAME, ADDRESS, CITY, STATE, ZIPCODE, BALANCE, ITEMNUMBER, DESCRIBE, TOTALCOST] as the field names for the joined file. Press <ret>.
5. Type [WHERE CUSTOMER.NAME=ORDERNO.NAME AND ORDERNO.ITEMNUMBER=ITEMS.ITEMNUMBER] as the conditions for retrieval. Press <ret>.
6. Type [ORDER NAME] as the ORDER clause for sorting the records.
7. Press <do> **F10** to accept the query and join the files. This displays the List screen with the joined file (Figure 6-17).
8. Use <arrows> to view all the fields from the joined files.
9. Press <menu> **F2** to return to the Database Operations menu.

```
 NAME                          ADDRESS
>DAVIS, JOHN                   85494 MAIN
>HAYES, WALTER                 78554 N. DIXIE
>HAYES, WALTER                 78554 N. DIXIE
>HAYES, WALTER                 78554 N. DIXIE
>LONG, M. DAVID                5895 PINEWOOD
>SCHULTZ, JAN                  32 A ST.
>SCOTT, RUBY                   4387 STATE
>SMITH, JACK                   543 NORTHWAY
>TOLLE, IVAN                   8549 DECATUR







                      record #1 of 9 records.
           (repeat factor)  <arrows> <change> <menu> <print>
```

FIGURE 6-17

Use caution when changing any data in the new file created by joining. A change made to a field here also changes the data in the fields in the original files. Although the joined file is a temporary one, you can use the Make command in the Operations menu to convert it to a permanent file. Changes to the new file will not affect the original files.

10. Choose "Make"; then name the new database JOIN.
11. Press <do>. (This process takes a minute or two on a two diskette-drive system.)
12. Press <menu>.
13. Select "Quit." Press <do> in response to the prompt to return to the Database Main menu.

After you used the Make command, the joined file (JOIN) appeared in a List screen rather than in a screen form. By knowing the fields (i.e., name, address, city, state, etc.) that are used in the join, you can create a screen form for the joined files. The file can then be displayed in a form that you set up. This is done by including the query to join the records in the screen form file.

Copying Records

When records are retrieved from a file, they are put into a temporary work file. Files can be copied from a temporary file to a permanent file with the Make command.

In the following hands-on exercise, select certain data from the ORDERNO file and copy it to a new file called HIPRICE.

Hands On

1. Select "Retrieve" from the Database Main menu.
2. Select "Compose."
3. Type the filename [ORDERNO] and press <ret> **Return**. In this case, you want a file of the items priced over $5.00 that have been ordered.
4. Type [WHERE ITEM_PRICE>5.00].
5. Press <do> **F10** to see the records retrieved in the List screen.
6. Press left <arrow> once to confirm these item prices are greater than $5.00.
7. Press <menu> **F2** to access the Database Operations menu.
8. Select "Make" to create the new file. The Make File Form Retrieval Data window appears.
9. Type [HIPRICE] as the name for the new file and press <do> for the program to accept the new filename. Records from ORDERNO file that meet the WHERE clause conditions are now copied to the new file HIPRICE. No screen form exists for the new file, so the records are displayed (Davis, Smith, and Scott) in the List screen. You can create a screen form with the Screen_Form command.
10. Press <menu> to display the Database Operations menu.
11. Select "Quit." Press <do> in response to the prompt to return to the Database Main menu.

There may be cases where you want to copy records from one file to another. This is called "appending a file" and it is done with the Append command. In order to Append a file, the fields of the first file must have the same name and be of the same type as the destination file, or the data will not be transferred. If there are fields that do not match exactly in name and type, no data can be transferred for those fields.

In the following hands-on exercise, add to HIPRICE those items costing from $1.00 to $2.00.

Hands On

1. Select "Retrieve" from the Database Main menu.
2. Select "Compose."
3. Type [ORDERNO] after the FROM clause as the name of the file and press <ret> **Return**.
4. Type [WHERE ITEM_PRICE IN <1:2>] as the retrieval condition and press <do> **F10** to accept the entry. This displays the records (Long and Teagarden) in the List screen.
5. Press <menu> **F2** for the Database Operations menu.
6. Select "Append." The Append Retrieval Data window appears.
7. Type [HIPRICE] as the name of the file into which the retrieved records will be copied; press <do>. A duplicate copy of the records is made and placed in the HIPRICE file. They still exist in the original ORDERNO file.
8. Press <menu> to display the Database Operations menu.
9. Select "Quit" and then press <do> to return to the Database Main menu.
10. Select "Retrieve" and then select "Compose."
11. Type [HIPRICE] after the FROM clause and press <do>. This displays the file appended with the new records.
12. Press <menu> to display the Database Operations menu.
13. Select "Quit." Press <do> in response to the prompt to return to the Main menu.

Summarizing Records

The Status command makes it possible to generate statistical information for a file. These statistics are calculations such as finding an average or standard deviation. The types of statistics that can be calculated are listed in the Status Command Functions, which are listed in Table 6-7.

TABLE 6-7 Status Command Functions

Function	*Description*
COUNT	Totals number of records.
SUM	Adds numeric values in a field for all records.
MIN	Finds the smallest numerical value in a field for all records.
MAX	Finds the largest numerical value in a field for all records.
MEAN	Finds the average of all numeric values in a field for all records.
STD.DEV	Finds the standard deviation for a field for all records.
VARIANCE	Finds the variance for a field for all records.

The Status Functions can be applied only to fields that are retrieved. Of these Status Functions, only text, date, and True/False fields can use the COUNT function. All the functions can be used with numeric, decimal, and scientific fields. In the next hands-on exercise, you will summarize some of the data fields in the CUSTOMER file.

Hands On

1. Select "Retrieve" from the Database Main menu.
2. Select "Compose."
3. Type [CUSTOMER] after the FROM clause as the filename.
4. Press <do> **F10** and the file is displayed in the List screen.
5. Press <menu> **F2** to access the Database Operations menu.
6. Select "Status." This bring up the Status File Specification window.
7. Press <ret> **Return** in response to the prompt "Template File:" since no Template file exists. Now type [CUSTOMER] in response to the "Output File:" prompt as your output file.
8. Press <do> and the Field Aggregate Status window is displayed.
9. Type [NAME] at the cursor position. Because this is a text field, you can use only the Count function. Press <ret> to enter and the cursor moves to the next line.
10. Type [PURCHASES]. To select another function, press the <change> **F6** key until SUM is displayed. Press <ret> and the cursor moves to the next line.
11. Type [PAYMENTS] and press <change> until MEAN is displayed. Press <ret> and the cursor moves to the next line.
12. Type [BALANCE] and press <change> until MAX is displayed.

```
                          Field Aggregate Status

NAME                 Count                         9.00       Up to Date
PURCHASES            Sum                         616.11       Up to Date
PAYMENTS             Mean                         29.44       Up to Date
BALANCE              Max                         169.76       Up to Date

          <do> <undo> <menu> <search> <change> <eval> <move_keys>
```

FIGURE 6-18

13. Press <eval> **Alt-F10** to calculate the status of the fields. This calculates and displays the values according to the functions that you selected (Figure 6-18).
14. Press <do> twice to save the Status file.
15. Press <menu> to display the Database Operations menu.
16. Select "Quit." Press <do> in response to the prompt to return to the Database Main menu.

TO QUIT: To exit this module and return to the Database Main menu later, select "Options" to return to the main Options window from which you may select another module or exit to the operating system. If you exit to the Operating System, you must reload OA.

RESTART: Reload OA. Select "Database" from the Options menu. The Database Main menu appears; continue with the next section.

Generating a Cross Reference Table

You can observe statistical information in more detail by cross referencing the records in a file than by using the "Status" command. In this section, you will generate a cross reference table to compare records to one another in an easy-to-read table format. First, you must create a table form that specifies what information is to be included in the cross reference table. The "Table" and "Table_Form" commands are used to do this.

The cross reference table will show the items each person bought, the total cost of the items, the total cost of each item bought by all the persons, and the cost for all items bought.

The table sums the cost of each product ordered by each customer. If a customer buys two of a certain product, the items are not listed separately but are added together and displayed as a total. The total individual-product cost is summed along the bottom of the table. The cost to each customer is summed along the right side of the table and a grand total is calculated in the lower right corner. Once the Cross Reference Table is on the screen, use <change> F6 to make modifications.

As the cross reference table is created, certain specifications must first be set. Practice in the following hands-on exercise.

Hands On

1. Select "Retrieve" from the Database Main menu.
2. Select "Compose."
3. Type [ORDERNO] after the FROM clause as the name of the file and press <do> **F10** to accept the query.
4. Press <menu> **F2** to access the Database Operations menu.
5. Select "Forms."
6. Select "Table_Form" from the menu.
7. Press <ret> **Return** in response to the prompt "Template File:" because you are not entering an existing Template Table.
8. Type [ORDERNO] after the prompt "Output File:" as the name of the new table form.
9. Press <do> twice to accept the table form name and the query composition. The Cross Table Specification window is displayed on the screen (Figure 6-19).
10. Type [ORDERNO Cross Reference Table] as the title for the table.
11. Press <ret> to enter the title name. The cursor will move down to the next line. The next entry is the field that will be computed.
12. Type [TOTALCOST].

```
C:ORDERNO.TBF                Cross Table Specification

       Title
       Field
       Function             Count  Sum  Min  Max  Mean  Variance  Std_Deviation
       Column Width        10
       Precision            2
Column Label
       Field
       Sorting Order        Label  Summary_Value
Row Label
       Field
       Width               10
       Precision            2
       Usage                Label  Interval
Interval
       Starts at
       Increment           1
       Date Increment       Day  Month
       How Many             0


        <arrows> <menu> gets submenu, <do> saves form, <undo> quits
```

FIGURE 6-19

13. Press <ret> four times to accept the field name and the default function, column width, and column precision. In this table, you will compare customers and how much of which product was ordered.
14. Type [ITEMNUMBER] as the name of the field in which the product numbers were stored under the Column Label heading.
15. Press <ret> to enter the field name. The cursor is now at the Sorting Order heading where you choose how you want the field sorted.
16. Press <ret> to sort by the product numbers (the product numbers were entered as labels) in this example. The cursor is now located opposite Field under Row Label.
17. Type [NAME] as the field name for the customer who put on order the items under the Row Label heading; press <ret> to accept the field name.
18. Type [20] for the width of the column to contain the names of the customers. The specifications are complete for your table.
19. Press <do> to enter these table form specifications. The records are again displayed in the List screen.

Now generate the Cross Reference Table itself in the next hands-on exercise.

Hands On

1. Press <menu> **F2** to display the Database Operations menu.
2. Select "Table." The Cross Table Form window appears. If ORDERNO is the default name press <do> **F10**. If not, enter [ORDERNO] and press <do>. The "Recalculating Table" prompt shows the progression of the recalculation. The Cross Reference Table is displayed on the screen (Figure 6-20) after recalculation is complete.

ORDERNO Cross Reference Table

SUM of TOTALCOST	ITEMNUMBER 1922	5445	6688	(1, 1) 7445	ALL(8)
N DAVIS, JOHN	----	----	----	----	23.56
A HAYES, WALTER	92.16	10.00	----	----	102.16
M LONG, M. DAVID	----	----	----	----	13.52
E SCHULTZ, JAN	----	----	----	----	12.42
SCOTT, RUBY	----	----	----	29.61	29.61
SMITH, JACK	----	----	----	----	20.82
TEAGARDEN, WILLIAM	----	----	3.78	----	3.78
TOLLE, IVAN	46.08	----	----	----	46.08
ALL	138.24	10.00	3.78	29.61	251.95

<print><change><move_keys> <eval> recalculates the table, <undo> quits

FIGURE 6-20

3. Use <arrows> to scroll across the columns to view the other product information that does not fit on the screen.
4. Press <undo> **Esc** and then <menu> to return to the Database Operations menu.
5. Select "Quit." Press <do> in response to the prompt to return to the Database Main menu.

Transferring Files

A file created with this module can also be used by other OA modules. But first, the file is converted into a form usable by the other programs. The database file must be converted to a Data Interchange Format (DIF) file. DIF files can be sent to another module, and the database module can receive files from other modules to be converted to a database file.

Files can be transferred to another module for use at a later time with the Export command, transferred to another module to be used immediately by the Context command, and transferred from another module into the database module by the Import_File command.

The data in a file might be exported, for example, to a graphics program to be incorporated as part of a chart or graph. In the next hands-on exercise, select a file to be exported and create a DIF file.

Hands On

1. Select "Retrieve" from the Database Main menu.
2. Select "Compose."
3. Type [ORDERNO] as file at the FROM prompt. Press <do> **F10** to accept the query.
4. Press <menu> **F2** to display the Database Operations menu.
5. Select "Export."
6. Type [ORDERNO] in response to the prompt, "Output to:". ORDERNO is the name you are assigning to the DIF file.
7. Press <ret> **Return**. By selecting to "Include_Header" an extra record containing the field names is output with the file. This is necessary when the DIF file is entered back to the database module. Press <do> to select "Include_Header."
8. Press <menu> for the Database Operations menu.
9. Select "Quit." Press <do> in response to the prompt to return to the Database Main menu.

A file from another software package or from another OA module may be transferred to a database file in the OA Database module with the "Import_File" command. Import the MERGE.DIF file from the data disk.

Hands On

1. Select "Design" from the Database Main menu. The File Design and Maintenance menu appears.

2. Select "Import_File."
3. Type [MERGE] as the name of the DIF file that is to be transferred to a database file. Press <ret> **Return** to enter the filename. With this database package, a file cannot be imported into a file that already exists; so you must create a new file.
4. Type [MERGE] at the prompt for the new database filename.
5. Press <do> **F10**. This transfers the file.
6. Select "Retrieve" from the Database Main menu.
7. Select "Compose."
8. Type [MERGE] at the FROM query.
9. Press <do> to display the records from the file that was transferred in the List screen.
10. Press <menu> **F2** for the Database Operations menu.
11. Select "Quit." Press <do> in response to the prompt to return to the Database Main menu.

With the Context command, data are sent directly to another module if it has been installed on the same menu system. By executing the Context command, the file is sent to the module that you select. Unless you are familiar with the other modules, just follow along with the hands-on exercise and do not actually perform the operations after step 6. With a single-diskette system, you have to interchange diskettes to accomplish this.

Hands On

1. Select "Retrieve" from the Database Main menu.
2. Select "Compose."
3. Type the filename [CUSTOMER] after the FROM prompt.
4. Press <do> **F10**. Other query condition clauses could be entered before pressing <do> to retrieve specific records.
5. Press <menu> **F2** to display the Database Operations menu.
6. Select "Context." If you do not have another module installed, stop by pressing <undo> **Esc**; then press <menu> to enter the Database Operations menu. Then select "Quit." Press <do> in response to the prompt to get back to the Database Main menu. Stop here if you do not wish to exit this module; to continue exits the Database module. The following steps are followed if you are going to transfer to another module. The Main Options menu is now displayed.
7. Select "Word Processor" as the module to which you are transferring the file.
8. Type [CUSTOMER] as the filename.
9. Press <ret> to transfer the file. When this is completed you will be in the Word Processor module (Figure 6-21). (If you have a two diskette-drive system, you will be prompted to "Insert OA Word/Comm diskette and press <do>.")
10. Press <menu> to access the Command Selection menu.
11. Select "Options" and press <do> to return to the Options menu. If the message "Update Changed Current File" appears, press <undo>.

```
L--------+1--------+--2------+------3--+---------4+--------+5--------+--6-----+------7--+
NAME--------------------- RATIN ADDRESS---------------- CITY-----------------!
BUCK, NIEL                04    614 CENTRAL AVE.        NORMAN               !
DAVIS, JOHN               01    85494 MAIN              PHOENIX              !
HAYES, WALTER             01    78554 N. DIXIE          PORTLAND             !
LONG, M. DAVID            01    5895 PINEWOOD           MIAMI                !
SCHULTZ, JAN              01    32 A ST.                TOLEDO               !
SCOTT, RUBY               02    4387 STATE              ST.PAUL              !
SMITH, JACK               01    543 NORTHWAY            NEW YORK             !
THOMAS, BOB C.            09    123 HIGH ST.            DAYTON               !
TOLLE, IVAN               01    8549 DECATUR            RALEIGH              !

[C:CUSTOMER.DOC]                    Insert                                 93%
INSERT: All characters are entered into text at the cursor position.

        <del><menu><search><print><format><change><line_del><line_ins>
```

FIGURE 6-21

Macros

A macro can simplify and speed the process of entering command sequences. You can create a macro by saving a series of keystrokes in a file that can be retrieved by pressing one key. Macros are useful in the Database module if you need to access certain files or parts of a file repeatedly over a long period of time. The <macro> Alt-F8 function key is used to create a macro. Review the procedure as described in Chapter 3, "Utilities."

Exiting the Database Module

When you finish working in the Database module, access the Database Main menu and select "Options." If you completed the previous Context command exercise, you are already at the Options menu. If you stopped at step 6, then do the following hands-on exercise. This displays the Options menu. Select another module or press "Operating System" to return to the DOS prompt.

Hands On

Select "Options." This displays the Options menu from which you can select another module or return to DOS.

Command Summary

The following is a brief summary of the commands listed in the main menus of the Database module.

Database Main Menu

Command	Description
Retrieve	Retrieves records from a file, either all records or specific ones determined by a query.
Browse	Displays all records by key field lists.
Enter_Data	Enters data into a file using a screen form.
Print	Prints a report by entering the proper print form name.
Design	Accesses commands to change or create database, screen, print, and table forms.
Macros	Selects and performs a macro instruction.
Options	Returns you to the Main Options Menu.

Data Retrieval Methods Menu

Command	Description
Form_Query	Retrieves records by specifying search conditions for fields.
Compose	Retrieves records using the structured query language.
Pre-defined	Retrieves records using previously stored queries within files.

Database Operations Menu

Command	Description
Order	Sorts records, like the Order clause.
Update	Updates all records retrieved for a given expression.
Browse	Functions same as Browse command in Database Main Menu.
Print	Prints retrieved records in a report.
Append	Copies and transfers data to a different database file.
Context	Sends data immediately to another OA II module.
Status	Generates summary information for retrieved records.
Table	Generates a cross reference table of relationships between selected fields.
Revise	Changes the query composition set using the Retrieve command.
Export	Transfers data from a file to a .DIF text file that can be used by another module.
Make	Retrieved records may be placed in a new file created with this command.
Delete	Used to erase specified records.
Forms	Used to create or change screen, print, and table forms.
Quit	Returns you to the Database Main Menu.

File Design and Maintenance Menu

Command	Description
Create_File	Creates a new screen form file for entering data into a file, also creates a database file for actual data.
Modify_File	Changes parameters in a database file; adding fields, changing field names, deleting fields, changing length of fields, changing or adding a database password, resetting Autoincrement value.
Screen_Form	Modifies or creates a screen form.
Print_Form	Modifies or creates a print form used to generate a report.
Import_File	Changes a .DIF file into a database file.
Table_Form	Changes or creates a table form used when creating a cross reference table.

Study Questions

1. Define the terms *database* and *file*.
2. What is the purpose of designating a field as a key field?
3. What is a screen form? Is there a particular order the fields must be placed in the form?
4. Is it possible to change data in a record or delete a record with the Browse command?
5. How does the Browse command differ from the Retrieve command?
6. What are the four clauses in the Structured Query Language? What is the purpose of each clause?
7. Which of the SQL clause(s) are mandatory and which are optional?
8. How do you specify that a record be sorted on a particular field in descending order?
9. Name and describe six different sections that a print form may contain in the database module.
10. What condition(s) must be met to join two or more files?

The following exercises use the files LOAN.DF, LOAN.IF, AND LOAN.SMK, which are located on the data diskette.

11. Load the file LOAN so that you can browse through all the records.
12. Use the <search> F4 key to search for the record for Rose Slys.
13. Enter this new record into the file LOAN:

Field	*Value*
LASTNAME	PARRISH
FIRSTNAME	LEMAR
ST_ADD	9942 BELLEVUE
CITY	INDIANAPOLIS
STATE	IN
ZIP	99999
LOAN_TYPE	A
BALANCE	5000
LATE_PAY	FALSE
CR_RATING	3

14. Use the Form_Query command to retrieve all records from the file LOAN that meet the following criteria:

    LOAN TYPE = A
    CR RATING = 3

    Which records are retrieved?

15. Use the Compose command to retrieve all the records from the file LOAN. How is the query worded? Which records are retrieved?
16. Use the Compose command to retrieve all records (the entire records should be retrieved) from the file LOAN in which the value in the field BALANCE IS GREATER THAN 25000. How is the query worded? Which records are retrieved?

17. Use the Compose COMMAND to retrieve only the fields LASTNAME, FIRSTNAME, CR RATING from the file LOAN where the value in the field CR_RATING is equal to the number one. How is the query worded? These fields are retrieved for which records?
18. Use the Compose command and enter the following query:

```
[FROM LOAN
 WHERE LATE_PAY = 'TRUE']
```

Now insert a new line containing [SELECT LASTNAME, FIRSTNAME, ST_ADD, CITY, STATE, ZIP] above the WHERE clause; then execute the query. How does the final query read? What is retrieved and displayed by this query?
19. Use the Compose command to retrieve only the fields LASTNAME and BALANCE from the file LOAN where the value in field BALANCE IS GREATER THEN 25000 and the value in field LATE_PAY IS EQUAL TO 'TRUE'. How is the query worded? The LASTNAME and BALANCE are retrieved from which records?
20. Using the Compose command, sort all the records in the file LOAN alphabetically by the LASTNAME field. How is the query worded?
21. Use the Compose command to select all the records in LOAN; then using the Order command from the Database Operations menu; sort all the records in the file LOAN in descending alphabetical order (from Z to A). What is your response to the prompt "Sorting Order:"?
22. Using the Browse command, update the following fields in the record for Jim Strong:

Field	*New Value*
ST_ADD	5634 Huron
CR_RATING	1

23. Use the Compose command to select all the records in LOAN; then update all FALSE entries to TRUE in the field LATE_PAY for all records in the file LOAN. Use <arrows> to scroll the LATE_PAY field onto the display screen to visually confirm the change. How many entries in the field LATE_PAY in the file LOAN now say FALSE?
24. Use the Browse command and delete the record for Ann Carlyle from the file LOAN.
25. Use the Compose command to retrieve the records for Steinberg and Kim; then use the Delete command from the Database Operations menu to delete those records. Browse the LOAN file to visually confirm the deletions.

The following exercises use the file EMP.DF that is created below. The file now contains only which records?

26. Create a new file called EMP. Stop when you see a blank screen (the Screen Definition window) and continue to the next exercise.
27. Create the screen form for the file EMP using the following entry attribute information. The general placement of the fields should be as follows:

LAST	FIRST
AGE	SEX
SALARY	SERVICE

Enter the following data in the appropriate fields.

Name:	*LAST*	*FIRST*	*AGE*	*SEX*	*SALARY*	*SERVICE*
Kind:	Key	Non-key	Non-key	Key	Key	Key
Type:	Text	Text	Number	Text	Decimal	Number
Justify:	Left	Left	Left	Left	Right	Left
Evaluate:	Normal	Normal	Normal	Normal	Normal	Normal
Video mode:	Normal	Normal	Normal	Normal	Normal	Normal
Must fill:	False	False	False	False	False	False
Disp. width:	25	10	2	1	10	2
Duplicate:	False	False	False	False	False	False
Must match:	False	False	False	False	False	False

After you are finished entering the data, save the screen form.

28. Modify the screen form EMP.SMK, created in the previous exercise as follows: change the Kind attribute for the AGE field from Non-key to Key. Save the screen form.
29. Enter the following data into the data file:

LAST	*FIRST*	*AGE*	*SEX*	*SALARY*	*SERVICE*
Frasier	Michael	45	M	48000	20
Bradley	Joan	41	F	32000	17
Simon	Don	30	M	28000	8
Cox	Susan	22	F	17500	1
Densmore	Stewart	50	M	42000	10

30. Create a database password for the file EMP. Use the word "pass" as the password. Then exit the database to the Options menu and reload the database and the file EMP so that it can be browsed.
31. Create a print form for the file EMP. The print form should contain only the fields LAST, FIRST, and SALARY where the value in the field SERVICE is greater than or equal to ten. In addition, sort in alphabetical order on the field LAST and set the display width to 80. How does the query read?
32. Enter Salary Survey as a centered header for the report.
33. Set the field SALARY so that it will have a width of ten, be right justified, and be displayed with two decimal places.
34. Type Accounting Department as a footer for the report.
35. In the Header section of the print form, move the field FIRST to position (0,2), LAST to position (15,2), and SALARY to position (45,2).
36. In the Record section of the print form, move the field FIRST to position (0,2), LAST to position (15,2), and SALARY to position (45,2).
37. Create a virtual field called WEEK at position (0,4) under the SALARY field using the formula SALARY/52 to show how much an employee makes per week.
38. In the Totals Screen, beneath the line that contains the SUM(SALARY) field, create a statistical field called AVERAGE that takes the mean, or average, of the values in the SALARY field.
39. Save the print form.
40. Print the report to the console using the print form file EMP.PMK so it can be previewed. Then print a hard copy of the report if a printer is available.

The following exercises use the files STUDENT.DF, STUDENT.IF, STUDENT.SMK, GRADE.DF, GRADE.IF, and GRADE.SMK.

41. Join all the records of the files STUDENT AND GRADE by the common field SOC_SEC and order the records alphabetically by the LASTNAME field. Use <arrows> to scroll the screen to visually confirm that all the requested fields are there. How does the query read?
42. Use the Make command to make a permanent file called RECORD from the temporary joined file.
43. Create a screen form for the file RECORD.
44. Add the following record to the file RECORD:

FIELD	*VALUE*
LASTNAME	MEYER
FIRSTNAME	JOE
SOC_SEC	555-44-3333
CLASS	MATH 101
GRADE	87

Return to the Database Main menu; use the Compose command to redisplay the file RECORD to visually confirm that the new record was added.

45. Use the statistical function COUNT on the LASTNAME field to determine the total number of records in the file; and use the statistical functions MAX, MIN, and MEAN on the GRADE field to determine the highest, lowest, and average grade respectively. What are the results of these calculations?

Chapter 7

Spreadsheet

Introduction

A spreadsheet is a table with rows and columns in which data are entered and calculated. The intersection of a row and a column creates a cell. In this electronic spreadsheet, 90 rows and

60 columns make a total of 5400 cells available for data entry. Each column is identified by a letter, and each row is identified by a number. So cell B3 would be located at column B and row 3. A spreadsheet can be created and used anywhere rows and columns of numbers are manipulated. After completing this chapter, you should be able to adapt some electronic spreadsheet applications to your own personal use.

Table 7-1 lists the spreadsheet function keys and their descriptions. Use this table as a guide when you complete the hands-on exercises throughout this chapter.

TABLE 7-1 Special Spreadsheet Function Keys

Name	*Key*	*Function*
<window>	F5	Advances to next spreadsheet window.
<edit>	F9	Puts cell into Edit mode.
<change>	F6	Changes field between text and numeric.
<query>	Alt-F9	Executes the current query for the internal database.
<ss-macro>	Alt-F10	Starts the spreadsheet macro.
<place>	Alt-F7	Places the current graph into the spreadsheet.
<justify>	Alt-F6	Changes justification of the current cell.
<tab>	Tab	Moves to a specific cell.
<backtab>	Back Space	Returns cursor to beginning of the next row or column.
<all>	F8	Selects all the cells when selecting range.
<graph1>	F7	Displays the current high-resolution graph if graphics are available.
<graph2>	Alt-F7	Displays graph in special character graph window.

The Work Area

The work area of a blank spreadsheet is shown in Figure 7-1. On a new spreadsheet, you'll find the column headings across the top, the row numbers at the left edge of the screen, and the status area at the bottom of the screen. The spreadsheet's cells in OA are labelled A1 through BH90, a total of 5400 cells.

The Status Area

The status area is the area on the screen where you will find information about the current spreadsheet. Use Figure 7-1 as a guide for locating the following information:

- The pathway on which the spreadsheet resides (represented by the nickname)
- The spreadsheet name, also called the model name, here labelled NEW
- The amount of memory available (100.0%)
- The identification of the current cell (A1)
- The direction in which the cursor, or pointer, will move (LR or TB for movement left-to-right or top-to-bottom)
- The window number (1). (This could be a number from 1 to 6 because up to six different windows can be shown on the screen at a time.)

```
 W1        A      |      B      |      C      |      D      |      E      |      F      |
  1
  2
  3
  4
  5
  6
  7
  8
  9
 10
 11
 12
 13
 14
 15
 16
 17
 18

Model C:NEW                     100.0%   Pointer:A1      Current:A1        LR   W:1  #0

         input:
```

FIGURE 7-1

- The channel number (#0) is used to associate another model that may be viewed and referenced while working with the current model.

The input area appears as a blank space since no data is being keyed. This is the line on which the keyed entry appears before it is actually entered into a particular cell.

You will get an idea of what a spreadsheet looks like by first selecting the Spreadsheet module and then selecting an existing spreadsheet.

Selecting the Spreadsheet Module

The Spreadsheet module is selected from the Main Options menu by pressing [s] or highlighting "Spreadsheet" and pressing <do> F10. Begin by selecting the Spreadsheet module.

Hands On

Select "Spreadsheet" from the Options menu. This displays the Spreadsheet Model Selection menu (Figure 7-2).

Selecting an Existing Spreadsheet

Figure 7-2 shows the Spreadsheet Model Selection menu. You can select an existing model with the Select command, create a new model with the New command, copy a model with the Copy command,

```
                 Open Access II Limited Version Spread_Sheet
 (c) Copyright 1984,1985,1986,1987 Software Products International, Inc.
                             All rights reserved


              Spreadsheet Model Selection Menu
        Select     New     Copy     Delete     Options
      Consolidate     Setup_Consolidation     Graph_Slides
                   <search>    <undo>
```

FIGURE 7-2

delete a model with the Delete command, and return to the Options menu with the Options command. With the Consolidate and Setup_Consolidation commands, it is possible to combine or summarize data from two or more models and put the results into a new model. The Graph_Slides command is discussed in the next chapter on graphics.

A Spreadsheet file is often referred to as a model. For this reason, the filename that identifies a spreadsheet file is often referred to as a model name. Filename and model name are synonymous in this case. For example, the model name of the sample spreadsheet you'll be examining first is SAMPLE. Select the spreadsheet model SAMPLE with the Select command in the following hands-on exercise.

Hands On

1. Select the Select command from the Spreadsheet Model Selection menu. The prompt "Select what model:" appears on the screen. You can either press <search> **F4** to look at a list of existing models, or proceed with step 2.
2. Type [SAMPLE] as the model name.
3. Press <ret> **Return** so the computer will find that model. A prompt "Make backup (<do><undo>)?" appears.
4. Press <do> **F10** to make a backup copy. The spreadsheet appears on the screen.
5. Use <arrows> to move the cursor to various cells in the spreadsheet.

You are looking at the Corsican Bros. Car Wash Second Quarter statement of sales and profits (Figure 7-3). Cell D17 shows a profit for the second quarter of $8,064.00.

```
 W1              A              |    B    |    C    |    D    |
  1                              Corsican Bros. Car Wash
  2                                  Sales/Profit
  3                                 Second Quarter
  4 Cost of Car Wash                     $5.50
  5 Cost of Supplies per wash            $0.50
  6 Other Costs                         40.00%
  7                                 April        May         June
  8 Cars washed                        850.00      986.00     1044.00
  9 Price                               $5.50       $5.50       $5.50
 10 -----------------------------------------------------------------
 11 Revenue                          $4675.00    $5423.00    $5742.00
 12 Costs (Less 40% Revenue)         $1870.00    $2169.20    $2296.80
 13 Expenses (Less .50 per car)       $425.00     $493.00     $522.00
 14 -----------------------------------------------------------------
 15 Profit                           $2380.00    $2760.80    $2923.20
 16 -----------------------------------------------------------------
 17 Total Profit--Second Quarter                             $8064.00
 18
R
Model A:SAMPLE                 97.3%   Pointer:D17    Current:D17     LR   W:1 #0

NUM [R   2$ -] +B15+C15+D15
        input:
```

FIGURE 7-3

Exiting/Saving a Spreadsheet

If you make a backup when the model is selected and make changes that you do not want to save, the Exit/Save command is used to discard the changes and use the backup model. In the next hands-on exercise, make a change to the model; then exit the model without saving the changes.

Hands On

1. Use <arrows> and place the cursor in cell B6 (40.00%).
2. Type [.3] and press <ret> **Return**. Notice that you entered the value at the blinking cursor, and it is transferred to the cell after you press <ret>; the cell value changes.
3. Press <menu> **F2** to display the Spreadsheet Command Selection menu.
4. Select "Exit/Save." The Exit/Save menu is now on the screen.
5. Select "Model_Selection"; the prompt "After_Saving Without_Saving" appears.
6. Select "Without_Saving" so you do not save the change made. The Spreadsheet Model Selection menu returns to the screen.

Making a Backup Copy

You should make a backup copy of the existing model before you begin working on it. A backup copy protects the original data contained in the model.

You made a backup copy of the model before you actually entered it when you were prompted to make a backup copy and you pressed <do> F10. However, if you try to make a backup and there

```
W1                 A               |    B    |    C    |    D    |
 1                                 Corsican Bros. Car Wash
 2                                       Sales/Profit
 3                                      Second Quarter
 4 Cost of Car Wash                         $5.50
 5 Cost of Supplies per wash                $0.50
 6 Other Costs                             40.00%
 7                                      April        May        June
 8 Cars washed                             850.00     986.00    1044.00
 9 Price                                    $5.50      $5.50      $5.50
10 --------------------------------------------------------------------
11 Revenue                                $4675.00   $5423.00   $5742.00
12 Costs (Less 40% Revenue)               $1870.00   $2169.20   $2296.80
13 Expenses (Less .50 per car)             $425.00    $493.00    $522.00
14 --------------------------------------------------------------------
15 Profit                                 $2380.00   $2760.80   $2923.20
16 --------------------------------------------------------------------
17 Total Profit--Second Quarter                                  $8064.00
 1
R                   Spreadsheet Command Selection Menu
Mo   Auto        Blank    Copy      Delete    Edit      Exit/Save  Format      #0
     Goal_Seek   Graph    Insert    Locate    Name      Order      Query
     Recalc      Setup    Table     Transfer  Update    Window     Xternal
           <move_keys>    <edit>   <print>  <graph#>  <query>   <change>
```

FIGURE 7-4

is no room for it on the disk, you will see the message "Not enough room to make backup. Any changes will be saved.". This means the model will be saved as it was changed in place of the original model file, but no backup will be created.

You can still make a backup even if you had selected not to originally; just select the Exit/Save command and choose Backup_Model from that menu. It is a good idea to make a backup of this model because you will be altering data in it later. Now, reselect the model SAMPLE and make a backup copy in the following hands-on exercise. This backup copy is saved separately with a .BCK extension and does not override the original model.

Hands On

1. Select the Select command from the Spreadsheet Model Selection menu. The prompt "Select what model:" appears on the screen.
2. Type [SAMPLE] for the model name.
3. Press <ret> **Return**. A prompt "Make backup (<do><undo>)?" appears.
4. Press <undo> **Esc**.
5. Press <menu> **F2** to display the Spreadsheet Command Selection menu (Figure 7-4).
6. Select "Exit/Save." The Exit/Save menu is now on the screen (Figure 7-5).
7. Select "Backup_Model." A backup copy is automatically made and the Command Selection menu returns to the screen.
8. Select "Exit/Save" to display the Exit/Save menu again.
9. Select "Model_Selection" to return to the Model Selection menu.

```
R
Model A:SAMPLE                 97.3%   Pointer:A1    Current:A1     LR  W:1 #0

 Exit/Save:  Model_Selection  Options  Context  Backup_Model  Copy_Model
```

FIGURE 7-5

Creating a New Spreadsheet

You've seen a completed spreadsheet; now it's time to create a new one. The Model Selection menu should still be on the screen.

Hands On

1. Select "New" from the menu. The prompt "Name of model to be created:" appears on the screen.
2. Type [NEW] to give the spreadsheet a model name. Model names must be eight characters or less.
3. Press <ret> **Return** to enter the model name. The prompt "Enter password for new model (<ret> if none):" appears.
4. Press <ret> to choose not to enter a password.

A blank spreadsheet with NEW as the model name is now on the screen. You may be wondering why you were not instructed to enter a password at the prompt. A password is a locking device whereby anyone who does not enter the specific password cannot access that spreadsheet model. This device is an effective measure that protects the model from unauthorized use when it contains private or confidential information. However, if *you* forget the password, neither you nor anyone else can access the spreadsheet. Bearing this in mind, you should probably create passwords only as instructed in these hands-on exercises.

Copying a Spreadsheet

There are two ways to make a copy of the spreadsheet model. The Copy command allows you to save the model under a different name so it can be changed or inserted in its entirety into another model. The first way to copy a spreadsheet model is directly from the Exit/Save choice in the Command Selection menu. Since your spreadsheet is on the screen, try this way first.

Hands On

1. Press <menu> **F2** to display the Command Selection menu.
2. Select "Exit/Save." The Exit/Save menu appears.
3. Select "Copy_Model." The prompt "Save to what model:" appears.

4. Type [COPY1] to label the copied model. (You must give the copied model a new name.)
5. Press <ret> **Return** to enter the copy's name; the prompt "Enter password for new model (<ret> if none):" appears.
6. Press <ret> to indicate that no password is being entered. The Command Selection menu appears on the screen.
7. Press <ret> twice to Exit/Save as previously described. The copy is now made and the Model Selection menu is on the screen.

A copy can be made from this menu, also. Now make a copy using the Copy command from the Model Selection menu.

Hands On

1. Select "Copy" from the menu. The prompt "Copy what model:" appears.
2. Type [NEW] as the name of the model you want to copy.
3. Press <ret> **Return** to enter the model name. The prompt "Copy NEW.FMD to what model:" appears.
4. Type [COPY2] to label this second copy of the spreadsheet model.
5. Press <ret> to enter the model name. The prompt "Enter password for new model (<ret> if none):" appears.
6. Press <ret> to avoid entering a password. The screen now shows a blank spreadsheet with the word "COPY2" in the model name space of the status line.
7. Use the Exit/Save procedure to exit this model before going to the next section. The Spreadsheet Model Selection menu is now displayed.

Deleting a Spreadsheet

A spreadsheet model can be deleted when it is no longer needed, or you can store that model on a floppy diskette if you want to remove it from hard-disk storage. The next hands-on exercise deletes the COPY2 spreadsheet model.

Hands On

1. Select "Delete" from the Model Selection menu. The prompt "Delete what model:" appears.
2. Type [COPY2] as the model to delete.
3. Press <ret> **Return** to enter the choice. The prompt "Verify delete: _:COPY2.FMD" appears.
4. Press <ret> to accept and verify the model to be deleted. The model COPY2.FMD is deleted. The screen returns automatically to the Model Selection menu.
5. Delete the other copied model using the above procedure. Remember to enter [COPY1] as the model name to delete.

TO QUIT: To exit this module, select "Options" to display the main Options menu. You can select another module or return to the operating system. If you exit to the Operating System, you must reload OA.

RESTART: Reload OA. Select "Spreadsheet" from the Options menu when you want to return to the Spreadsheet Model Selection menu.

Working with an Existing Spreadsheet

Now, look at some of the choices in the Command Selection menu. In the next hands-on exercise, you will make selections from this menu to work on the existing spreadsheet called SAMPLE. But first, copy the SAMPLE spreadsheet model before making any changes to it. Then if you make a mistake during any of the exercises, you can select the original model and begin again. Label the copy SAMPLE1.

Hands On

1. Select "Copy" from the Spreadsheet Model Selection menu. The prompt "Copy what model:" appears.
2. Type [SAMPLE] as the model name that you want to copy.
3. Press <ret> **Return** to enter the model name. The prompt "Copy SAMPLE.FMD to what model:" appears.
4. Type [SAMPLE1] to label this second copy of the spreadsheet model.
5. Press <ret> to enter the model name. The prompt "Enter password for new model (<ret> if none):" appears.
6. Press <ret> to avoid entering a password. The screen now shows a spreadsheet with the word "SAMPLE1" appearing in the model name space of the status line.

Asking "What If" Questions

With the copied SAMPLE1 spreadsheet on the screen, notice that the car wash price, found in cell B4, is $5.50. What if the owners increased the price to $5.75? This kind of situational question is ideal for a spreadsheet program. The subtotal and grand total amounts change, too. Instead of getting an eraser, calculator, and a sharpened pencil, you can put the computer to work to answer the question and recalculate the values.

In the next few hands-on exercises, you will see the effect on the entire spreadsheet when you change the car wash price from $5.50 to $5.75.

Hands On

1. Use <arrows> to move the highlighted cursor to cell B4, the cell containing the car wash price--$5.50. (Another way to move to a specific cell location is to press <tab> **Tab** and arrive at the prompt "Move to what coordinate:". Type [B4] to override the default characters and press <ret> **Return** to move the cursor directly to that cell. A blinking box appears on the input line.)

2. Type [5.75] as the "what if" price.
3. Press <ret> to put that entry into cell B4.

Recalculating a Column

Now look at cell B4. The number changed to $5.75, but the totals have not been adjusted. Calculations are done in a separate step that is activated from the Command Selection menu. So, now recalculate the April totals.

Hands On

1. Press <menu> **F2** to access the Command Selection menu.
2. Select "Recalc" (recalculate) from the menu to arrive at the prompt "Recalculate: expressions over area: B4."

A range of cells is designated by using a colon between two cell coordinates. For example, A1:C2 designates the rectangular area that includes cells A1, A2, B1, B2, C1, and C2.

Notice on the display screen that B4 automatically appears as the default when "Recalc" was selected in the previous exercise. The default position is the last cell coordinate the cursor was on. To assure that all affected rows and columns of the spreadsheet for the April totals are recalculated, designate a range of cells to be acted upon in the next hands-on exercise.

Hands On

1. Type [:] as a delimiter in designating the range of cells. The default "B4" appears again.
2. Type [B17] to include all the cells in the B column in a range of cells from B4 to B17 (B4:B17). Notice the B4 entry was written over.
3. Press <ret> **Return** to start the recalculation process.

Column B has been recalculated and the April numbers are changed as a result of this recalculation.

Recalculating the Entire Spreadsheet

The only recalculation occurred in column B. The total in cell B15 should now read $2507.50.

Sometimes a column-by-column recalculation is appropriate. However, if other totals are affected, the entire spreadsheet should be recalculated. In the next hands-on exercise, recalculate all the spreadsheet columns. Watch carefully and you will see the recalculations ripple through the spreadsheet. The SAMPLE1 spreadsheet and the Command Selection menu should still be on the screen.

Hands On

1. Select "Recalc" from the Command Selection menu.
2. Press <all> **F8** to recalculate all the rows and columns of the spreadsheet. The range of cells is shown as A1:E17; therefore, all the rows and columns are quickly recalculated.

The "what if" question has been answered; the total three-month profit reads $8496, an approximate $500 profit increase.

Updating

Constant numerical values in a spreadsheet can also be changed with the Update command. This command temporarily changes the value of a cell so its effects can be seen on others cells; then it restores the cell to its original value.

You may, upon updating a cell, choose to recalculate the entire model with the updated value. But if you choose to do this, you will not be able to restore the original value of the cell.

When using the Update command, the exclamation point symbol (!) is used to represent the value to be updated. In the next hands-on exercise, see what effect a 10 percent decrease in April's number of cars washed would mean to April's profits; then restore the original value.

Hands On

1. Select "Update" from the Command Selection menu. The prompt "Update: values over area:" appears.
2. Type [B8] and press <ret> **Return**. The prompt "Update: expression (=restores)" appears.
3. Type [!*.9] (The value in cell B8 times (*) 90% to calculate a 10% decrease) and press <do> **F10**. The value is changed to 765 cars washed.
4. Select "Recalc."
5. Type [:B17] and press <ret>; April's profit is now $2256.75. Now restore the original value.
6. Select "Update" from the Command Selection menu again.
7. Type [B8] and press <ret> as the area to be restored.
8. Press <do> to enter = as the default to restore the original value.
9. Select "Recalc."
10. Type [:B17] and press <ret> to restore April's profit to $2507.50.

TO QUIT: Press <menu> **F2** and use exit procedures to return to the Model Selection menu. Select "Options" to return to the main Options menu. From here you may exit to the operating system or use another module. If you exit to the Operating System, you must reload OA.

RESTART: Reload OA. Select "Spreadsheet." Select "Select" and load SAMPLE1 model. Press <menu>.

G O A L S E E K I N G			
DEPENDENT Entry	TARGET Value	INDEPENDENT Entry	REQUIRED Value
B4			

FIGURE 7-6

Goal Seeking

Goal seeking is a way to determine values necessary to meet a certain goal. For example, a goal might be to find out how many cars Corsican Bros. would have to wash in June to make a profit of $3500 in June. You can select a dependent variable (one whose value is determined by other values from other cells, i.e., the number of cars to be washed) and set a target value (what you would like it to be, i.e., a profit of $3500 in June). The target value is used to calculate a required value for an independent variable (one in which the value does not rely on the values in other cells). In the following hands-on exercise, see how many cars you would have to wash in June to make a profit of $3500 in June.

Hands On

1. Select "Goal_Seek" and the Goal Seeking window appears (Figure 7-6).
2. Type [D15], the cell containing June's profit, as the dependent entry and press <ret> **Return**.
3. Type [3500] as the target value and press <ret>. A prompt asks "Enter another target value?".
4. Press <undo> **Esc** because you don't want to enter another target value.
5. Type [D8], the number of cars washed, as the independent value and press <ret>. You would have to wash 1187 cars to make the $3500 profit. The prompt "Save New Independent Entry Values?" appears.
6. Press <undo> and the prompt "Do you wish to Goal Seek again?" appears.
7. Press <undo> to end goal seeking.

Locating Text

You may want to access a particular heading or text area. The Locate command moves the cursor to the cell where the specified text is located. However, the program locates cells from the current cursor position only. To locate the first occurrence, the cursor should be at the beginning of the model, cell A1. This option is helpful in finding an entry in a large spreadsheet where the entire model cannot fit on the screen.

Hands On

1. Press <undo> **Esc** to remove the Spreadsheet Command Selection menu from the screen.
2. Use <arrows> to move the cursor to the beginning (cell A1) of the SAMPLE1 model.
3. Press <menu> **F2** to access the Command Selection menu.
4. Select the Locate command. The prompt "Locate what:" appears.
5. Type [May] and press <do> **F10**. The text to be located must be entered exactly as it appears in the model. The cursor moves to the first occurrence of May at cell C7.

Naming Cells

For convenience, a cell or group of cells can be given a descriptive name to identify the data in those cells. The cell names can be used to represent that data in calculating a formula or be used when a prompt asks for a name for an area. For example, the data contained in cell B4 could be given the name PRICE to represent the cost of the car wash.

Hands On

1. Press <undo> **Esc** to access the Command Selection menu.
2. Select "Name." The prompt "Name: What name:'" appears. The name must be preceded by an apostrophe; it is already placed there.
3. Type [PRICE] as the name of area and press <do> **F10**. The prompt "Name: What area:" will appear.
4. Type [B4] as the area to be represented by the name PRICE and press <do>.
5. Select "Exit/Save" and then select "Model_Selection." The screen should show the Spreadsheet Model Selection menu when completed.

TO QUIT: To exit this module, select "Options" to display the main Options menu. From here you can select another module or return to the operating system. If you return to the Operating System, you must reload OA.

RESTART: Reload OA. Select "Spreadsheet" from the Options menu; the Spreadsheet Model Selection menu appears.

Entering Data into a Spreadsheet

In this section, you will create a new spreadsheet and enter data. The data will take the form of text, numbers, and formulas. The model is simple so that you can concentrate on data-entry methods. First, create a spreadsheet model called TIMES.

Hands On

1. Select "New" from the Spreadsheet Model Selection menu. The prompt "Name of model to be created:" appears on the screen.

2. Type [TIMES] to give the spreadsheet a model name.
3. Press <ret> **Return** to enter the model name. The prompt "Enter password for new model (<ret> if none):" appears.
4. Press <ret> to choose not to enter a password. The blank spreadsheet model "TIMES" appears.

Entering Text and Numbers

In the following hands-on exercise, enter data into a "times table." Once the blank spreadsheet labelled TIMES is on the screen, you can begin the exercise.

Hands On

1. Use <arrows> to move the cursor to cell C1 (or press <tab> **Tab** and enter C1 and press <ret> **Return**).
2. Type [TIMES] to indicate a heading for this model.
3. Press <ret> to enter the word as a heading.
4. Move the cursor to cell B3.
5. Type [Facts] as a heading for this column.
6. Press <ret> to enter the heading.
7. Move the cursor to cell E3.
8. Type [Solution] as the heading for this column.
9. Press <ret> to enter the heading.
10. Move the cursor to cell A4.
11. Type [1] and press <ret> to enter data. Press down <arrow> once.
12. Type [2] and press <ret> to enter data. Press down <arrow> once.
13. Type [3] and press <ret> to enter data.
14. Move the cursor to cell B4.
15. Type [times] as an explanation of the action being taken in this table.
16. Press <ret> to enter the word "times."
17. Move the cursor to cell C4.
18. Type [3] and press <ret> to enter the multiplier.

Your spreadsheet looks like the one in Figure 7-7 now. Some rows and columns still need data entries, and there is an easy way to do this--by copying cells.

Copying Cells. Sometimes it is easier to copy cells than to reenter data. This times table can be completed by copying some cells. Make sure the TIMES spreadsheet is still on the screen. Practice using the Copy command to enter values in a cell.

Hands On

1. Move the cursor to cell B4.
2. Press <menu> **F2** to display the Command Selection menu.

```
W1      A     |     B     |     C     |     D     |     E     |     F     |
 1                          TIMES
 2
 3             Facts                              Solution
 4         1.00times               3.00
 5         2.00
 6         3.00
 7
 8
 9
10
11
12
13
14
15
16
17
18
R
Model C:TIMES                    99.9%   Pointer:C4     Current:C4      LR  W:1 #0

NUM [R   2  -] 3
        input:
```

FIGURE 7-7

3. Select "Copy." A screen prompt "Copy: From B4" appears.
4. Press <ret> **Return** and the prompt appears as "To: B4."
5. Type [B5] to indicate that cell B5 should receive the copied data.
6. Press <ret>. The cursor moves to "Repeat 1." Type [2], to indicate you want the copy repeated twice.
7. Press <do> **F10** to complete the copy. (The repeat choice is convenient for copying to many cells. Or, a larger range of cells could be designated in step 5.)

The Spreadsheet Command Selection menu is still on the screen. In the next hands-on exercise, copy the number 3 in column C.

Hands On

1. Select "Copy" from the menu.
2. Use <arrows> to move the cursor to cell C4. The prompt on the status line reads "Copy: From C4."
3. Press <ret> **Return** to copy. The prompt at the cursor now states "To: C4."
4. Type [C5:] to include cell C5.
5. Type [C6] to include cell C6 in the range of cells.
6. Press <ret> to enter the range of cells. The prompt moves to "Repeat 1."
7. Press <do> **F10** to execute the command. A prompt appears "Copy: All Values." "Copy: All" is highlighted.
8. Press <do> to copy the number into the designated cells.
9. Press <undo> **Esc** to remove the Command Selection menu.

```
 W1      A    |    B    |    C    |    D    |    E    |    F    |
  1                       TIMES
  2
  3            Facts                           Solution
  4        1.00times            3.00
  5        2.00times            3.00
  6        3.00times            3.00
  7
  8
  9
 10
 11
 12
 13
 14
 15
 16
 17
 18
R
Model C:TIMES               99.9%   Pointer:B4     Current:B4      LR   W:1 #0

TXT [L        ] times
        input:
```

FIGURE 7-8

TO QUIT: Press <menu> **F2**. Use Exit procedures to return to the Model Selection menu. Select "Options" and the main Options menu appears. From here you may exit to the operating system or use another module. If you exit to the Operating System, you must reload OA.

RESTART: Reload OA. Select "Spreadsheets"; select "Select" and load TIMES as the spreadsheet model.

The spreadsheet now looks like the one in Figure 7-8.

Entering Formulas. A spreadsheet manipulates, totals, and acts upon numbers through formulas. A formula entry must be preceded by a plus (+) sign. The affected cells' coordinates are identified and the mathematical operators (+, -, *, and /; add, subtract, multiply, and divide, respectively) indicate what action is taken.

In the times-table model, the mathematical formula to arrive at a solution at cell E4 would be "multiply 1.00 times 3.00." After you enter the formula A4*C4 in cell E4, the computer makes the necessary calculation. Now enter this single formula into the TIMES model.

Hands On

1. Move the cursor to cell E4.
2. Type [+A4*C4] to put the formula on the input line. Remember that the plus (+) sign indicates entry of a formula.
3. Press <do> **F10** to enter the formula and calculate the value for cell E4.

Notice that the solution, 3.00, is automatically entered in the spreadsheet. However, it is the formula, not the number, that appears on the status line when the cursor is at that coordinate. In the next hands-on exercise, you will learn how to copy formulas for the solutions to the other two rows of problems (cells E5 and E6).

Copying Formulas. Formulas can be copied in several different ways--with absolute, relative, and prompted (or mixed) references. The best way to show you the ramifications of using different cell references is to give you examples.

If the formula to multiply the first row of numbers (+A4*C4) were copied to row 5 (where the problem is 2 times 3) using absolute cell references, the formula would remain +A4*C4. It would give the same solution as for row 4's problem 1.00 times 3.00, or 3.00. That answer is obviously incorrect for the problem 2.00 times 3.00.

If the formula were copied to row 5 using relative cell references, it would relate to the new cells and would read +A5*C5, and give 6 as the solution. Formulas can also be copied using prompted, or mixed, cell references, where each cell coordinate could be chosen as being either absolute or relative.

Now enter the formulas, copying the one currently in cell E4 to cells E5 and E6 using relative cell references. The TIMES spreadsheet should be on the screen.

Hands On

1. Position the cursor in cell E4.
2. Press <menu> **F2** to access the Spreadsheet Command Selection menu.
3. Select "Copy" and the prompt "Copy: From: E4" appears on the screen.
4. Press <ret> **Return** to indicate that data in cell E4 should be copied. The prompt "To: E4" appears.
5. Use <arrows> to move the cursor to cell E5.
6. Press <ret> to enter E5. The prompt is on "Repeat: 1."
7. Type [2] and press <do> **F10** and the prompt "Copy: All Values" appears.
8. Select "All." The prompt "Copy Expression: Relative Absolute Prompted" appears.
9. Select "Relative" (the cursor may already be there). The formulas are copied and solutions are entered using the relative cell reference.

The formula was automatically copied to the designated cells as you can tell by the correct numbers now appearing in column E, the solution.

Your completed TIMES spreadsheet looks like the one in Figure 7-9 now. Remember that when cells are copied or moved from one part of the spreadsheet to another, the formulas in those cells are also moved. Solutions throughout the spreadsheet can be affected. The spreadsheet program's accuracy depends on the validity of formula entries.

Blanking an Entry

Blanking simply means erasing the contents of a cell or group of cells. This is done with the Blank command in the Command Selection menu. You can choose to blank a single cell (e.g., B5), a

```
W1      A    |    B    |    C    |    D    |    E    |    F    |
 1                       TIMES
 2
 3              Facts                           Solution
 4          1.00times          3.00                 3.00
 5          2.00times          3.00                 6.00
 6          3.00times          3.00                 9.00
 7
 8
 9
10
11
12
13
14
15
16
17
 1 ┌──────────────────────────────────────────────────────────────┐
R  │               Spreadsheet Command Selection Menu             │
Mo │ Auto       Blank     Copy     Delete    Edit    Exit/Save  Format   │ #0
   │ Goal_Seek  Graph     Insert   Locate    Name    Order      Query    │
NU │ Recalc     Setup     Table    Transfer  Update  Window     Xternal  │
   │      <move_keys>  <edit>  <print>  <graph#>  <query>  <change>     │
   └──────────────────────────────────────────────────────────────┘
```

FIGURE 7-9

range of cells (e.g., B5:D9), a whole row (e.g., 3), a whole column (e.g., C), or a named area (e.g., 'PRICE). Practice with this hands-on exercise.

Hands On

1. Press <undo> **Esc** to remove the Spreadsheet Command Selection menu.
2. Use the <arrows> to move to cell B10.
3. Type [34] and press <ret> **Return** to enter the data.
4. Press <menu> **F2** to access the Spreadsheet Command Selection menu.
5. Select "Blank." The prompt "Blank what area: B10" appears as the default cursor position setting.
6. Press <do> **F10**. The value in cell B10 is blanked, or erased, from the cell.

If you try to blank more than one cell, a prompt appears asking you to verify that you, indeed, want the cells blanked.

Editing Data

Sometimes spreadsheets require editing; that is, text labels need to be changed, or entries updated, or entire rows and columns inserted or deleted. You can edit the TIMES spreadsheet, which should still be on the screen, using the Edit command from the Command Selection menu. In the following hands-on exercise, you will edit, or change, a heading.

Hands On

1. Select "Edit" from the Command Selection menu. The prompt "Edit: what area:" appears.
2. Move the cursor to cell B3; the prompt reads "Edit: what area: B3."
3. Press <do> **F10**. The Edit window containing the word "Facts" appears and is now ready for editing.
4. Type [Problems] to make the edit. (If you are in the Insert mode, the word "Facts" is pushed to the right. Press <del> **Del** five times to delete the word "Facts." Or you could also deselect the Insert mode as soon as you notice that it's on by pressing <ins> **Ins** one time. Then delete only the extra characters.)
5. Press <do> to enter the word "Problems" into the spreadsheet.
6. Press <undo> **Esc** to remove the Command Selection menu from the screen.

TO QUIT: Press <menu> **F2**. Use Exit procedures to return to the Model Selection menu. Select "Options" and the main Options menu appears. From here you may exit to the operating system or use another module. If you exit to the Operating System, you must reload OA.

RESTART: Reload OA. Select "Spreadsheet"; select "Select" and load TIMES as the spreadsheet model.

Formatting

There are many ways to change the look of the spreadsheet. You can see from Figure 7-9 that there are a couple of ways it could be changed so that it will be easier to read. The headings, for example, are too close to the body of the table, and the second column of words ("times") crowds into the first column of numbers.

One way to format, or change, the physical appearance of a spreadsheet is to insert blank rows or columns. These blank spaces could also be formatted with underlines or other characters to divide the rows and columns for easier reading. Now insert a blank line in the TIMES spreadsheet.

Hands On

1. Press <menu> **F2** to access the Command Selection menu.
2. Select "Insert." The prompt "Insert: Row Column" appears.
3. Select "Row" and a prompt appears: "Insert: Row(s) starting at:".
4. Type [4] to designate where a blank row should be inserted.
5. Press <do> **F10** to enter the number. The prompt "How many rows/columns?: 1" appears.
6. Press <do> to insert only one row. (If you want more than one blank row, you would enter another number before pressing <do>.)
7. Press <undo> **Esc** to remove the menu. A blank row now appears between the heading and the rest of the table.

Other problem areas can be corrected by formatting. Some of the modification choices include changing column width, assigning attributes to the various numerical entries, adding blank rows or columns, and underscoring headings or totals.

Changing Column Width

Entries to a specific column will sometimes require more or less than twelve characters, the allotted default setting. When this is the case, you can still enter the data in the spreadsheet; the excess letters will spill over to the next cell. Then adjustments to the column width can be made from the formatting choices. With the TIMES spreadsheet on the screen, change the width of two middle columns in the following hands-on exercise.

Hands On

1. Move the cursor to column C.
2. Press <menu> **F2** to access the Spreadsheet Command Selection menu.
3. Select "Format." The prompt "Format: Width, Attributes, Filler_char, Data_type, Translate_macro" appears.
4. Select "Width" and the prompt "Set width of this column to: 12" appears.
5. Type [5], overwriting the default setting of 12, to set the column width to five characters.
6. Press <do> **F10 to** enter the choice. The prompt "Format Width: Set how many columns to this width? 1" appears.
7. Type [2] to change adjoining columns (C and D) to five characters.
8. Press <do> to change the width of columns C and D.
9. Press <undo> **Esc** to remove the menu.

Check the grid showing the column headings at the top of the screen. Columns C and D are now only five characters wide.

Setting Filler Characters

You can put a filler character into any of the cells, rows, or columns. In the following hands-on exercise, put a row of asterisks between the headings and the numeric columns; the TIMES spreadsheet should be on the screen.

Hands On

1. Position the cursor in cell A4.
2. Press <menu> **F2** to access the Spreadsheet Command Selection menu.
3. Select "Format." The prompt "Format: Width Attributes Filler_char Data_type Translate_macro" appears.
4. Select "Filler_char." The prompt "Set filler to:" appears.
5. Type [*] to specify that a row of asterisks should be added. Another prompt "Format applies to area: A4" appears.
6. Type [:] to indicate that a range of cells is being designated. The cursor position at cell A4 is repeated.

```
R
Model C:TIMES                          99.9%    Pointer:A4     Current:A4       LR  W:1

TXT [L       ]
LCR1[????????]  <left>  <right>  <change>/[space]  <backspace>  <do>  <undo>
                Justification:  Left, Center, Right, left padded
```

FIGURE 7-10

7. Type [E4] to set the end of the range of cells.
8. Press <do> **F10** to enter the row of asterisks.
9. Press <undo> **Esc** to remove the menu.

The spreadsheet now has a row of asterisks to set off the columns from the headings.

Designating Attributes

You can specifically choose other formatting features for the spreadsheet's data entries, for example, type enhancements such as boldface print and underlined characters. The data in a cell can be positioned in the center of the cell, right or left justified, or padded--that is, left justified with one blank space at the left. Other choices are including a comma in numbers over 999; using the percent sign, dollar sign, or foreign currency notation; protecting cells from change; and making cells invisible. Figure 7-10 shows just one of the screen Attribute Selection menus. Each question mark offers its own series of choices listed at the bottom of the menu. For this example, the choices for justifying the data entries in each cell include placing them at the left, center, right, or left padded with one blank space. In this next hands-on exercise, you will format using the underline attribute.

Hands On

1. Position the cursor at cell C1.
2. Press <menu> **F2** to access the Spreadsheet Command Selection menu.
3. Select "Format."
4. Select "Attributes" from the list of options.
5. Press the right <arrow> three times. Watch the bottom of the menu as you space across to see the selections change to reflect the menu choices available. The choices listed here are "Bold, Underline, Italics, Shadow, Title, Prompt, Error, 1, 2, 3."
6. Press <space> **Space Bar** twice to choose the underline. Notice that the question mark under the flashing cursor changes to "U" (the first letter of "Underline," the second selection).
7. Press <do> **F10** to select the Underline attribute. The prompt "Format applies to area: C1" appears. Make sure that the data at coordinate C1 is that which you want to underline.
8. Press <do> to execute the action. The Spreadsheet Command Selection menu automatically returns to the screen.
9. Press <undo> **Esc** to delete the menu.
10. Use <arrows> to move the cursor so you can see that the word "TIMES" has been underlined. (It may be in reverse video on a color monitor.)

```
W1      A     |    B     | C | D |     E     |    F     |    G     |
 1                         TIMES
 2
 3            Problems                Solution
 4 ****************************************
 5        1.00times      3.00           3.00
 6        2.00times      3.00           6.00
 7        3.00times      3.00           9.00
 8
 9
10
11
12
13
14
15
16
17
18
R
Model C:TIMES              99.9%   Pointer:C3     Current:C3      LR  W:1 #0


       input:
```

FIGURE 7-11

Figure 7-11 shows the reformatted TIMES spreadsheet. Compare how it looked before with partial formatting (Figure 7-8).

Practice another formatting command by deleting the ".00" that appears for each numerical entry on the TIMES spreadsheet.

Hands On

1. Press <menu> **F2** to access the Spreadsheet Command Selection menu.
2. Select "Format."
3. Select "Attributes." Press <arrows> four times to select "Precision."
4. Press <space> **Space Bar** once to indicate 0 (no decimal places).
5. Press <ret> **Return** to enter that setting. The prompt "Format applies to area:" appears.
6. Move the cursor to cell A5 to indicate the beginning of a range of cells.
7. Type [:] to delimit the range of cells.
8. Move the cursor to cell E7 to indicate the end of a range of cells.
9. Press <do> **F10** to delete all the extra zeros. The Spreadsheet Command Selection menu returns to the screen.

Another formatting attribute involves centering data within a cell. In this hands-on exercise, center the word "times."

Hands On

1. Select "Format."
2. Select "Attributes." The first attribute listed is "Justification: Left, Center, Right, Left Padded."
3. Press the <space> **Space Bar** twice to select to "center" data. Notice the question mark becomes a C (center).
4. Press <ret> **Return** to choose to center data. The prompt "Format applies to area:" appears on the screen.
5. Move the cursor to cell B5 to set the beginning of a range of cells.
6. Type [:] to delimit the range of cells.
7. Move the cursor to B7 to set the end of the range of cells.
8. Press <do> **F10** and the word "times" is automatically centered in all three cells; the Spreadsheet Command Selection menu returns to the screen.
9. Press <undo> **Esc** to remove the menu from the screen.

TO QUIT: Press <menu> **F2**. Use exit procedures to return to the Model Selection menu. Select "Options" and the main Options menu appears. From here you may exit to the operating system or use another module. If you exit to the Operating System, you must reload OA.

RESTART: Reload OA. Select "Spreadsheet"; select "Select" and load TIMES as the spreadsheet model.

You may continue to examine all the attributes by selecting Format and place the cursor on each of the question marks. On each question mark, press <change> F6 or the <space> key to view the selections.

Question mark number 3 allows you to set cells to a Form mode. The Form mode is used in conjunction with the Auto command in the Command Selection menu. The Auto command allows you to automatically jump to previously designated "Form" cells. This is handy if you have widely separated data or repeated steps to enter.

Printing a Spreadsheet

Figure 7-12 shows the Print Command Setup window as it appears at the bottom of the spreadsheet when you choose the print option. You can select and set the parameters shown in Table 7-2 from this window, which is accessed by the <print> F3 key. Screens can also be printed directly using the <prt_scr> Alt-F3 key. The following hands-on exercise prints the TIMES spreadsheet model.

```
                         Print Command Setup Window
Report type:  Normal  Preview  Merge  Expression_dump  Dump/Cross-ref
Area:                                   Output device: IBM QUIETWRITER
Titles:   None                          Page Numbers:   None
Grid labels:   None                     Paper eject:  True
Header:
Footer:
Mail-Merge Data Area:                   Record #:    0
           <arrows>  <change>   <print> or <do> to start printout
```

FIGURE 7-12

TABLE 7-2 Print Command Window

Option	*Description*
Report type	Selects the following report type for the designated area: ■ Normal Prints the screen as it appears ■ Preview Previews a report by printing to the screen ■ Merge Completes a Mail-Merge with the specified area and records from the Mail-Merge Data Area ■ Expression_Dump Prints the area contents, expressions, and attributes ■ Dump/Cross-ref Same as Expression_Dump, but prints a list of cells that refer to any cells in the area
Area	Specifies either all or part of the model to be printed.
Output Device	Selects the output device. The <search> F4 key can be used to list those devices.
Titles	Selects a title to be printed as None, Row, Column, or Both by pressing <change> F6.
Page Numbers	Selects page numbers to be printed at the Top, Bottom, or not at all--None.
Grid Labels	Selects to print None, Row, Column, or Both of the grid labels.
Paper eject	Selects True or False to generate a page feed after reports or Mail-Merge records.
Header	Enters as many as 68 characters at the top of the page.
Footer	Enters as many as 68 characters at the bottom of the page.
Mail-Merge Data Area	Selects area when Merge is selected as the report type.
Record #	Enters a record number, for Normal reports, from the Mail-Merge Data Area to be used in merged text files.

Hands On

1. Press <print> **F3** to access the Print Command Setup window.
2. Press <ret> **Return** to select "Normal." The cursor moves to the Area field.
3. Press <all> **F8** to indicate to print the entire model. The cursor moves to "Output device."
4. Press <search> **F4** to select either "Console" or the appropriate printer device; press <ret>.
5. Press <ret> four times to move to the Header field.
6. Type [yourcoursename] and press <ret>.
7. Press <ret> twice to bypass the mail-merge fields.
8. Press <do> **F10** to print the model.
9. Press <undo> **Esc** twice to remove the Print Command Setup window; both the TIMES spreadsheet and the Command Selection menu are on the screen.

10. Select "Exit/Save" and then select "Model_Selection" to return to the Spreadsheet Model Selection menu.

TO QUIT: To exit this module, select "Options" to display the main Options menu. From here you can select another module or return to the operating system. If you exit to the Operating System, you must reload OA.

RESTART: Reload OA. Select "Spreadsheet" from the Options menu and return to the Spreadsheet Model Selection menu.

Macros

A macro is a set of commands that can be executed by one keystroke or one command. The macro in the next hands-on exercise is created right in the spreadsheet model simply by entering macro text commands or macro function keys in a column. A macro can be created in a spreadsheet model and then executed by pressing the <ss_macro> Alt-F10 key and entering the cell number where the macro starts.

An alternate method of executing the macro is to set up a named field called 'AUTOMAC' for the cell that contains the first instruction in the macro. The macro is then automatically executed when the named cell is selected; it could be executed, for example, as soon as the model is selected. The specific keys in spreadsheet macros are listed in Table 7-3.

TABLE 7-3 Spreadsheet Macro Function Keys

Name	*Key*	*Function*
<edit>	F9	Puts cell into Edit mode.
<query>	Alt-F9	Executes the current query for the internal database.
<window>	F5	Advances multiple windows.
<justify>	Alt-F6	Changes justification of the current cell.
<graph1>	F7	Displays the current high-resolution graph if supported.
<graph2>	Alt-F7	Displays graph in special-character graph window.

The spreadsheet macro uses commands in the following format:

<command,operand1,operand2,operand3,{operand4}>

The command is enclosed in angle brackets < > and any optional parts are enclosed in {} brackets; for example, <move,4,2> means to move to cell B4.

The command language includes the following operands:

- x-pos Specifies left margin distance
- y-pos Specifies top margin distance
- length Specifies length of a window or entry
- height Specifies height in rows of a window
- time Specifies time duration in tenths of a second

The spreadsheet command language and a brief description of each command is summarized in Table 7-4.

TABLE 7-4 Spreadsheet Macro Commands

Command	*Function*
<?>	Interrupts the macro until <ss_macro> key is pressed.
<beep,frequency,duration>	Sets an audible beep at a specified frequency and time.
<beep>	Produces a beep.
<case,area1{,area2}>	Produces menus and determines the path to take from the menu.
<env,option1,option2>	Sets the environment for the macro.
<If,expression,coord1,coord2>	Evaluates an expression as true or false and continues the macro at the coordinate for true or false.
<msg,1,area,x-pos,y-pos{,length,height}>	Produces a message that must be answered by <do> or <undo>.
<msg,2,area,time,x-pos{,length,height}>	Produces a message for a specific time on the screen.
<msg,3,constant/coord,x-pos,y-pos.length>	Creates a window where the macro prompts the user for input.
<goto,coordinate>	Causes the macro to jump to a new location and begin execution at that cell.
<pause,time>	Pauses the macro for a specified time.
<let,1,text/expression,coordinate>	Assigns a text entry, numeric entry, numeric cell entry, or calculation results to a specific cell.
<let,2,row,column,coordinate>	Copies the contents of the cell to a new cell.
<let,3,row1,col1,row2,col2>	Copies the value of a cell to a new cell.
<set,coordinate/expression>	Sets the "integer register," which can store only whole numbers.
<jump,row,column,{model number}>	Causes the macro to jump to the specified cell and continue execution.
<move,row,column>	Moves the cursor to a specified row and column.

In the following hands-on exercise, create a macro that will enable you to change the cost of the car wash and recalculate the entire model based on that cost. The explanation following each entry tells you what the macro will do.

Hands On

1. Select "Select" and enter [SAMPLE1] as the model name.
2. Press <ret> **Return** twice and the model appears on the screen.
3. Position the cursor in cell A24 where you will enter the macro commands.
4. Type [<tab>a1<ret>] and press <ret>; when the macro is executed, this moves the cursor to cell A1.
5. Move to cell A25 and enter [<menu>sgn] and press <ret>; this turns off the grid display by selecting Setup, then Grid, then No_Grid.
6. Move to cell A26 and enter[<move,4,2> <undo>] and press <ret>; this moves the cursor to cell B4.
7. Move to cell A27 and enter the following:

   [<msg,3,"Cost of Car Wash ",2,20,7> <ret>]

   Now press <ret>; this prompts for a selection from a menu that you will create as part of the macro and enters that data into cell B4.
8. Move to cell A28 and enter [<menu>ra1:d17<ret>] and press <ret>; this recalculates the model.
9. Move to cell A29 and enter [<case,b29:c29>] and press <ret>; this displays the menu choices and executes according to the choice selected.
10. Move to cell B29 and enter [NEW_COST] and press <ret>. This is one of the menu choices.
11. Move to cell C29 and enter [STOP] and press <ret>. This is the other menu choice.
12. Move to cell A30 and enter [<menu>sgd] and press <ret>; this redisplays the grid after the macro has finished executing. The menu choices that you created in steps 10 and 11 must have statements associated with them that execute the desired choice. The statements must appear directly below them in the macro listing.
13. Move to cell B30 and enter [<goto,a24>] and press <ret>; this executes the macro when a new price is entered.
14. Move to cell C30 and enter [<goto,a30>] and press <ret>; this causes execution to start at line cell A30, which ends the macro.

The model now looks like Figure 7-13, with the macro statements included. You will execute the macro with the <ss_macro> Alt-F10 key. In the following hands-on exercise, change the car wash price and recalculate the model with this macro. Notice what happens to the grid in the example.

Hands On

1. Press <ss_macro> **Alt-F10** and the prompt "Start Macro at what coordinate:" appears.
2. Type [A24] and press <do> **F10**. The prompt "Cost of Car Wash:" appears in a box.
3. Type [6.00] and press <do>. The new price is entered and the model is recalculated. The total profit is $8928.00.
4. Select "NEW_COST" from the menu you created.

```
W1                A                  |    B     |     C    |     D    |
15 Profit                               $2507.50   $2908.70   $3079.80
16 ----------------------------------------------------------------------
17 Total Profit--Second Quarter                                $8496.00
18
19
20
21
22
23
24 <tab>a1<ret>
25 <menu>sgn
26 <move,4,2><undo>
27 <msg,3,"Cost of Car Wash ",2,20,7><ret>
28 <menu>ra1:d17<ret>
29 <case,b29:c29>                  NEW_COST    STOP
30 <menu>sgd                       <goto,a24>  <goto,A30>
31
32
Model A:SAMPLE               96.0%   Pointer:A32    Current:A32     LR  W:1 #0

        input:
```

FIGURE 7-13

5. Type [5.75] and press <do>. Notice that all calculations are now back to the original values in the model.
6. Select "STOP" and the model SAMPLE1 is redisplayed.

Setting Default Parameters

After entering the name of a new spreadsheet, you can change the default parameters for the spreadsheet module. To view or change the default parameters, select the Setup command from the Spreadsheet Command Selection menu. For now, look at the Setup options listed in Table 7-5.

TABLE 7-5 Setup Command Options

Option	*Function*
Order	Determines the movement of the cursor after pressing <ret> or <do>.
Advance	Determines whether or not the cursor automatically advances after pressing <ret> or <do>.
Attributes	Determines the default values for text or numeric cells.
Menu	Determines whether the Spreadsheet Command menu is displayed or if you are prompted for a command.
Modes	Determines the mode after a command is executed, either Insert or Command.

TABLE 7-5 (continued)

Option	*Function*
Margin	Determines left and right margins and paragraph indentions.
Grid-Labels	Determines whether or not the grid displayed around the model is seen.
Suffix	Determines whether the default file suffix is .FMD (normal) or .CMP (compressed).

In the following hands-on exercise, change the way the cursor moves on the screen when the <ret> Return key is pressed. Watch the screen to see the different cursor movements.

Hands On

1. Press <menu> **F2** to access the Spreadsheet Command Selection menu.
2. Select "Setup."
3. Select "Order."
4. Use <arrows> to highlight "Top_to_Bottom." Press <do> **F10** and then press <undo> **Esc** twice.
5. Press <ret> **Return**. Notice how the cursor moves from top to bottom on the screen.
6. Press <menu>.
7. Select "Setup."
8. Select "Order."
9. Use <arrows> to highlight "Left_to_Right" and press <do>.
10. Press <undo> twice.
11. Press <ret>. Notice how the cursor now moves from left to right.

Windows

Throughout this chapter you have been working with only one window displayed on the screen. As you become more proficient with spreadsheets, you can work with multiple windows.

With the Window command, you can split the screen into as many as six windows. Windows enable you to view the data in another portion of the same spreadsheet or in another spreadsheet while working in the current model. The options in the Window command are shown in Figure 7-14 and are discussed in Table 7-6.

```
TXT [L       ] Revenue
 Window:   Split  Unsplit  Connect  Titles  Edge  View
```

FIGURE 7-14

TABLE 7-6 Window Command Options

Option	Function
Split	Splits the current window into from one to six horizontal or vertical windows.
Unsplit	Unsplits the current window--merges them into one.
Connect	Connects windows so that they scroll together.
Titles	Sets titles for the top row and left column to remain on the screen as the model is scrolled.
Edge	Moves the pointer to the top left position in a window to be redrawn.
View	Enables you to change the contents of a window to another spreadsheet, graph, or expression.

With the View option in the following hands-on exercise, you will see how each cell value in the SAMPLE1 model was calculated.

Hands On

1. Press <menu> **F2** to access the Command Selection menu.
2. Select "Window."
3. Select "View."
4. Press <do> **F10** to select "Expressions." The expressions used to calculate the cell values in the model are displayed (Figure 7-15).
5. Repeat steps 2 through 4 to toggle the values back into the model cells.
6. Press <undo> **Esc** to remove the Command Selection menu.

The next hands-on exercise splits the current window W1 horizontally into two windows, W1 and W2. (Note that window W1 appears in the upper left corner of the window.)

Hands On

1. Select <menu> **F2** to display the Command Selection menu.
2. Select "Window." The prompt "Window Split: Split Unsplit Connect Titles Edge View" appears.
3. Select "Split." This displays the prompt "Window Split: Horizontally Vertically."
4. Select "Horizontally." The prompt "Window Split: at what row/column:" is displayed. The current row number of the cursor is displayed since you are splitting the window horizontally.

```
W1              A              |    B    |    C    |    D    |
 1                              Corsican Bros. Car Wash
 2                                   Sales/Profit
 3                                 Second Quarter
 4 Cost of Car Wash                     5.75
 5 Cost of Supplies per wash             .50
 6 Other Costs                            .4
 7                                 April        May        June
 8 Cars washed                          850         986        1044
 9 Price                              +B4*1       +B4*1       +B4*1
10 -----------------------------------------------------------------
11 Revenue                            +B8*B4      +C8*B4      +D8*B4
12 Costs (Less 40% Revenue)          +B11*B6     +C11*B6     +D11*B6
13 Expenses (Less .50 per car)        +B8*B5      +C8*B5      +D8*B5
14 -----------------------------------------------------------------
15 Profit                      +B11-B12-B13+C11-C12-C13+D11-D12-D13
16 -----------------------------------------------------------------
17 Total Profit--Second Quarter                          +B15+C15+D15
 1
R                   Spreadsheet Command Selection Menu
Mo   Auto       Blank     Copy      Delete    Edit      Exit/Save   Format      #0
     Goal_Seek  Graph     Insert    Locate    Name      Order       Query
TX   Recalc     Setup     Table     Transfer  Update    Window      Xternal
           <move_keys>  <edit>  <print>  <graph#>  <query>  <change>
```

FIGURE 7-15

5. Use <arrows> to move the cursor to row 10. Press <do> **F10**. The window is now split horizontally into two windows, W1 and W2. Each window is identified with a window number in the upper left corner of the window. The Command Selection menu is displayed.
6. Press <undo> **Esc** to remove the Command Selection menu. The cursor is currently in W2.
7. Press <window> **F5** once to move the cursor to W1. This function key jumps the cursor back and forth between windows.
8. Press <end> **End** once. The cursor is now on cell A9 of window W1.
9. Press the down <arrow> three times. Notice that the top window scrolled, but the bottom window did not.

It is possible to connect two windows so that when one window scrolls, the other also scrolls. The windows can be connected in these ways: (a) vertically, so they will scroll together only when scrolling vertically; (b) horizontally, so they will scroll together only when scrolling horizontally; or (c) both, so they will scroll together when scrolling either horizontally or vertically. The following hands-on exercise connects the two windows so that they scroll together vertically.

Hands On

1. Press <menu> **F2** to display the Command Selection menu.
2. Select "Window." The prompt "Window Split: Split Unsplit Connect Titles Edge View" appears.

3. Select "Connect." The prompt "Window Connect: to which window:" appears. The prompt asks for the window number of the window to be connected.
4. Type [2] and press <do> **F10**. The prompt "Window Connect: Horizontally Vertically Both" appears.
5. Select "Vertically." The Command Selection menu is displayed.
6. Press <undo> **Esc** to remove the Command Selection menu.
7. Press the down <arrow> three times. Notice that both windows now scroll together vertically.

The contents of a window can be changed to another spreadsheet model with the Xternal_channel option, to a graph with the Graph option, or to show the expressions used to calculate a spreadsheet model with the Expressions option. To use the Xternal_channel option, a channel (or link) must first be defined using the Xternal command found in the Command Selection menu. Three channels--1, 2, or 3--can be defined. Channel 0 is the current model. The next hands-on exercise defines an external channel to the spreadsheet model WINDOWEX.

Hands On

1. Press <menu> **F2**.
2. Select "Xternal." The prompt "Xternal: open/close channel#:" appears.
3. Enter [2] and press <do> **F10**. The prompt "Open to model:" is displayed.
4. Type [WINDOWEX] and press <do>. The channel is open to the model WINDOWEX. The Command Selection menu is displayed.

We can now return to the Window command and use the Xternal_channel option to display the WINDOWEX model in window number two.

Hands On

1. Press <window> **F5**. The cursor should be in window two (W2).
2. Select "Window." The prompt "Window Split: Split Unsplit Connect Titles Edge View" appears.
3. Select "View." The prompt "Window View: Expressions Xternal_channel Graph" appears.
4. Select "Xternal_channel." The prompt "Window Xternal: View which model channel in this window?:" appears.
5. Type [2] and press <do>. The model WINDOWEX is displayed in window number two. The Command Selection menu is also displayed.

The top row and/or the left column of a window can be set so that either or both always remain on the screen when the spreadsheet is scrolled. This option is called "titles." The following hands-on exercise sets the top row as titles in window number one.

Hands On

1. Select "Window." The prompt "Window Split: Split Unsplit Connect Titles Edge View" appears.
2. Select "Titles." The prompt "Window: No_titles Row_titles Column_titles Both" appears.
3. Select "Column_titles." The top row is now set as a title and will remain on the screen when the window is scrolled. The Command Selection menu is displayed.
4. Press <undo> **Esc**.
5. Press the down <arrow> until window number one begins scrolling. Notice that in window number two, the years on the top row of titles remains on the screen.
6. Press <menu> **F2**.
7. Select "Window." The prompt "Window Split: Split Unsplit Connect Titles Edge View" appears.
8. Select "Titles." The prompt "Window: No_titles Row_titles Column_titles Both" appears.
9. Select "No_titles" to turn off the Titles option. The Command Selection menu is displayed.
10. Press <undo> to remove the Command Selection menu.

The Edge option moves the spreadsheet model so that the cell that is currently highlighted will be in the upper left corner of the window. The following hands-on exercise uses the Edge option to reposition the spreadsheet model.

Hands On

1. Press <arrows> to move the cursor to the number 164.00 in the column under 1987 and across from April.
2. Press <menu> **F2** to display the Command Selection menu.
3. Select "Window." The prompt "Window Split: Split Unsplit Connect Titles Edge View" appears.
4. Select "Edge." The model is now repositioned with the number 164.00 in the upper left corner of the W2 window.

The Unsplit option is used to merge the windows back into one so that only W0 is displayed. The following hands-on exercise unsplits the windows.

Hands On

1. Select "Window." The prompt "Window Split: Split Unsplit Connect Titles Edge View" appears.
2. Select "Unsplit." The windows are unsplit and the Command Selection menu is displayed.

Sorting

Sorting can be accomplished in the spreadsheet model with the Order command. Areas of the spreadsheet can be sorted in ascending (lowest to highest) or descending (highest to lowest) order. You can also sort by either rows or columns and sort for both numbers and letters. Once you have sorted, however, you cannot return the list to its unsorted state. The next hands-on exercise sorts a list of items.

Hands On

1. Press <undo> **Esc**.
2. Press <arrows> and move the cursor to cell H1.
3. Type [c] in cell H1, type [b] in cell H2, and type [a] in cell H3.
4. Press <menu> **F2**. The Command Selection menu is displayed.
5. Select "Order." The prompt "Order: Area:_ By: Column Row" appears.
6. Type [:H1] and press <ret> **Return**.
7. Select "Column" and press <do> **F10**. The prompt "Order: row/column:_ Type: Ascending Descending" appears.
8. Type [H] and press <ret>.
9. Select "Ascending" and press <do>. The list is now ordered in ascending order.
10. Press <undo> to remove the Model Selection menu.

Transferring Files

As with some of the other modules, files can be transferred in and out of the spreadsheet module. This is done with the Transfer command in the Command Selection menu. You can import and export data to and from a Data Interchange File (DIF). Data can be defined by setting query conditions using the structured query language when importing from an existing database file. Review the Structured Query Language in the Database module if you attempt the Query command.

A database can be created in the spreadsheet by using the Query command in the Command Selection menu. The data in the database can be defined, entered, and retrieved using a query. Table 7-7 summarizes the commands in the Data Management menu.

TABLE 7-7 Data Management Menu Commands

Command	*Function*
Data_Form	Selects the area in the model for the data base, defines the layout of each record; used to enter data.
Query_Form	Sets the search conditions.
Output_Form	Sets the area of the model that is to receive the data from a database list, etc.
Status	Allows expressions to be set and compares records against the expression. Results can be displayed in a Status window.

TABLE 7-7 Data Management Menu Commands

Command	*Function*
Sort	Sorts the database by a selected field.
List	Presents a list of records that meet the query.
Unique_List	Lists only unique records that meet the query condition.
Find	Locates a record(s) with a query.
Highlight	Presents a list of all records, but highlights only those that meet a query condition.
Delete	Erases a record(s) that meets the query condition.
Join_List	Presents a list of records from joined databases.
Joined_Unique	Lists unique records in the output area from joined databases.

Creating a Goal-Seeking Table

When working with "what if" conditions, you can set goal-seeking conditions in table form with the Table command. With this command, you can calculate multiple "what if" conditions. You can choose to set a "one-way" table in which you specify a number of independent variable values and any number of dependent variables.

The other option is to create a "two-way" table in which you designate two independent variables and a single dependent variable.

In the following hands-on exercise, create a one-way table in which revenues and profits are calculated for varying car wash prices. Tables are usually created for calculating "what ifs" from existing data and defined formulas in a model; they are usually developed at the bottom half of the spreadsheet window. If you are not sure how to enter data into a cell, review the section on entering data into a spreadsheet. The SAMPLE1 (Corsican Bros.) spreadsheet should still be on your screen.

Hands On

1. Type the following values into columns B through D and rows 19 through 23 in the SAMPLE1 model. These values are part of the goal-seeking table.

	B	C	D
19		Revenue	Profit
20	Price	+B11	+B15
21	5.50		
22	6.00		
23	6.25		

Column B represents the independent variable Price. Columns C and D are values dependent on the value of PRICE. The Revenue and Profit entries in row 20 are the current values. As <ret> **Return** is pressed after entering +B11 or +B15, the actual value is entered in the table.

```
W1                  A                 |       B       |       C       |       D      |
17 Total Profit--Second Quarter                                              $8496.00
18
19                                                   Revenue      Profit
20                                  Price                  4887.50       2507.50
21                                            5.50         4675.00       2380.00
22                                            6.00         5100.00       2635.00
23                                            6.25         5312.50       2762.50
24
25
26
27
28
29
30
31
32
33
3 ┌──────────────────────────────────────────────────────────────────────────────┐
R │                     Spreadsheet Command Selection Menu                          │
Mo│  Auto        Blank     Copy      Delete     Edit      Exit/Save   Format      │ #0
  │  Goal_Seek   Graph     Insert    Locate     Name      Order       Query       │
NU│  Recalc      Setup     Table     Transfer   Update    Window      Xternal     │
  │         <move_keys>  <edit>  <print>  <graph#>  <query>  <change>              │
  └──────────────────────────────────────────────────────────────────────────────┘
```

FIGURE 7-16

2. Press <menu> **F2** to access the Spreadsheet Command Selection menu.
3. Select "Table" from the Command Selection menu. The Table Command Setup window appears.
4. Press <ret> to select "One-Way."
5. Type [B20:D23] as the area for the table and press <ret>.
6. Type [B4], where Price is defined, as the independent row. Do Not press <ret>.
7. Press <do> **F10**. The table is calculated showing revenues and profits for the different prices (Figure 7-16). The Command Selection menu appears.
8. Select "Exit/Save" and then select "Model_Selection."
9. Select "After_Saving." The SAMPLE1 model is saved and the Spreadsheet Model Selection menu appears.

Returning to the Options Menu

The Model Selection menu offers an Options command choice. If you select this item, the Options menu appears on the screen. From this menu you can select another Open Access module or return to the operating system.

Hands On

Select "Options" from the Spreadsheet Command Selection menu. This selection returns you to the Main Options menu.

Command Summary

Here is a brief summary of the commands listed in the main menus of the spreadsheet module.

Spreadsheet Model Selection Menu

Select	Selects and displays an existing model.
New	Creates a new spreadsheet model.
Copy	Copies and saves an existing model with a new name.
Delete	Erases a model from storage.
Options	Returns you to the Main Options menu.
Consolidate	Takes data from two or more models, summarizes the results, and stores them in a separate model.
Setup_Consolidation	Sets parameters for the model used when consolidating models.
Graph_Slides	Creates, changes, or displays a slide show; used for graphics.

Spreadsheet Command Selection Menu

Auto	Moves quickly to cells with the Form attribute.
Blank	Erases data from a cell or area of cells.
Copy	Copies the contents of a cell to other cells.
Delete	Deletes a column or row.
Edit	Accesses the text editor.
Exit/Save	Exits the current model and returns you to either the Model Selection menu or the Main Options menu.
Format	Defines the attributes assigned to the cells and how the model will appear physically, such as column width, filler characters, data type, and various attributes.
Goal_Seek	By identifying dependent and independent variables, calculations are made to show what is needed to meet desired results.
Graph	Accesses the Graphics Configure menu defined in Chapter 8, Graphics.
Insert	Inserts any number of rows or columns into the model.
Locate	Searches text cells for a character string and moves the cursor to that location.
Name	Gives a name to a cell or area of cells.
Order	Sorts a row or column in ascending or descending order.
Query	Accesses the Data Management menu.
Recalc	Recalculates the model cell values after changes are made.
Setup	Sets various parameters for the model such as cursor movement, margins, and various attributes.
Table	Creates a one-way or two-way table of dependent and independent variables.
Transfer	Imports a DIF file into the model or saves all or part of the current model to a DIF file to be exported to another file or module.
Update	Makes changes to constant values, often used for "what-if" analysis.
Window	Allows the creation of multiple windows on the screen.
Xternal	Allows establishment of a link to other models and the current model.

Data Management Menu

Data_Form	Selects the area in the model for the database, defines the layout of each record; used to enter data.
Query_Form	Sets the search conditions.
Output_Form	Sets the area of the model that is to receive the data from a database list, etc.
Status	Allows expressions to be set and compares records against the expression. Results can be displayed in a Status window.
Sort	Sorts the database by a selected field.
List	Presents a list of records that meet the query.
Unique_List	Lists only unique records that meet the query condition.
Find	Locates a record(s) with a query.
Highlight	Presents a list of all records, but highlights only those that satisfy a query condition.
Delete	Erases a record(s) that meets the query condition.
Join_List	Presents a list of records from joined databases.
Joined_Unique	Lists unique records in the output area from joined databases.

Study Questions

1. C3 is a cell designation. What does "C" represent and what does "3" represent?
2. What word is often used instead of "file" to describe a spreadsheet?
3. What is the purpose of the colon in the designation B6:E7?
4. Which command loads and displays an existing spreadsheet model?
5. How can the contents of a text cell be edited after they have been entered?
6. Which command erases the contents of a cell?
7. Is it possible to increase the width of a column? If so, how?
8. Three ways a formula can be copied to another cell are ____________ , ____________ , and ____________ .
9. What is goal seeking?
10. In which two ways can a macro be executed in a spreadsheet?

The following exercises use the spreadsheet model INV.FMD.

11. Load the model INV.FMD into the spreadsheet module.
12. Enter the formulas to calculate the In Stock Jan 31 quantity for each item in column E and center the values in cells E8, E9, E10, and E11. In Stock Jan 31 = In Stock Jan 1 -(Sold + Damaged). What are the formulas?
13. Enter the label [Totals] in cell A13.
14. Enter a formula in cell B13 to calculate the total number of all items In Stock for Jan 1. What is that formula?
15. Copy the formula in cell B13 to cells C13, D13, and E13 and then center the values in cells B13, C13, D13. What are the formulas in cells C13, D13, and E13?
16. Change the number of washers sold to 27 and the number of dryers damaged to 3 and recalculate the entire spreadsheet. What are the new totals--total SOLD, total DAMAGED, and total In Stock JAN 31?
17. Format all the numbers in the spreadsheet so that they have no decimal places and appear as whole numbers.

18. Insert a blank row above line 8 so that there is a blank line between the headings ITEM, JAN 1, SOLD, etc., and the data.
19. With the Filler_Char option, fill cells A8:E8 with the minus (-) character.
20. Print the entire model INV.FMD to the console or to a printer if one is available.

The following exercises use the model SALES.FMD that you will create.

21. Create a new blank spreadsheet model called SALES.FMD. Do not enter a password.
22. Change the width of column A to 15.
23. Enter the following data in the indicated cells:

Cell	*Label*	*Number*
A1	Retail Price	
B1		200
D1	Cost Percent	
E1		27% (.27)
B2	Q1	
C2	Q2	
D2	Q3	
E2	Q4	
F2	Totals	
A3	Units Sold	
B3		50
C3		75
D3		65
E3		65
A4	Revenues	
A5	Cost of Sales	
A6	Fixed Expenses	
B6		1000
C6		1000
D6		1000
E6		1000
A7	Profit	

Enter the formula to calculate revenues (units sold * retail price) in cell B4. What is the formula?

24. Copy the formula in cell B4 to cells C4, D4, and E4. Hint: You will need to copy the formula using prompted cell references. What are the formulas in cells C4, D4, and E4?
25. Enter the formula to calculate cost of goods sold (Revenue * Cost percent) in cell B5. What is that formula?
26. Copy the formula in cell B5 to cells C5, D5, and E5. What are the formulas in those cells?
27. Enter the formula to calculate profits for quarter 1 (Revenue - Cost of Sales - Fixed Expenses) in cell B7. What is that formula?
28. Copy the formula in cell B7 to cells C7, D7, and E7. What are the formulas in those cells?
29. Enter the formula to total the number of units sold for all four quarters (units sold Q1 + units sold Q2 + units sold Q3 + units sold Q4) in cell F3. What is the formula?
30. Copy the formula in cell F3 to cells F4, F5, F6, and F7. What are the formulas in those cells?
31. Insert two blank rows at the top of the spreadsheet.

32. Enter the heading [Sales] in cell C1.
33. Use the Edit command to edit the text in cell C1 to read [Sales and Profit].
34. Center the range of cells B4:F4.
35. Insert a single blank row starting at row 4.
36. Insert a single blank row starting at row 6.
37. With the Filler_Char option, fill cells B6:F6 with the minus (-) character.
38. Format the value 0.27 in cell E3 so that it displays as 27%. Now what appears in cell E3? How do you delete ".00"?
39. Save the model.
40. Reload the model SALES.FMD.
41. With the Update command, perform a temporary "what if" analysis to see the effect of a 10% increase in the Cost Percent [!*1.1] using the Update command. Recalculate the entire spreadsheet and record the total profit for all four quarters; then restore cell E3 to its original state and recalculate the entire spreadsheet. What is the effect of a 10% increase? What is the total profit for the four quarters after recalculation?
42. Use the Goal Seeking command to determine how many units need to be sold in Q4 to generate a profit of $15,000. How many units must be sold? What are the entries in the Goal Seeking window?
43. Create a macro starting at cell A14 that will change the Retail Price and recalculate the entire model based on that cost. Execute the macro.

The following exercises use the models INV.FMD and WINDOWEX.FMD found on the Open Access data diskette.

44. Load the model INV.FMD.
45. Split the model INV.FMD into two horizontal windows at row 10.
46. Open an Xternal channel to the model WINDOWEX.FMD.
47. Display the model WINDOWEX.FMD in window #2.
48. Set the titles in row A of window #2 so that they remain fixed when window #2 is scrolled.
49. Connect window #1 and window #2 so that they scroll together horizontally.
50. Remove window #2 so that only window #1, containing the model INV.FMD, remains; then exit the Spreadsheet module.

Chapter 8

Graphics

Introduction

With Open Access Publisher's Version software, you can create, modify, and produce graphics from data contained in a spreadsheet. If you have not already read the spreadsheet module in this workbook, you should study it first.

The graphs created from the data in a spreadsheet model can be displayed on the monitor, output directly to a printer or plotter, saved in an image file that can be incorporated into a document for later printing, or saved as a slide file to be incorporated into a slide show. These options will be explained in more detail as we progress.

OA displays graphs in color if your system has the appropriate hardware card and a color monitor. It allows both high-resolution and text-resolution graphics. High resolution lets you draw images by controlling the individual pixels on a screen. High-resolution graphics require that the computer be equipped with a graphics card and a high-resolution monitor. All the graphs discussed in this section can be produced using a high-resolution system. However, if your system does not have high-resolution capabilities, OA provides a Text-Resolution mode that enables some graphs to be created using ASCII text and special characters. Pie graphs, surface graphs, and 3-D graphs cannot be created, however, in this mode.

Table 8-1 lists the keys that are used throughout this chapter.

TABLE 8-1 Keys Used in Open Access Graphics Workbook

Name	*Key*	*Function*
<graph1>	F7	Displays text or high-resolution graphs.
<graph2>	Alt-F7	Displays only text graphs.
<do>	F10	Accepts command or last entry.
<undo>	Esc	Cancels entry or returns to previous menu.
<ret>	Return	Accepts entry.
<menu>	F2	Displays submenus.
<arrows>	Arrows	Moves cursor and highlights.
<change>	F6	Selects data to be changed.
<move_keys>	PgDn, PgUp Home, End	Cursor-movement keys.
<search>	F4	Displays file directory.
<print>	F3	Initiates output.
<line_ins>	Crtl-Return	Inserts a line.
<line_del>	Crtl-Backspace	Deletes a line.

Entering Data

Before a graph is created, the data to be graphed must be entered into the spreadsheet. Select the spreadsheet model called GR1 for this hands-on exercise.

Hands On

1. Select "Spreadsheet" from the Options menu. The Model Selection menu appears.
2. Use <arrows> to highlight "Select" from the Model Selection menu and press <do> **F10**. You are prompted: "Select what model:".
3. Enter [GR1] and press <ret> **Return**. You are prompted: "Make backup (<do>/<undo>)?".
4. Press <do>. A backup is made and the spreadsheet is displayed.

The GR1 spreadsheet model is displayed on the screen (Figure 8-1). This model shows sales figures for products A, B, and C during the years 1986, 1987, and 1988.

Accessing the Graphics Configure Menu

The graph portion of the spreadsheet visually displays the relationships between the values in a model. The Graph command accesses the Graphics Configure menu, and the Command Selection menu must first be activated as done in the following hands-on exercise.

```
 W1       A       |     B       |     C     |     D       |     E       |     F       |
  1                                 Sales Figures
  2
  3   Product          '86          '87          '88
  4   -------        -------      -------      -------
  5      A            6000         5500         5000
  6      B            5000         4500         4000
  7      C            3000         3500         4500
  8
  9
 10
 11
 12
 13
 14
 15
 16
 17
 18
R
Model A:GR1                        70.8%   Pointer:D3     Current:D3      LR  W:1 #0

TXT [C        ] '88
        input:
```

FIGURE 8-1

```
                     Graphics  Configure  Menu
     Data      Display    Title     Scale     View     Position    Output
        Load     Copy_Chart    Pause    Palette    Graph_Window    Mode
                        <do>        <undo>        <graph#>
```

FIGURE 8-2

Hands On

1. Press <menu> **F2** to access the Command Selection menu.
2. Select "Graph" and the Graphics Configure menu appears (Figure 8-2).

The Graphics Configure menu contains commands to create, modify, and produce graphs using the spreadsheet data. These commands are shown in Table 8-2.

TABLE 8-2 Graphics Configure Menu Commands

Command	*Description*
Data	Defines the areas of the spreadsheet containing data to be graphed.
Display	Defines the type of graph (bar, line, or pie) and the presentation.

TABLE 8-2 (continued)

Command	*Description*
Title	Allows titles for a graph to be entered.
Scale	Allows the definition of maximum and minimum scale values and the number of divisions along an axis.
View	Changes the display parameters of a graph.
Position	Changes the color and texture of the "slices" of a pie chart and "explodes" a pie chart.
Output	Defines the output parameters to produce hard copy, slide, or image file output.
Load	Allows a chart file (.CHT) to be loaded containing the parameters for Display, Title, Scale, View, Position, and Palette and applies these to the current Data.
Copy_Chart	Saves the current parameters for Display, Title, Scale, View, Position, and Palette to chart file for later use.
Pause	Allows you to define the time a graph is displayed on the screen if displayed by a macro using <graph1> F7.
Palette	Changes the colors of the graph and the background color.
Graph_Window	Changes the size and position of the Text Graph window. The Text Graph window is accessed by pressing <graph2> Alt-F7.
Mode	Determines whether the graph produced by <graph1> F7 will be high resolution or text resolution.

The following sections let you practice each of these commands. All of the examples are applicable to your computer if you have a high-resolution system. The sections that cannot be completed without high-resolution capabilities are identified.

Defining the Data to be Graphed

Data to be graphed must be selected from a spreadsheet model. The data to be graphed must be defined in order to create a graph. You will do this with the Data command, which brings up the Graphics Data Selection window shown in Figure 8-3. There are four different fields (two required, two optional) that can be defined in this window. The two required fields are

```
                       Graphics  Data  Selection  Window

  Row Labels:  A5:A7                           Column Labels:  B3:D3
 Data levels are:   Rows  Columns
Data:  1.B5:D7         2.                3.                4.
       5.              6.                7.                8.

          <arrows>  <change>  <graph#>  <line_del>  <undo>
```

FIGURE 8-3

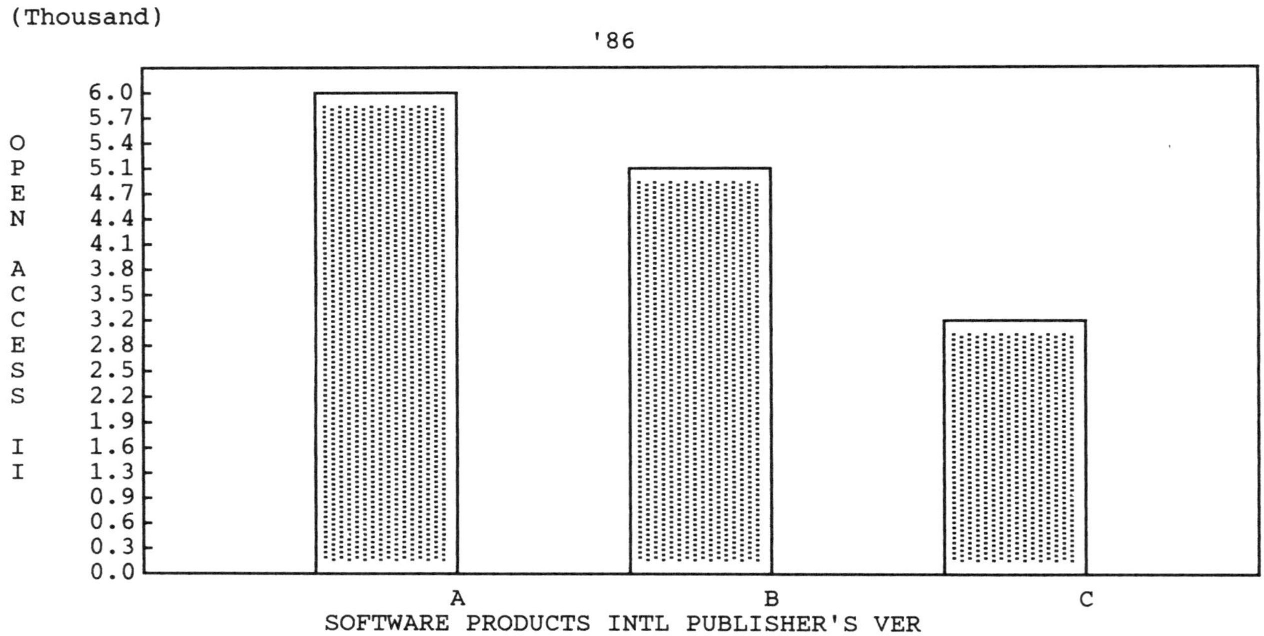

(a)

FIGURE 8-4a

1. *Data.* This field allows you to define in the spreadsheet up to eight rectangular areas for the data to be graphed.
2. *Data levels.* This field indicates whether the data presented for graphing are across rows or down columns. For example, look at the GR1 model. If the defined data are B5:D7 in the Data field and if you want to compare all three products during a given year such as in Figure 8-4a, you would choose Columns as the data levels. The values in the data area are graphed on the y-axis, and each bar represents a particular product. Using the same data area, if you want to see how a particular product progressed for each of the three years such as in Figure 8-4b, choose Rows for the data levels. The values in the data area are graphed on the y-axis, and each bar represents a particular year.

The two optional fields are

1. *Row Labels.* This field allows a range of cells that contain row labels to be entered.
2. *Column Labels.* This field allows a range of cells that contain column labels to be entered.

The row labels in Figure 8-1 are A5:A7; these labels identify the rows in the selected data area. The column labels are B3:D3; these labels identify the columns in the selected data area.

The graph in the following hands-on exercise compares how products A, B, and C sold relative to each other in each of the three years.

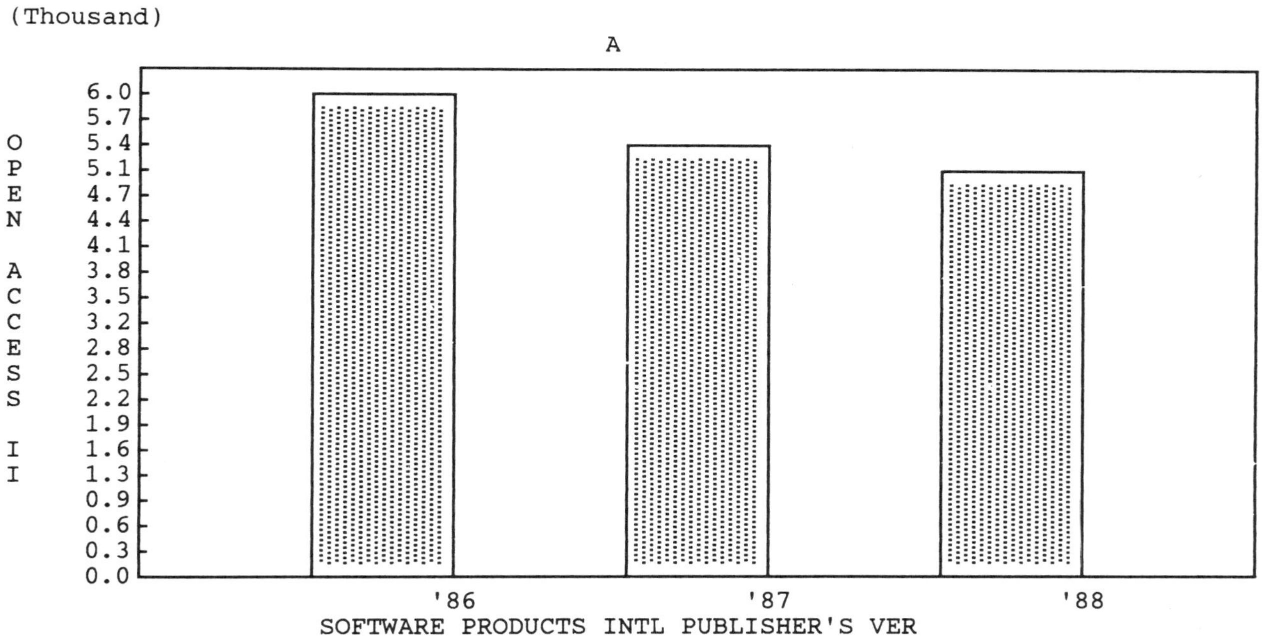

(b)

FIGURE 8-4b

Hands On

1. Select "Data" in the Graphics Configure menu. The Graphics Data Selection window appears and the cursor is in the "Data: 1" field.
2. Enter [B5:D7] in the "Data: 1" field and press <ret> **Return**. This defines the data to be graphed. (If you make a mistake, highlight the Data field and press <lin_del> **Ctrl-Backspace** to erase the field and then reenter the range.) You can enter data by one of the following ways:

   a. Type the sequence of characters [B5:D7] and press <ret>.
   b. Type the characters [B5:]; then use <arrows> to position the cursor in the spreadsheet at the desired location, D7 for this example, and press <ret>.
   c. Press <change> **F6**; then, use <arrows> to position the cursor at the desired starting location, B5. Type [:], a colon. Then, use <arrows> to position the cursor at the end of the desired block, D7, and press <ret>. (This area could have been defined as D7:B5.)

3. Press up <arrow> once to move to the Data Levels field.
4. Highlight "Columns" using the left or right <arrows>. This compares all three products (A, B, and C) in a given year.
5. Press up <arrow> once to move to the Row Labels field.
6. Enter [A5:A7] the same way you did in the Data field. This defines the labels that identify the data in rows.
7. Press <ret> or right <arrows> to move to the Column Labels field.

8. Enter [B3:D3]. This defines the labels that identify the data in columns.
9. Press <do> **F10** to accept these values. The Graphics Configure menu appears on the screen.

You have now finished defining the data for the first graph. Let's decide how to display the graph.

Defining the Chart Type, the Graph Type, and Presentation Format

Selecting the Display command from the Graphics Configure menu causes the Display window (Figure 8-5) to appear. Graphics data must be defined using the Data command before using this command as accomplished in the previous exercise.

The Display command allows you to

- Select a Chart Type. This selection determines the kind of chart that will be displayed. The nine different Chart Types are described in Table 8-3.
- Specify the type of graph--either bar, line, or pie--for each level of data. For example, in Figure 8-1 there are three levels of graphs when comparing products A, B, and C to a given year. One level is shown in the graph in Figure 8-4a where products A, B, and C are compared for the year 1986. The second level is another graph that compares products A, B, and C for the year 1987. The third level is a graph that shows products A, B, and C for the year 1988. When the "Chart Type" is selected as "simple," each year will be a separate graph; and you will be able to toggle between the graphs using the PgUp and PgDn keys. Other "Chart Type" selections, such as "Overlay," allow

```
W1       A      |     B     |     C    |     D     |     E     |     F     |
 1                               Sales Figures
 2
 3    Product
 4    -------       --+-----------------------------------------------------+
 5       A            |                     Display                          |
 6       B            |Chart Type :                                          |
 7       C            |     Overlay  Windowed  Three-D  Simple  Scatter      |
 8                    |     Hi/Low/Close  Stack-Bar  Surface  Stacked-Line   |
 9                    |Transpose  :   Not Applicable                         |
10                    |Level Name                   Type                     |
11                    |                                                      |
12                    | 1    '86                Bar   Line   Pie             |
13                    | 2    '87                Bar   Line   Pie             |
14                    | 3    '88                Bar   Line   Pie             |
15                    |                                                      |
16                    |                                                      |
17                    |                                                      |
18                    |                                                      |
R                     |                                                      |
Model A:GR1           |   <change> <arrows> <move_keys> <graph#>             | 1 #0
                      +------------------------------------------------------+
```

FIGURE 8-5

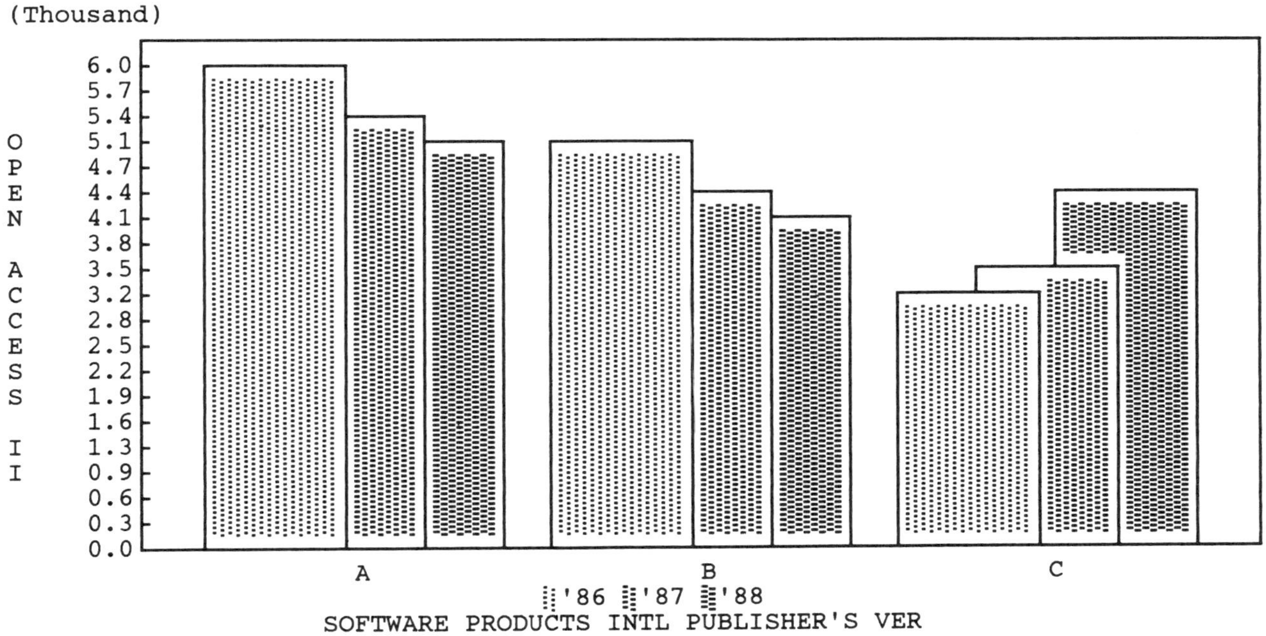

FIGURE 8-6

you to see all the data in one graph in which case there is only one level of graph. Figure 8-6 shows these levels combined in a single graph.

- Transpose. This determines if the x-axis and y-axis are to be transposed. Toggle Yes or No for transpose. The Transpose function can be used only in High-Resolution mode with Overlay, Windowed, Simple, Stack-Bar, and High/Low/Close chart types. It is bypassed for all other chart types.

TABLE 8-3 Chart Types

Type	*Description*
Overlay	All levels of the graph will be displayed at the same time if they are bars or lines, giving an overlayed bar graph or line graph. Pie charts cannot be overlayed.
Windowed	All levels are displayed at the same time but in different windows. The levels can be bar, line, or pie.
Three-D	All levels are displayed as three-dimensional bars. Available on high-resolution monitors only.
Simple	Only the highlighted level in the Display window is displayed on the screen in whichever graph is chosen.
Scatter	Creates an x-y graph using paired values where the x value comes from level 1 and the y value comes from all subsequent levels. A different symbol is used for each set of these levels.

TABLE 8-3 (continued)

Type	*Description*
High/Low/Close	Graphs Dow Jones-type data where the data presented for graphing is high price (level 1), then low price (level 2), then closing or last price (level 3).
Stack-Bar	Creates a bar graph with each level "stacked" on the previous level.
Surface	Creates a 3-D graph with data points joined to produce a surface. Available on high-resolution monitors only.
Stacked Line	Creates a line chart with each level stacked on the previous level and the areas between the lines shaded. Available on high-resolution monitors only.

The levels and the names are shown in the lower left portion of the Display window. A level will have a name if one was defined for it in the Graphics Data Selection window with the Row Labels or Column Labels fields. Each level has three graph types available--bar, line, and pie:

- Bar Command used to draw a bar graph
- Line Command used to draw a line graph
- Pie Command used to draw a pie chart; high resolution only

Each level can be a different graph type. For example, level 1 might be a bar graph, level 2 a line graph, and level 3 a pie graph (high resolution needed for pie graph). The validity of the combination of types selected is determined by the Chart Type selected. For example, pie graphs cannot be overlayed; therefore, you would not select the chart type "Overlay" if you want to use pie graphs.

Now look under the Level heading in the Display window. Notice that one of the levels is highlighted. This is the level that will be displayed first. Pressing the <move_keys> PgDn or PgUp will change the highlighted level and, thus, the level of the graph that will be displayed first. The <move_keys> also toggle through each graph level when the graphs are displayed as shown next. Define the display in the next hands-on exercise.

Hands On

1. Select "Display" from the Graphics Configure menu. Press <do> **F10** if the message "CHART1.CHT not found. Creating new chart with same name" appears. The Display window appears.
2. Use <arrows> to highlight the chart type "Simple" if it is not already highlighted.
3. Press down <arrow> once to move to the Transpose field of the Display window. Highlight "No" using <arrows>. This choice is available for high-resolution monitors only. Press down <arrow> once to move to the Type portion of the Display window. The cursor on monitors without high resolution goes directly to the Type portion of the Display window.
4. Highlight the graph type "Bar" for level 1 using left and right <arrows>.

5. Press down <arrow> once to move to level 2.
6. Highlight the graph type "Bar" for level 2 using left and right <arrows>.
7. Press down <arrow> once to move to level 3.
8. Highlight the graph type "Bar" for level 3 using left and right <arrows>.
9. Highlight "1" under the Level heading using <move_keys> **PgUp** or **PgDn**.
10. Press <graph1> **F7** to view the graph showing sales volumes of products A, B, and C in 1986.
11. Press the <move_keys> **PgDn** key to view the second level of the graph showing how products A, B, and C sold in 1987.
12. Press the <move_keys> **PgDn** key to view the third level of the graph showing sales volumes of products A, B, and C in 1988.
13. Press the <move_keys> **PgDn** key to return to the level 1 graph.
14. Press <undo> **Esc** to return to the Display window.

The <graph1> F7 key is used to display text or high-resolution graphs. The <graph2> Alt-F7 key combination displays only text graphics. In addition, only the highlighted level will be displayed in the <graph2> window. You cannot use the <move_keys> PgUp and PgDn to toggle through the levels in the <graph2> window. To view other levels, you must return to the Display window and highlight the level you want to view. Either the <graph1> or <graph2> key can be pressed at any time to see the effect changes in the display parameters have on a graph.

Hands On

1. Press <graph2> **Alt-F7**. This is the graph for level 1. Later you will learn how to change the size and position of this window.
2. Press <undo> **Esc** to return to the Display window.

To see all the levels of a graph in the same chart, use the chart type Overlay. Each level must be either a bar graph or a line graph to use the Overlay chart type. Pie charts cannot be overlayed. The current Display window has the graph type Bar selected for each level. Now change the chart type to Overlay.

Hands On

1. Press up <arrow> to move the pointer to the chart type options.
2. Press left or right <arrow> until the chart type "Overlay" is highlighted.
3. Press <graph1> **F7** to view the graph. All three levels are displayed in one graph by overlaying the bars. The legend at the bottom of the screen identifies the year each bar represents.
4. Press <undo> **Esc** to return to the Display window.

Now reset the Display options and exit the Display window. The Graphics Configure menu is on the screen.

Hands On

1. Highlight the chart type "Simple" using <arrows>.
2. Press <do> **F10** to accept the window values and return to the Graphics Configure menu.

Entering Titles

The Title command allows you to add descriptors to graphs, such as a title summarizing the contents of the graph. Graphics data must be defined under the Data command before using this command. The Title command displays the Titles window (Figure 8-7), which offers three titles-- one at the top, one at the side, and one at the bottom of the graph. In OA, only the top title can be entered by the user, but the foreground and background colors of a title can be specified. The foreground color is the color of the letters of the title. The background color is the color to appear behind the letters of the title. Depending on your system, you may have up to fifteen colors to choose from. Now add a title to the graph.

Hands On

1. Select "Title" from the Graphics Configure menu. The Titles window appears on the screen and the pointer is located in the Top field.
2. Enter the title [Sales Figures] in the Top field and press <ret> **Return**. The pointer jumps to "Fore," the field used to define the foreground color for a title.
3. Select the foreground color for the top title using left or right <arrows> and press <ret>. The pointer will jump to the Back field (the field used to select the background color of a title). Remember, the computer system must have color capabilities in order to see color. Be aware of the colors you choose for both the foreground and background. Some color combinations make it impossible to read any wording for the title.
4. Select the background color for the top title using left or right <arrows> and press <do> **F10** to return to the Graphics Configure menu. (If you should press <ret>, an error

```
                                Titles
                       Title                            Colors
                                                      Fore    Back
Top    :                                              3       0
Side   :   OPEN ACCESS II                             3       0
Bottom :   SOFTWARE PRODUCTS INTL PUBLISHER'S VER     3       0

                     <arrows> <move_keys> <graph#>
```

FIGURE 8-7

message is displayed. Press <do> or <undo> to exit the error message and continue. Press <do> again to return to the Graphics Configure menu.)

5. Press <graph1> **F7** to see the results. Notice the title on the top of the graph. Remember, the side and bottom titles are inserted by OA.
6. Press <undo> **Esc** to return to the Graphics Configure menu.

The top title can be changed at any time and the result of the change can be viewed using the <graph1> F7 or <graph2> Alt-F7 function keys.

Defining the Scale

The Scale command allows you to

- Adjust the scale of the y-axis by defining the minimum and maximum values to be graphed
- Define the number of axis divisions on the y-axis
- Change the size of the window of the <graph1> display

Graphics data must be defined before using this command. Figure 8-8 shows the Scale window. Examine the effects of changing the minimum and maximum values to be graphed in this hands-on exercise.

Hands On

1. Select "Scale" from the Graphics Configure menu. The Scale window appears. Notice that the actual data limits for the example are given--the maximum of 6000 and the minimum of 3000.
2. Press <graph1> **F7** to view the graph once more.
3. Press <move_keys> **PgDn** until the Sales Figures graph for '86 is displayed if it is not already displayed. Notice the current scale on the y-axis. In High-Resolution mode, the base is zero and extends up to 0.9. Note that the numbers on the scale are multiplied by 10,000--that's what the "10 thousand" in parentheses means above the y-axis. In Text-Resolution mode, the base is zero and the scale extends up to 6.0. The numbers on this scale are multiplied by 1000 as indicated by the "Thousand" in parentheses.

```
                         Scale

Data Limits : Desired             Actual
Maximum :                         6000.0000
Minimum :                         3000.0000

Axis Divisions :   10

           <arrows> <graph#> <change>
```

FIGURE 8-8

4. Press <undo> **Esc** to return to the Scale window.
5. Enter [4500] as the maximum limit in the Maximum field and press <ret> **Return**.
6. Enter [4000] as the minimum value in the Minimum field and press <ret>.
7. Press <graph1> to see the effect of the changes. Notice that the y-axis scale stops at 4.50 (Remember, it's really 4500). The word "thousand" now appears in parentheses above the y-axis. This means each scale value is multiplied by 1000. The tops of the first two bars are cut off and because the graph now has a base of 4000, Bar C (which is less than 4000) does not show up on the graph.
8. Press <undo> to return to the Scale window.
9. Press up <arrow> twice to position the pointer on the Maximum field.
10. Enter a space to clear the Maximum field and press <ret>. The pointer jumps to the Minimum field.
11. Enter a space to clear the Minimum field and press <ret>.
12. Press <do> **F10** to accept the changes and return to the Graphics Configure menu.

TO QUIT: Press, <undo>. The Command Selection menu appears. Select "Exit/Save." Select "Model_Selection." The Model Selection menu appears. Select "Options" and the main Options menu appears. From here, you may exit to the operating system or use another module. If you exit to the Operating System you must reload OA.

RESTART: Reload OA. Select "Spreadsheet." The Spreadsheet Model Selection menu appears. Select "Select." Enter [GR1]. Press <ret>. Press <undo>. Press <menu> **F2**. The Command Selection menu appears. Select "Graph." The Graphics Configure menu appears.

Now examine the effects of changing the axis divisions on the y-axis. This option of the Scale command affects only graphs in High-Resolution mode.

Hands On (High-Resolution mode only)

1. Select "Scale" from the Graphics Configure menu.
2. Press down <arrow> twice to place the pointer in the Axis Divisions field. Notice that the current value is 10. Ten is the maximum number of divisions; one is the minimum.
3. Press <graph1> **F7** to view the graph. Notice the y-axis has ten axis divisions, 0.0 through 0.9.
4. Press <undo> **Esc** to return to the Scale window.
5. Enter [5] in the Axis Divisions field.
6. Press <graph1> to view the effects of the change. Notice the y-axis scale has only five divisions now: 0.2, 0.4, 0.6, 0.8, and 1.0.
7. Press <undo> to return to the Scale window.
8. Enter [10] in the Axis Divisions field.
9. Press <do> **F10** to accept the change and return to the Graphics Configure menu.

The Scale command also changes the size and position of the <graph1> window in which a graph is displayed. If the window is too small to display a graph, the error message "Window too small" flashes in the window. Try changing the size and position of the <graph1> window in the following hands-on exercise.

Hands On

1. Select "Scale" from the Graphics Configure menu.
2. Press <change> **F6**. An empty <graph1> window appears and is in the Size mode. The <move_keys> **Home** and **End**, and <arrows> are used to change the size of the window.
3. Press <move_key> **Home** twice.
4. Press <graph1> **F7** to see how the change of window size affected the appearance of the graph.
5. Press <undo> **Esc** to leave the graph and return to the empty <graph1> window.
6. Press <change>. The filled-in <graph1> window appears in reverse video. This is the Position mode. The <move_keys> **Home** and **End**, and, <arrows> are used to change the position of the window.
7. Press <move_keys> **End** once.
8. Press <graph1> to see the effects of the change. Notice the <graph1> window is now centered in the screen.
9. Press <undo> to leave the graph.
10. Press <undo> to return to the Scale window.
11. Press <do> **F10** if the "Abandon changes?" window appears. Changes made to the <graph1> window are not saved. If you wanted to save the changes, you would press <do> in step 10 instead of <undo>. For now, keep the full screen <graph1> window.
12. Press <do> to accept the Scale window values and return to the Graphics Configure menu.

Changing the Display Parameters

The View command allows you to change the colors, textures, window position, and a number of other parameters of a graph. This command operates only in High-Resolution mode. The functions performed by this command vary depending on the chart type and graph type selected in the Display command. Each chart type is described in Table 8-4. Graphics data must be defined before you use this command.

When the View command is selected from the Graphics Configure menu, the View window appears. A series of options appears at the bottom of the View window. These options vary depending on the chart type selected and are selected in the same way as other menu options. Once an option is selected, the pointer does one of two things:

1. Moves to the appropriate pattern on the right side of the window to allow you to select a new color, texture, symbol, or line type.
2. Moves to the window display so you can resize or change the window's position.

In some cases, the options are determined by the type of graph defined at each level in the Display command. For example, if some levels have bar graphs, some line graphs, and others pie charts, the options available in the View window depend on the level that is active. The <move_keys> PgUp and PgDn keys are used to scroll through the levels. Now examine the options for each type of chart in Table 8-4.

TABLE 8-4 View Options

Chart Type	*Function*
Overlay	■ In a bar graph, it is possible to change (a) type of outline bars, (b) color of bars, and (c) texture of "fill" of the bars. ■ In a line graph, it is possible to change (a) color of the line, (b) symbol at the plot points, and (c) texture of the line. ■ In a pie graph, it is possible to determine if the values shown on graph are actual data values or pie slices as a percentage of the whole pie.
Windowed	■ The Windows option allows you to change the position or size of any window. ■ The Graphs option provides the same options as for the Overlay chart type.
Three-D	■ The Data option allows you to change (a) the presentation of the data; (b) the outline, color, and texture of the top, left, and right facets of the data bars; and (c) the width and depth of the columns. ■ The Grid option allows you to (a) change the outline, color, and texture of the bottom, left, and right facets of the grid; and (b) tilt and rotate the grid. ■ The Copy option allows you to copy the parameters from level 1 to all other levels.
Simple	Same as options for the Overlay chart type.
Scatter	■ The Color option changes the color of the symbols or lines. ■ The Symbol option changes the symbol character for each level. ■ The Connect option connects the plot points with lines. ■ The Copy option copies parameters for level 1 to all other levels.
High/Low/Close	Options change the color of the plots in the graph.
Stack-Bar	Options change the outline, color, and the texture of the bars.
Surface	Same as options for Three-D chart type except you cannot change the left and right facets because there are no bars.
Stacked-Line	Options change the outline, color, and texture of the lines and fills.

Try changing a few parameters in the example graph in the next hands-on exercise. The graph should presently indicate a Simple chart type, and all three levels should be defined as Bar graphs. Verify this from the display window. Refer to the hands-on exercises in the section titled "Defining the Chart Type, the Graph Type, and Presentation Format" if you're unsure how to do this. Be aware of the colors you choose when changing colors. For example, if you choose black for the bar color and the background color is black, the bar will be indistinguishable from the background.

Hands On (High-Resolution mode only)

1. Select "View" from the Graphics Configure menu. The View window appears. Notice the arrow-shaped pointer over the word "Outline" at the bottom left corner of the screen. It may be hard to see at first.
2. Press <do> **F10** to select "Outline." The pointer jumps to the color bar on the right.
3. Press up and down <arrows> to select a new color for the outline and press <do>. Notice the outline around the bar has changed color (if your system has color capabilities), and the pointer has jumped back to "Outline."
4. Press right <arrow> once to move the pointer over the word "Color" and press <do>. The pointer again jumps to the color bar, but this time the color chosen changes the color of the bar.
5. Press up or down <arrows> to select a new color for the bar and press <do>. Notice the bar has changed color and the pointer has jumped back to "Outline."
6. Press right <arrow> twice to move the pointer over the word "Texture" and press <do>. This time the pointer jumps to the second bar, which contains different texture patterns.
7. Press up or down <arrows> to select the desired texture and press <do>. The cursor again jumps to the word "Outline." Notice the change in the appearance of the bar. Each graph level can be changed this way. The other levels can be reached by pressing <move_keys> **PgUp** or **PgDn**.
8. Press <undo> **Esc** to accept the changes and return to the Graphics Configure menu.
9. Press <graph1> **F7** to view the effect of the changes made in the View window.
10. Press <undo> to return to the Graphics Configure menu.

Enhancing a Pie Graph

The Position command allows slices of a pie chart to be "exploded"--that is, set off from the rest of the pie for emphasis (Figure 8-9). The Position command from the Graphics Configure menu activates the Position window (Figure 8-10). Because this command works with pie charts, it requires high-resolution graphics.

The Position window lists the names of the slices of a pie graph. The names for our example are A, B, and C. Each slice can be either exploded by selecting ON or moved back into the pie after being exploded by selecting OFF from the Explode option. In addition, the color and texture of each slice can be changed by using the left and right <arrows> keys by placing the pointer in the correct row under the Pies Color and Texture options.

Effects of the changes can be viewed immediately by pressing <graph1> F7. Before you use the position command, change the graph types to "pie" in the following hands-on exercise.

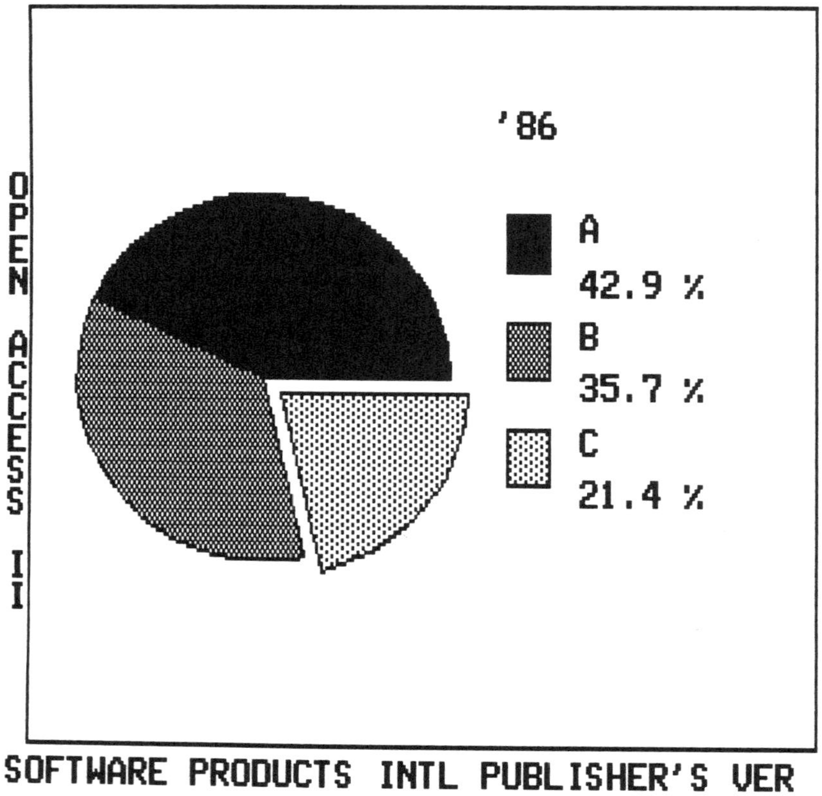

FIGURE 8-9

```
W1       A     |    B     |    C     |    D     |    E     |    F     |
 1
 2                                   Position
 3    Product
 4    -------              Name                          Pies
 5       A                                   Explode     Color    Texture
 6       B
 7       C          1  A                     Off   On      1         1
 8                  2  B                     Off   On      2         2
 9                  3  C                     Off   On      3         3
10
11
12
13
14
15
16
17
18                          <arrows> <move_keys> <graph#>
R
Model A:GR1                   97.9%   Pointer:D3     Current:D3      LR   W:1 #0
```

FIGURE 8-10

Hands On (High-Resolution mode only)

1. Select "Display" from the Graphics Configure menu.
2. Press <arrows> to position the pointer to the chart type "Simple."
3. Press down <arrow> twice to position the pointer to the Type area.
4. Press left or right <arrows> to position the pointer to "Pie."
5. Press down <arrow> to go to level 2.
6. Press left or right <arrows> to position the pointer to "Pie."
7. Press down <arrow> to go to level 3.
8. Press left or right <arrows> to position the pointer to "Pie."
9. Press <do> **F10** to accept the changes and return to the Graphics Configure menu.

Now that you have pie graphs to work with, select the Position command to explode a slice of a pie. In this next hands-on exercise, you will explode the pie slice representing product C for each graph level.

Hands On (High-Resolution mode only)

1. Select "Position" from the Graphics Configure menu.
2. Press down <arrow> twice or press <move_keys> **End** to move the pointer to the explode Off parameter for slice 3 (C).
3. Press right <arrow> once to turn On the Explode option for slice 3 (C).
4. Press <graph1> **F7** to see the effect. Notice that slice 3 (C) is drawn away, "exploded," from the rest of the pie.
5. Press <move_keys> **PgDn** once to see the level 2 graph for 1987.
6. Press <move_keys> **PgDn** once to see the level 3 graph for 1988.
7. Press <move_keys> **PgDn** once to return to the level 1 graph for 1986.
8. Press <undo> **Esc** to return to the Position window.
9. Press <undo> to return to the Graphics Configure menu.

Defining the Output Parameters

Once you have created a graph, you can use the Output command to access several output options. Selecting Output from the Graphics Configure menu activates the Output window (Figure 8-11).

The Output window has four parameters for you to define:

1. *Hardcopy*. This parameter defines the size of the graph when it is output. The options include Normal and Double. Double increases the printout to twice the Normal size.
2. *Device*. This parameter selects the output device you want for the Hardcopy or Image options of the Output To parameter. The <search> F4 key displays a list of printers or plotters. Ask your instructor which file to choose to match the equipment.

```
 W1        A      |     B      |     C     |     D      |     E      |     F      |
  1                                 Sales Figures
  2
  3    Product        '86          '87          '88
  4    -------      -------      -------      -------
  5       A          6000         5500         5000
  6       B          5000         4500         4000
  7       C          3000         3500         4500
  8                       ┌──────────────────────────────────────────────────┐
  9                       │                     Output                       │
 10                       │                                                  │
 11                       │Hardcopy     :   Normal  Double                   │
 12                       │Device       :  IBM QUIETWRITER                   │
 13                       │Output to    :   None  Slide  Image  Hardcopy     │
 14                       │Page Eject   :   False  True                      │
 15                       │                                                  │
 16                       │                                                  │
 17                       │                 <arrows> <search>                │
 18                       └──────────────────────────────────────────────────┘
R
Model A:GR1                     70.8%   Pointer:D3     Current:D3      LR  W:1 #0
```

FIGURE 8-11

3. *Output To.* The Output To parameter provides four options from which to choose: None, Slide, Image, and Hardcopy.

- The None option is selected when no hard copy output is desired. The graph can be viewed only on the screen.
- The Slide option saves a graph on a disk in a format so that it can be incorporated into a slide show; the slide show is displayed on the monitor by the Graph_Slides command in the Spreadsheet Model Selection menu. The graph is saved automatically with a .PHO suffix. The Graph_Slides command is discussed later in this chapter.
- The Image option creates an image file that can be incorporated into a report or document for output to a printer or plotter. An image file is saved automatically with an .IMA suffix.
- The Hardcopy option directs the output of a graph directly to the printer or plotter selected in the Device parameter.

4. *Output Name.* This option appears only when the Slide or Image options are chosen. The output for both the Slide and Image options are disk files. The Output Name parameter allows the disk filenames to be specified for these files.

The Output window is used to determine the output parameters. When the graph is displayed in the window after pressing <graph1> F7, output can be obtained by pressing <print> F3. The graph must be displayed on the screen using <graph1> for output to occur.

The following hands-on exercise will show you how to set up the output parameters for Hardcopy output to a printer or plotter. Ask your instructor which printer or plotter file is appropriate for your system. If your system is not connected to a printer, do steps 1 through 10 and then skip to step 12.

Hands On

1. Select "Display" from the Graphics Configure menu and set the graph type for each level to "Bar"; then press <do> **F10**.
2. Select "Output" from the Graphics Configure menu. The Output window is displayed.
3. Press left or right <arrows> to highlight "Normal" for the Hardcopy field if it is not already highlighted.
4. Press down <arrow> once to position the pointer to the Device field.
5. Enter the appropriate device filename, for example, the printer file [EPSON FX-86E]. Your instructor can tell you which device file is appropriate for your equipment. Use <search> **F4** to display the available device files.
6. Press down <arrow> once to position the pointer to the Output To field.
7. Press right or left <arrows> to highlight "Hardcopy."
8. Press right or left <arrows> to highlight "False" if the Page Eject field appears.
9. Press <do> **F10** to accept the changes and return to the Graphics Configure menu.
10. Press <graph1> **F7** to display a graph. (Go to step 12 if not printing hard copy.)
11. Press <print> **F3** to print a hard copy of the graph.
12. Press <undo> **Esc** to return to the Graphics Configure menu.

Now set the Output To parameter to create slide files of each of the three graphs that will be used later in the section about of the Graph_Slides command.

Hands On

1. Select "Output" from the Graphics Configure menu.
2. Press down <arrow> twice to position the pointer to the Output To field.
3. Highlight "Slide" using left or right <arrows> and press <ret> **Return**. If the Paper Eject: field appears, use the left or right <arrows> to highlight "False" and then press the down <arrow> once to position the cursor to the Output Name field.
4. Enter [SLIDE01] as the Output Name and press <ret>. This file name is self-incrementing. If you want to make several slide files from a multilevel graph, the filename will automatically increment to SLIDE02 and so on as you will see.
5. Press <do> **F10** to return to the Graphics Configure menu.
6. Press <graph1> **F7** to display a graph.
7. Press <print> **F3** to save the slide file of the level 1 graph to disk as SLIDE01.PHO.
8. Press <move_keys> **PgDn** to see the level 2 graph.
9. Press <print> to save the slide file of the level 2 graph to disk as SLIDE02.PHO.
10. Press <move_keys> **PgDn** to see the level 3 graph.
11. Press <print> to save the slide file of the level 3 graph to disk as SLIDE03.PHO.
12. Press <move_keys> **PgDn** to return to the level 1 graph.
13. Press <undo> **Esc** to return to the Graphics Configure menu.

Image files are defined in the same fashion as Slide files. If no output is desired, the Output parameter Output To is reset to None.

Saving the Current Parameters in a Chart File

You may want to display the data in a variety of ways. This may require modifying one or more of the parameters for the Display, Title, Scale, View, Position, and Palette commands. The Copy_Chart command allows you to save the parameters for those commands in a file. The files can then be recalled later with the Load command, so you can use it later, as discussed in the next section.

The Copy_Chart command in the Graphics Configure menu activates the Copy_Chart window. The Chart parameter allows you to enter the name of the chart file to be saved. The default is the current file chart. The default name can be accepted or another name can be entered. If the default name is used, the contents of that file are overwritten with the current parameter settings. You can use <search> F4 to display a list of the names of the chart files that already exist.

In the following hands-on exercise, create a chart file in which you can save the current parameters selected.

Hands On

1. Select "Copy_Chart" from the Graphics Configure menu. The Copy_Chart window appears with the current chart filename displayed.
2. Enter [CHART2] and press <do> **F10**. The current chart is saved under the filename CHART2.CHT, and the program returns to the Graphics Configure menu.

Loading a Chart File

With the Load command, you can load a previously created chart file containing the parameters for Display, Titles, Scale, View, Position, and Palette and apply these to the current data. Selecting the Load command from the Graphics Configure menu activates the Change Current Chart window, and you can then enter the name of the chart file to be loaded.

When a data model is used more than once, the parameters set earlier can be conveniently saved and used again. This saves time and makes the use of graphics more convenient. In the next hands-on exercise, first change some of the current parameters and then load the chart file created in the previous section to change them back.

Hands On

1. Select "Display" from the Graphics Configure menu. Notice that the graph types are all Bar.
2. Press down <arrow> to move to the Type option.
3. Select the graph type Line for each level.
4. Press <do> **F10** to accept the changes. This returns you to the Graphics Configure menu.

5. Press <graph1> **F7** to display the graph. Notice that the data are presented in a line graph instead of a bar graph.
6. Press <undo> **Esc** to return to the Graphics Configure menu.

You've changed the graph type in the Display command. However, to return to the previous parameters, load the chart file CHART2.CHT created in the last section. Practice with the following hands-on exercise.

Hands On

1. Select "Load" from the Graphics Configure menu.
2. Enter [CHART2] and press <do> **F10**. The old chart is loaded and those parameters take effect.
3. Press <graph1> **F7** to see the effect of the new chart. Notice the graph type is back to Bar.
4. Press <undo> **Esc** to return to the Graphics Configure menu.

Setting Graph Display Time from a Macro

A macro is a series of keystrokes and commands stored on a disk; it can later be called up and executed automatically. You may want to first review macros in Chapter 3, Utilities, before continuing here.

The Pause command from the Graphics Configure menu activates the Pause window. Here you enter the pause seconds, that is, the number of seconds the graph is to be displayed. The maximum pause length allowed is 999 seconds. The Pause command allows you to define in a macro the length of time a graph will be displayed on the screen using the <graph1> F7 key. The following hands-on exercise shows you how to use the Pause command.

Hands On

1. Select "Pause" from the Graphics Configure menu.
2. Enter [20] as the desired pause length in seconds. Up to 999 seconds can be entered.
3. Press <do> **F10** to accept the pause length. (When the <graph 1> **F7** key is included in a macro, the graph will be displayed for the number of seconds that you entered.)

Changing the Colors

To add impact to your graph, you can specify colors for the foreground and the background. The Palette command is used to define the foreground palette and the background color for a graph. To change colors, however, your system must support color. Each foreground palette consists of three colors. Selecting Palette from the Graphics Configure menu activates the Palette window.

The <arrows> are used to change the palette number for the chart and the background color for the screen. The <graph1> F7 key and the <graph2> Alt-F7 key combination are used to view the effect of changes to the palette and background before leaving the Palette command. The <do> F10 key accepts the changes and returns you to the Graphics Configure menu. Now try to change the foreground palette and background color of the current graph. The following hands-on exercise requires that your system has color capabilities.

Hands On (Requires color capabilities)

1. Select "Palette" from the Graphics Configure menu.
2. Press <graph1> **F7** to view the current foreground palette and background color of the graph.
3. Press <undo> **Esc** to return to the Palette window.
4. Press left or right <arrows> to change the palette. (If the palette doesn't change, use the opposite direction arrow.)
5. Press <graph1> to view the change.
6. Press <undo> to return to the Palette window.
7. Press down <arrow> once to move the pointer to the Background field.
8. Press the left or right <arrows> to change the background color. (If the background color doesn't change, use the opposite direction arrow.)
9. Press <graph1> to view the change.
10. Press <undo> to return to the Palette window. Reset the palette and background to the colors of your choice.
11. Press <do> **F10** to accept the changes and return to the Graphics Configure menu.

Changing the Size and Position of the Text Graph Window

The Text-Resolution Graph window can be displayed by pressing <graph2> Alt-F7. The Graph_Window command from the Graphics Configure menu activates the Graph_Window window from which you can change the size and position of this window. When you first enter this window, you can use the <move_keys> Home and End and the <arrows> to change its size. The pointer will be in the lower right corner for size changes. You can also change the position of the window. Pressing <change> F6 key toggles between these two functions. After you press <change>, the pointer moves to the upper left corner and the window will be filled in. The <move_keys> Home and End can then be used to change the window's position. The <graph2> Alt-F7 key can be pressed at any time to view the effect of any changes made. Pressing <do> F10 accepts the current parameters and returns you to the Graphics Configure menu.

Try changing the size and position of the <graph2> window in the next hands-on exercise. The <graph2> window can display only text-resolution graphics. In this case, use a bar graph since the current graph is of type Bar. Now let's use the Graph_Window command and observe its effects.

Hands On

1. Select "Graph_Window" from the Graphics Configure menu. The empty <graph2> **Alt-F7** window appears and is in the Size mode. The <move_keys> **Home** and **End** and <arrows> are used to change the size of the window.
2. Press the <move_keys> **Home** once.
3. Press <graph1> **F7** (in this case <graph1> displays the graph in the <graph2> window that is currently on the screen) to see the effects that the change in window size has on the appearance of the graph. If the window is too small to display a graph, the error message "Window too small" flashes in the window.
4. Press <undo> **Esc** to leave the graph and return to the empty <graph2> window.
5. Press <change> **F6**. The filled-in <graph2> window appears. This is the Position mode. The <move_keys> **Home** and **End** and <arrows> are used to change the position of the window.
6. Press <move_keys> **End** twice.
7. Press <graph1> to see the effects of the change. Notice the <graph2> window is now at the bottom right corner of the screen.
8. Press <undo> to leave the graph.
9. Press <undo>.
10. Press <do> **F10** if the "Abandon changes?" prompt appears. The Graphics Configure menu appears. The changes made to the <graph2> window are not saved. If you wanted to save the changes, you would press <do> **F10** in Step 9 instead of <undo>. For now, keep the same <graph2> window.

Selecting High-Resolution or Text-Resolution Modes

The Mode command gives you the option of selecting either High-Resolution or Text-Resolution mode if your system is capable of both. If your system is capable of only Text-Resolution mode, this window does not activate and you are always in Text-Resolution mode.

By selecting Mode from the Graphics Configure menu, you will activate the Mode window. Remember, the chart types Three-D, Surface, and Stacked-Line as well as the graph type Pie can be displayed only in high resolution. Select the mode in the following hands-on exercise.

Hands On (High-Resolution mode only)

1. Select "Mode" from the Graphics Configure menu.
2. Press left or right <arrows> to highlight the desired mode. In this case highlight "High-Res."
3. Press <do> **F10** to accept the mode and return to the Graphics Configure menu.

All the graphics commands available from the Graphics Configure menu have been discussed. Now return to the Spreadsheet Model Selection menu so that you can examine the Graph_Slides Command.

```
                         Slide Show

        Display   Edit  Output  Pause  Palette  Mode

Carousel Name :

              <arrows> <move_keys> <search>
```

FIGURE 8-12

Hands On

1. Press <undo> **Esc** to return to the Command Selection menu.
2. Select "Exit/Save." This displays five choices.
3. Select "Model_Selection." If you've made any changes, this will display two more options: "After_Saving Without_Saving." If no changes were made, it will leave you at the Model Selection menu.
4. Select "After Saving" if the additional options are displayed. The Model Selection menu appears.

The Graph_Slides Command

In the discussion of the Output command, you learned that graphs could be output in a slide format. The Graph_Slides command from the Spreadsheet Model Selection menu activates the Slide Show window (Figure 8-12). The Graph_Slides command contains the options that allow you to create a slide show from a series of graphic slides. These slides are placed in a "carousel" file. After a carousel has been created, the Graph_Slides command allows you to edit a carousel of an existing slide show, display a slide show, and output the slides to an output device such as a printer or plotter. The length of time a slide is displayed can be controlled by inserting the specified Pause in a macro when the slide show is displayed by a macro. You can also change the color of the slides when they are displayed on the screen.

Creating a Slide Show

The Edit command is used to create a slide show. By selecting the Edit command, you access the Edit carousel window (Figure 8-13). From here you can name the slide show and then load existing

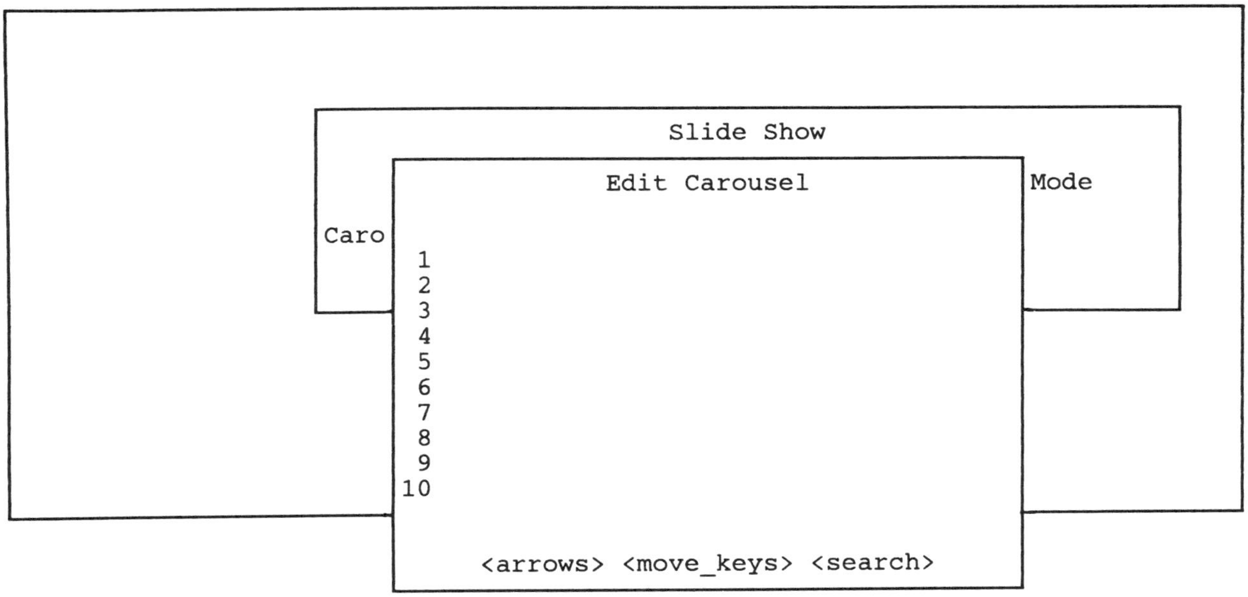

FIGURE 8-13

slides into a carousel. A carousel can contain thirty-two slides. Use the slides you created earlier in this slide show. They are SLIDE01.PHO, SLIDE02.PHO, and SLIDE03.PHO. In this hands-on exercise, you will put these slides into a carousel.

Hands On

1. Select "Graph_Slides" from the Model Selection menu.
2. Select "Edit." The cursor jumps to the Carousel Name: field.
3. Enter [CAR1] as the carousel name and press <do> **F10**. The Edit Carousel window appears.
4. Enter the names of the three slide files you created: [SLIDE01], [SLIDE02], and [SLIDE03] in positions 1, 2, and 3 respectively, pressing <ret> **Return** after each entry. (Or, use <search> **F4** to view and enter the name of files.)
5. Press <do> to accept the slide files and create the completed carousel file. The Slide Show window appears.

Displaying a Slide Show

Now display the slide show you just created using the Display command.

Hands On

1. Select "Display" from the Slide Show window. The cursor jumps to the Carousel Name: field.

2. Enter [CAR1] as the carousel name (it may already be displayed) and press <do> **F10**. The first slide is displayed.
3. Press <arrows>, <ret> **Return**, or <do> **F10** to scroll through the carousel, displaying the other slides.
4. Press <undo> **Esc** to exit the slide show and return to the Slide Show window.

Editing a Slide Show

A slide show can be edited using the Edit command to add or remove slides or rearrange the order in which the slides are displayed. The <line_ins> Ctrl-Return key inserts a line between two slide names in the Edit window so an additional slide name can be inserted. The <line_del> Ctrl-Backspace key deletes the slide name at the current pointer position. Now delete SLIDE02.PHO from the carousel and display the remaining slides in the following order: SLIDE03.PHO, and SLIDE01.PHO.

Hands On

1. Select "Edit" from the Slide Show window. The cursor jumps to the Carousel Name: field.
2. Enter [CAR1] as the carousel name (it may already be displayed) and press <do> **F10**.
3. Press down <arrow> once.
4. Press <line_del> **Ctrl-Backspace** to delete the slide file SLIDE02.PHO.
5. Press up <arrow> once.
6. Press <line_ins> **Ctrl-Return** to insert a line above SLIDE01.PHO.
7. Enter [SLIDE03] and press <ret> **Return**.
8. Press down <arrow> once to place the pointer in line 3.
9. Press <line_del> to delete the slide file.
10. Press <do> to save the carousel and return to the Slide Show window.
11. Select "Display" from the Slide Show window. The cursor jumps to the Carousel Name: field.
12. Enter [CAR1] as the carousel name (it may already be displayed) and press <ret>. The slides are now displayed in the desired order, with SLIDE03 (Sales Figures for '88) being displayed first.
13. Press <arrows>, <ret>, or <do> to display the second slide.
14. Press <undo> **Esc** to return to the Slide Show window.

The Output, Pause, Palette, and Mode Commands

These commands function in exactly the same manner as discussed under the Graphics Configure menu. Refer to those sections for a discussion of their effects.

Exiting the Program

The following hands-on exercise shows you how to return to the main Options menu, from which you can select another module or return to the operating system.

Hands On

1. Press <undo> **Esc** to return to the Model Selection menu.
2. Select "Options" to return to the Options menu.

Command Summary

The following is a brief summary of the major commands in the Graphics module.

Graphics Configure Menu	
Data	Defines the spreadsheet data to be graphed.
Display	Defines the type of graph--bar, line, pie--and the presentation.
Title	Inserts titles for the graph.
Scale	Sets divisions on an axis and the minimum and maximum values of the axis.
View	Changes various graph display parameters, such as color, lines, and 3-D perspective.
Position	Explodes a pie chart and changes the color and texture of a slice of the pie.
Output	Defines the output parameters to hard copy or image files.
Load	Loads a chart file, .CHT, of stored graph parameters.
Copy_Chart	Saves graphic parameters to a chart file.
Pause	Sets graph display time when displayed with a macro with the <graph1> key.
Palette	Changes graph and background color.
Graph_window	Changes position and size of a text graph.
Mode	Sets the mode for a graph made with the <graph1> key, either text or high resolution.

Study Questions

1. What is the difference between high-resolution and text-resolution graphics?
2. How is the Graphics Configure menu accessed?
3. Data for a graph are selected from a(n)__________.
4. List the nine chart types that may be selected from the Display window by selecting the Display command; give a brief description of each.
5. What is the difference between the <graph1> and <graph2> function keys?
6. What command is used to set the minimum and maximum scale values of the x- and y-axis?
7. What does it mean to explode part of a pie chart?
8. What is the purpose of the Palette command?
9. What command allows you to change between high resolution and text resolution?
10. The______________ command allows you to create a slide show from a series of graphic slides.

The following exercises use the spreadsheet model SALESREP.FMD.

11. Load the model SALESREP.FMD and access the Graphics Configure menu.
12. Select the Data command and define the Data, Data levels, Row labels, and Column labels for a graph that will compare each sales representative's sales for all four quarters and total year sales. What are your entries?
13. Define the chart type as Simple and the graph type as Bar. What command did you use to do this?
14. Display each level of the graph and then return to the first level and press <undo> **Esc**. Which key did you use to display each level?
15. Enter the text [Sales Performance] as the top title of the graph. Foreground and background colors should be chosen so that the title is readable. Display the graph and then return to the Graphics Configure menu.
16. Change the Scale of the graph so the minimum is 5000. View all levels of the graph and then reset the Scale.
17. Save the current parameters to a Chart File called MYCHART. Which command did you use?
18. Change the Chart Type so that all levels of the graph are displayed in a single display window. View the graph. Which chart type did you use? Which key did you use to then display the graph?
19. Change the Chart Type to display all three graphs at the same time on the display screen in separate windows. Which chart type did you use? Which key did you use to then display the graph?
20. Change the Chart Type to Simple and display the data as a pie graph if you have high-resolution capabilities or as a line graph if you do not have high-resolution capabilities. View all levels of the graph. Which command did you use to change the chart type? Which key did you use to then display the graph?
21. Load the Chart file MYCHART created in Exercise 17. Which command did you use?
22. Display and output the level 1 graph to a printer if one is available.
23. Display and output each level of the graph to a Slide file so that they can all be incorporated into a Slide Show. Use the default name MYCHART01.PHO as the file name. The filename will automatically be incremented for each slide made. Which steps did you take to do this?
24. Create a carousel file called DISPLAY and load the slides MYCHART01.PHO, MYCHART02.PHO, and MYCHART03.PHO created in exercise 23 and display them in the following order; level 1 first, level 2 second, and level 3 third. What are the steps you took to do this?
25. Edit the slide carousel so that level 3 is first, level 1 is second, and level 2 is third and then display the slides. What are the steps you took to do this?

Chapter 9
Communications

Introduction

With the Open Access II Communications module, you can use your computer to communicate with other computers. When proper communications criteria are met, the amount of accessible information is almost limitless. Major services include CompuServe, MCI MAIL, the Source, Dow Jones News Retrieval, and many others. There are also local services such as those provided by some colleges and local computer clubs.

Telephone lines and a modem are necessary to connect to these services. A modem is a device that converts the digital signals produced by the computer into analog signals that can be used by the telephone lines. At the receiving end, another modem converts the analog signals back into digital signals the computer understands. There are many kinds of modems, each with a different set of characteristics; so when the modem is used, those characteristics must first be described to the computer.

One way to use a modem efficiently is to create a modem file to define the parameters of the modem. This file is then saved and reused instead of reentering the parameters each time the modem is used.

Each computer information service requires a different sequence of access commands. These commands include entering the proper phone number, operating conditions, entering and exiting procedures (often called log-on and log-off procedures), among others. By creating and saving these access commands in a service file, you merely recall the individual service file rather than reenter all the sequences each time you access a service.

There are commands that make your computer a bulletin board, but these are not available with the Publisher's Version of Open Access II. If you access any of the bulletin board commands, a message explains that this feature is not available on this version of the software package.

In the last section of this chapter, you will use both the service file and the modem file to simulate communication with an information service. To actually communicate, however, you must be connected to a modem and be a subscriber to the service. For future reference, though, follow along to learn the basic procedures.

Selecting the Communications Module

The Communications module can be used to create and store modem and service files used when communicating with other devices and services. The Communications module uses the same basic function keys as the other modules with the exception of three special function keys. These keys and their functions are listed in Table 9-1.

TABLE 9-1 Function Keys Unique to Communications

Name	*Key*	*Function*
<change>	F6	Alternately displays six sets of prompt/status lines at the bottom of the screen.
<format>	Alt-F6	Displays the Format Parameters window for changing baud rate, parity, data bits, and stop bits.
<status>	Alt-F7	Displays the Status window, which contains the current operating conditions.

The following hands-on exercise loads the Communications module.

Hands On

Select "Communications" from the Options menu. This displays the Communications Options menu (Figure 9-1) from which you create the modem and service files.

```
              Open Access II Limited Version Communications
 (c) Copyright 1984,1985,1986,1987 Software Products International, Inc.
                          All rights reserved



                      Communications Options Menu

  Terminal        Invoke          Modem           Service         Xmit
  Receive         Get_Log         Quit            Hangup          Window
  Edit            Load            Data_Save       Clear           Archive
  Print           Utilities       Bulletin_Brd    BB_Config       Options

          <do><arrows><undo><print><status><format><change>
```

FIGURE 9-1

Creating a Modem File

A modem file describes the configuration setup for a particular brand of modem. After the file is created and saved, the configuration process does not have to be repeated each time you use the modem.

Configuring the modem means describing to the communications program each aspect of the operating conditions necessary to operate the particular modem. This ensures that data will be transmitted and received properly.

In the following hands-on exercise, set up an example modem file for the Hayes Smartmodem 1200. When setting parameters for other modems, consult the class instructor or the modem manual for the proper settings.

Hands On

1. Select "Modem" from the Communications Options menu. The Select Modem File window (Figure 9-2) appears.
2. Type [HAYES12.MDM] if it is not already the default. (If other modem files had been previously created, you could press <search> **F4** to view and select from a list of those files.)
3. Press <do> **F10**. A prompt appears asking if you would like to create a new configuration.
4. Press <do>. This answers the prompt and accesses the Configure Modem menu (Figure 9-3). (When selecting a file already created, press <change> **F6** to access the Configure Modem menu.)
5. Select "Format" (Format can also be selected by pressing <format> Alt-F6). The Modem Format Parameters window (Figure 9-4) appears.

```
      Select Modem File    [HAYES12.MDM]

 Modem file:    HAYES12.MDM

   <do><undo><menu><change><search><print>
```

FIGURE 9-2

```
                  Configure Modem    [HAYES12.MDM]

  Configure:     Format     Misc_Params  Startup     Init       Dial
                 Post_Dial  End_of_Line  Hangup      Restore    Break

          <do><undo><arrows><print><format><status><change>
```

FIGURE 9-3

```
                  Configure Modem    [HAYES12.MDM]

  Configure:     Format     Misc_Params  Startup     Init       Dial

             Modem Format Parameters     [C:HAYES12.MDM]

     Baud Rate:    110   150   300   600  1200  2400  4800  9600
     Parity:       NONE  ODD   EVEN  MARK IGNORE
     Data Bits:    7  8
     Stop Bits:    1  2

                  <do><undo><arrows><status>
```

FIGURE 9-4

6. Use <arrows> to highlight a Baud Rate of "1200" if it is not already highlighted; press <ret> **Return**.
7. Use <arrows> to highlight "NONE" for parity bits (an error-checking bit) if it is not already highlighted; press <ret>.
8 Use <arrows> to highlight "8" bits to represent each character if it is not already highlighted; press <ret>.

```
                                                              
  Config     Miscellaneous Modem Parameters   [HAYES12.MDM]    Dial
                                                               Break
            Modem Description:            HAYES12
            Select COMM Port to use:      COM1  COM2
            Translate Modem Character:    YES  NO
            Modem Command Character:
            Modem Character Translation:
            Dial Pause Character:
            Timeout:                        300
            Character Timeout:              200
            Time Between Redial:              0
            Delay After Each Character:       0

                  <do><undo><arrows><status><change>
```

FIGURE 9-5

9. Use <arrows> to highlight "1" as the number of stop bits, which signals the end of a character if it is not already highlighted; press <ret>.
10. Press <do> to enter these modem format parameters. This also returns you to the Configure Modem menu.

The Miscellaneous Modem Parameters window is shown in Figure 9-5. The parameters are described in Table 9-2. The actual settings chosen are different for each modem. Consult the modem manual for the specific parameters to use. In the next hands-on exercise, set the Miscellaneous Parameters for the Hayes 1200 modem file.

TABLE 9-2 Miscellaneous Parameters

Parameter	*Description*
Modem Description	Names or describes the modem file.
Select COMM Port to Use	Selects the serial communications port to use. The most common port is COM1.
Translate Modem Character	Chooses to send out each character "as is" (NO); or to replace the Modem Command Character with a translation (YES).
Modem Command Character	A character inserted before all modem commands to indicate that what follows is a command rather than data.

TABLE 9-2 (continued)

Parameter	*Description*
Modem Character Translation	Sends a character string instead of the Modem Command Character if you selected YES for Translate Modem Character. (For example, if the Modem Command Character was a "%," you would have to send "%%" as the Modem Translation Character.)
Dial Pause Character	A character inserted to create a pause during dialing. The actual length of the pause is a function of the modem.
Timeout	The period of time, in 1/10-second increments, to wait for a response in a command sequence.
Character Timeout	A period of time, again in 1/10-second increments, to wait for outgoing characters to reach the modem.
Time Between Redial	A period of waiting, set in 1/10-second increments, between redialing a phone number or dialing an alternate number.

Hands On

1. Select "Misc_Parameters" from the Configure Modem menu.
2. Type [Hayes12] if not entered as the default.
3. Use <arrows> to select "COM1" as the serial port designation; press <ret> **Return**.
4. Use <arrows> to select "NO" for the Translate Modem Character; press <ret>.
5. Press <ret> twice to enter the Dial Pause Character field. This bypasses the Modem Command Character and Modem Character Translation because this modem does not use them.
6. Type [,] which is the Hayes Smartmodem 1200 character for initiating a pause. Press <ret>.
7. Type [300] for a thirty-second (1/10 times 300) delay for Timeout; press <ret>.
8. Type [100] for a ten-second delay for Character Timeout, which is a delay for each outgoing character to reach the modem; press <ret>.
9. Type [30] for a three-second delay before redialing.
10. Press <do> **F10** to accept all the entries. The Configure Modem menu returns to the screen.

Control sequences must be set to initiate certain commands. A control sequence is the sequence of characters used by a modem to perform such operations as reading the modem file, dialing, and hanging up. Consult the specific operating manual for each modem for its exact control sequences. The modem also sends specific responses that indicate that it has completed a particular task. The exact sequences needed for each modem control command vary from modem to modem, but the purpose of the sequence is the same as described in Table 9-3.

TABLE 9-3 Modem Control Commands

Modem Control Command	*Sequence Description*
Startup	Sets defaults and readies the modem for use.
Init	Activates modem once the format parameters are initialized.
Dial	Sent before a phone number is dialed.
Post_Dial	Sent after the phone number is dialed.
End_of_Line	Sent at the end of each line of a modem sequence to indicate the end of a line. Maximum length one line.
Hang_Up	Hangs up the modem.
Restore	Returns the modem switches to a previous state or condition.
Break	Sends a line break or may be a user-defined sequence.

You must enter the appropriate command sequence to put the modem in Command mode. The Command mode is the mode in which all characters sent by the computer to the modem are recognized as modem commands. In the Data mode, all characters are recognized as data rather than a command.

In the next hands-on exercise, set some of the sequences that are appropriate for the Hayes 1200-baud modem. These sequences are different for each modem. In these sequences, items in parentheses are responses from the modem; other items are commands to the modem. Some modems do not use all of the sequences.

Hands On

1. Select "Startup" from the Configure Modem menu. The Startup Sequence window (Figure 9-6) appears.
2. Type [ATE1S0=0], the command sequence for the startup sequence. Press <ret> **Return**. "AT" starts every Hayes Smartmodem 1200 command. This sequence causes all characters to be echoed (sent to the modem) in the Command mode.
3. Type [("OK(13)(10)")]. This means that the computer waits for the modem to send the word "OK," which is followed by a carriage return (ASCII 13) and a line feed (ASCII 10).
4. Press <do> **F10** to accept the sequence and return to the Configure Modem menu.

Not all modems use all the sequences, and they are different for each modem. The sequences entered here are examples of the type of sequences you will enter for actual situations. Now set the initialization sequence for the modem.

```
                 Configure Modem    [HAYES12.MDM]

   Configure:    Format     Misc_Params  Startup     Init        Dial
[HAYES12.MDM]                 Startup Sequence                [Inserting ]
________________________________________________________________________

        <do><undo><status><change><home><end><ins><edit_keys>
```

FIGURE 9-6

Hands On

1. Select "Init."
2. Type [ATE1S0=0], the command sequence for the startup sequence. Press <ret> **Return**. "AT" starts every Hayes Smartmodem 1200 command. This sequence causes all characters to be echoed (sent to the modem) in the Command mode. All commands sent by the computer to the modem are recognized as modem commands. In the Data mode, all characters are recognized as data rather than as commands.
3. Type [("OK(13)(10)")]. This tells the computer to wait for the modem to send the word "OK," followed by a carriage return (ASCII 13) and a line feed (ASCII 10).
4. Press <do> **F10** to accept the sequence and return to the Configure Modem menu.
5. Select "Dial" for the Dial Sequence from the menu to enter the sequence sent before dialing the phone.
6. Type [ATDT(D2)]. This sequence enters a delay of 2/10 of a second before dialing.
7. Press <do> to accept the entry.
8. Select "End_of_Line" from the menu to set the modem End of the line sequence.
9. Type [(13)] if it is not already there. This sequence is sent by the modem to indicate the end of a line, in this case a carriage return.
10. Press <do> to accept the entry and return to the Configure Modem menu.
11. Select "Hangup" from the menu.
12. Type [(D11)+ + +(D11)AT]; press <ret>. This sequence causes a pause of 1.1 seconds, sends the characters "+ + +," and pauses for another 1.1 seconds. This is this modem's way of switching from the Data mode to the Command mode to be able to hang up. The characters "AT" indicate that characters that follow are interpreted as commands, not data.

13. Type [("OK(13)(10)")(D5)ATHO]; press <ret>. The computer waits for an "OK," a carriage return, and a line feed. "ATHO" is the command sequence that tells the modem to behave as if the telephone were hung up.
14. Type [("OK(13)(10)")(D5)]. The modem waits for an "OK" followed by a carriage return and a line feed. Then there is a delay of one-half second to verify the hang up. Remember, the exact sequence and codes depend on the modem used.
15. Press <do> to accept the entry and return to the Configure Modem menu. If sequences are not entered exactly, the prompt "Invalid hang-up sequence" appears. Press <undo> **Esc** and carefully reenter the sequence.
16. Press <undo> twice to return to the Communications Options menu.

TO QUIT: To exit this module, select "Options" to return to the main Options menu. From here you may exit to the operating system or use another module. If you exit to the Operating System, you must reload OA.

RESTART: Reload OA. Select "Communications" from the Options menu. The Communications Options menu appears and you can continue with the next section.

Creating a Service File

Information services offer numerous and varied services. You can connect to other computers, local bulletin boards, or major national services. A service file is used to configure, or describe, different remote computers or computer services to the communications program. It is used to format and describe operating procedures, log-on and log-off procedures, and to insert phone numbers that access the service. With a service file, you need only to describe a particular computer or service once. Then, access the file by reloading the specific service configuration. Now set up a service file for a fictitious service called NEWS.

Hands On

1. Select "Service" from the Communications Options menu. The Select Service File window appears.
2. Type [NEWS] and press <change> **F6**. You are prompted to create a new service file configuration.
3. Press <do> **F10**. The Password window appears. Passwords are discussed later in the chapter. For now, do not enter one.
4. Press <undo> **Esc** to return to the Configure Service menu (Figure 9-7).
5. Select "Format" to access the Service Format Parameters window (Figure 9-8).
6. Use <arrows> to set the Baud Rate: to "1200" and press <ret> **Return**; set Parity: to "MARK" and press <ret>; set Data Bits: to "7" and press <ret>; set Stop Bits: to "1."
7. Press <do> to accept and return to the Configure Service menu.
8. Select "Misc_Params." The Service Miscellaneous Parameters window (Figure 9-9) appears.
9. Type [NEWS] in the Service Description field if not already there as the default.
10. Press <ret>.
11. Use <arrows> to set the parameters to the settings shown in Table 9-4.
12. Press <do> when you have completed the entries to return to the Configure Service menu.

```
                    Configure Service   [NEWS.SRV]

   Configure:     Format    Misc_Params      Phone_No   Logon    End_of_Line
                  Quit      1User            2User      3User    4User
                  5User     6User            7User      8User    Ansback
                  CFilter   X_Password

            <do><undo><arrows><print><format><status><change>

 TIME: 11:04:26 AM  ELAPSED: 00:00:00   WORK USED: 0   WORK LEFT: 12,200
```

FIGURE 9-7

```
                    Configure Service   [NEWS.SRV]

   Configure:     Format    Misc_Params      Phone_No   Logon    End_of_Line
              Service Format Parameters    [C:NEWS.SRV]

     Baud Rate:    110   150   300   600  1200  2400  4800  9600
     Parity:       NONE  ODD   EVEN  MARK  IGNORE
     Data Bits:    7  8
     Stop Bits:    1  2

                      <do><undo><arrows><status>

 TIME: 11:04:26 AM  ELAPSED: 00:00:00   WORK USED: 0   WORK LEFT: 12,200
```

FIGURE 9-8

```
             Service Miscellaneous Parameters    [NEWS.SRV]

   Service Description:                  NEWS
   Xmit/Receive Protocol:                KERMIT  XMODEM  TEXT
   Emulation:                            NONE  VT100
   Display of Unprintable Chars:         IGNORE  DISPLAY  ASCII  ^CHAR
   Input Translation File:
   Output Translation File:
   Log Device:
   Log Filename:
   Auto Logging to Log Device:           YES  NO
   Translate on Input:                   YES  NO
   Translate on Output:                  YES  NO
   ASCII text into Workarea:             YES  NO
   Local Echo:                           YES  NO
   Terminal Window Framed:               YES  NO

<do><undo><search><arrows><pg_up><pg_down><home><end><status><change>

TIME: 11:04:26 AM  ELAPSED: 00:00:00   WORK USED: 0   WORK LEFT: 12,200
```

FIGURE 9-9

TABLE 9-4 Service Miscellaneous Parameters

Service Parameter	*Set To*	*Description*
Xmit/Receive Protocol	TEXT	Sets the protocol, or the rules, by which data are transferred. Protocol options include KERMIT = Kermit protocol; XMODEM = XModem protocol; TEXT = ASCII character by character send and receive, with or without XON/XOFF.
Emulation	NONE	NONE selects the standard "dumb terminal" mode; VT100 selects the VT100 Emulation mode.
Display of Unprintable Characters	IGNORE	Determines what is done with unprintable characters. IGNORE will discard; DISPLAY will display without translating; ASCII will display in (nnn) format; and ^CHAR will display the control character format.
Input Translation File	<ret>	Translation file (.XLT) used to translate ASCII text received.
Output Translation File	<ret>	Translation file (.XLT) used to translate ASCII text being sent.

TABLE 9-4 Service Miscellaneous Parameters

Service Parameter	*Set To*	*Description*
Log Device	<ret>	Logs or records all ASCII transmissions with this selection and the next two parameters. This is the default log device. Pressing <ret> maintains the current default log device. PRINTER = default log device is a printer configuration. FILE = default log device is a text file.
Log Filename	<ret>	The log file or printer configuration.
Auto Logging to Log Device	NO	If NO, incoming text is not copied to a log device. If YES, it is copied to a log device.
Translate on Input	NO	YES activates the Input Translation File and translates all ASCII characters received. NO does no translation.
Translate on Output	NO	YES activates the Output Translation File and translates all ASCII characters being sent. NO does no translation.
ASCII Text into Workarea	YES	If YES, incoming and outgoing text is copied into the edit work area. If NO, incoming and outgoing text are not copied.
Local Echo	NO	NO does not echo outgoing characters to the screen. YES and all characters sent to the modem will echo.
Terminal Window Framed	YES	YES displays the Terminal Window with a border around it. NO and no border will be displayed.
Expansion of Blank Lines	NO	NO sends blank lines as they occur. YES and a space will be inserted at the end of the line. Some services view a blank line as the end-of-text symbol.
Auto Dial of Phone Numbers	YES	YES includes autodial and log-on when using the Invoke command. NO and no dial or log-on occurs during Invoke.
Convert Lower to Upper Case	NO	NO does not convert the text before sending. YES and lowercase letters will be converted to uppercase letters before sending.
Hangup from Service upon Exit	YES	YES and Modem is hung up automatically when you leave the Communications module. NO and the modem is not automatically hung up.
Report Errors	YES	YES reports any errors in framing, parity, and overruns in the Terminal mode. If NO, the errors are not reported.
XON/XOFF on read (in)	YES	YES responds to XON/XOFF characters received from remote computers. NO ignores.

TABLE 9-4 Service Miscellaneous Parameters

Service Parameter	*Set To*	*Description*
XON/XOFF on send (out)	YES	YES sends XOFF when the receive buffer is full and sends XON after the receive buffer is emptied. NO does not.
Ignore CTS	NO	NO reports any Clear-to-Send errors. If YES, it acts as if a Clear-to-Send signal is present even if it is not.
Ignore Line Feeds	YES	YES inserts a line feed after each carriage return. If NO, no line feeds are inserted after a carriage return. This will depend on how the service sends the data to the modem.
Tab Spacing	8	Tab spacing for receive, send, and edit, and adds spaces to line up on the next tab.
Delay after each character	0	If you need to slow a transmission because of a slow service without XON/XOFF, enter a value in 1/10 seconds; otherwise zero.
Number of Times to Redial	3	The number of times to redial.
Timeout	200	The amount of time to wait in 1/10 seconds to receive service command sequences. 200 = 20 seconds.
Connect Timeout	300	The time in 1/10 seconds for waiting to successfully connect when performing an autodial.
Input Screen Width	255	Maximum number of characters for each line when receiving ASCII text files.
KERMIT Checksum Characters	1	The number of bytes used in computing checksums when using KERMIT protocol.
INS and DEL Key Translation	(0) and (27)	The INS and DEL keys can translate to any ASCII code. This allows ASCII 0 and 27 (^@ and ESC) to be entered which otherwise cannot be entered directly.
End of Text File Character	(.)	Signals the end of the text file when used on a line by itself in a text file. This value cannot be a space.
VT100 Keypad	Appl	Appl sends VT100 application codes. Numeric sends VT100 numeric codes and ANSI cursor control codes.
VT100 Cursor Keys	Appl	If this mode is set *and* the keypad is in Application mode, the cursor keys will send ANSI cursor control codes rather than DEC application control codes.
VT100 Wraparound	ON	If this mode is set, the cursor will automatically advance to the next line upon reading the end of the line. The reset state causes the characters on the right margin to be replaced by each additional character until an explicit return is received.

TABLE 9-4 Service Miscellaneous Parameters

Service Parameter	*Set To*	*Description*
VT100 NL/LF		If the Line Feed mode is selected, line feeds received will cause only vertical movement of the cursor to the next line, and the return key will send the single code CR. If New Line mode is selected, line feeds received will cause movement of the cursor to the first position of the next line and the return key will send out both CR and LF.

You must have the phone number of the service before you can access that service. The number can be manually dialed, or it can be entered in the Service Phone Number List and automatically dialed. The following hands-on exercise shows how to do this using a fictitious service number.

Hands On

1. Select "Phone_No" from the Configure Service window. The Service Phone Number List window (Figure 9-10) appears.
2. Type [1p (777) 555-1234] for the service phone number. All punctuation is ignored; only the numbers are dialed. The small "p" is a pause determined by the modem after dialing 1.
3. Press <do> **F10** to access the Configure Service window.

The Configure Service window includes these service commands.

Logon	Sequence to access a service
End_of_Line	Sequence sent after each line
Quit	Sequence that ends or quits the connection
1User to 8User	Sequence may be defined by the user to represent control sequences that can be sent to the service
Ansback	Code required by some phone networks, like Telenet, as you send back an answer when accessing them
C_Filter	Sequence in which you designate certain characters be removed from an incoming transmission

```
                  Configure Service    [NEWS.SRV]

   Configure:    Format    Misc_Params     Phone_No    Logon    End_of_Line

                   Service Phone Number List    [NEWS.SRV]

 Phone No. 1:
 Phone No. 2:
 Phone No. 3:

                  <do><undo><arrows><status><change>


 TIME: 11:04:26 AM  ELAPSED: 00:00:00   WORK USED: 0   WORK LEFT: 12,200
```

FIGURE 9-10

Service files allow you to set various service control sequences, for example, the log-on sequence. These service control sequences are entered manually the first time, but they can be saved for use later. The purpose of the control sequences is to send messages to the service you want to access. The exact sequences for a particular service are learned upon subscribing to that service. In the following hands-on exercise, enter a new service control sequence, using the same NEWS service file created in the previous exercise.

Hands On

1. Select "Logon" from the Configure Service menu. The Logon Sequence menu (Figure 9-11) appears.
2. Type [(D30)("logon:(32)")NEWS("FILES??(13)(10)")LOCAL] and press <ret> **Return.**
3. Type [(S30)PASSWORD] and press <ret>. This is the log-on sequence for this fictitious service. In this example, the service waits three seconds after receiving the signal from the modem and waits until the word "logon:" is received and then sends NEWS with no carriage return. After the reply "WHAT??," it sends "LOCAL" with a carriage return. After a wait of three seconds, it sends "PASSWORD" with a carriage return.
4. Press <do> **F10** to accept the sequence.
5. Select "End_of_Line" from the Configure Service menu.
6. Type [(13)], if it is not already there. This indicates a carriage return. Press <do>.
7. Select "Quit" from the menu.
8. Type [BYE] as the quit sequence and press <ret>.
9. Type [(S50)]; this discontinues service and waits for five seconds.
10. Press <do> to enter and return to the Configure Service menu.

```
                        Configure Service    [NEWS.SRV]

   Configure:     Format     Misc_Params     Phone_No    Logon    End_of_Line
[NEWS.SRV]                         Logon Sequence                      [Inserting ]
________________________________________________________________________________


         <do><undo><status><change><home><end><ins><edit_keys>



   TIME: 11:04:26 AM  ELAPSED: 00:00:00   WORK USED: 0   WORK LEFT: 12,200
```

FIGURE 9-11

Some services charge a flat rate for using their service; others charge for the time that is used. To prevent unauthorized use of your service file, you may want to insert a password. When the password is entered, it is not echoed (shown) onto the screen; so it is not seen by others. The procedure for entering a password is demonstrated in the next hands-on exercise.

Hands On

1. Select "X_Password" from the Configure Service menu to access the Password window.
2. Type [PASS] as the password. The password can contain up to ten characters. Notice you do not see the word as it is typed.
3. Press <do> **F10**. You are asked to verify the password.
4. Type [PASS] to verify the password.
5. Press <do>. If the two passwords match, the password is accepted. You are then returned to the Configure Service menu.
6. Press <undo> **Esc** twice to return to the Communications Options menu.

TO QUIT: To exit this module, select "Options" to return to the main Options menu. From here you may exit to the operating system or use another module. If you exit to the Operating System, you must reload OA.

RESTART: Reload OA. Select "Communications" from the Options menu. The Communications Options menu appears and you can continue with the next section.

Communicating with a Service

Before communicating with a service, you must specify the modem and service file you intend to use. If you have inserted a phone number and set it for automatic dialing, the service can be automatically called; or you can dial manually. Many of the log-on and other commands are learned through actually using the service. Once you know exactly what is required, it is most efficient to enter the command sequences into a file.

In the next hands-on exercise, use the modem and service files created previously. The exercise stops at the point where dialing begins.

Hands On

1. Select "Invoke" from the Communications Options menu. The Select Modem File window appears.
2. Type [HAYES12.MDM] if not already entered as the default modem file. <search> **F4** can be used to display all modem files that have been created. (If you need to change anything in the modem file, press <change> **F6** or <menu> **F2**, which returns the Configure Modem menu. From this menu, you can change format parameters and modem command sequences.
3. Press <do> **F10** to accept the modem file as is and access the Select Service File window.
4. Type [NEWS] if not already entered as the default service file name.
5. Press <do> and the Password window appears.
6. Type [PASS]. Notice that the password is not echoed on the screen.
7. Press <do> and the Verify Modem window appears (Figure 9-12). This window shows the modem and service files chosen and asks if your modem is attached.

```
        Modem: C:HAYES12.MDM
         Service: C:NEWS.SRV
       Verify Modem is attached
  <do> to continue, <undo> returns
```

FIGURE 9-12

8. Press <do> to send the startup sequence. If you do not have a modem or if it is not connected properly, you will see (after a few seconds) at the top of the screen an error message saying "Unable to send character - Timeout."
9. Press <undo> **Esc** unless the Communications Options menu is on the screen.

If the modem were attached, you would have made the connection to the service. You must enter your password and once verified, you are connected. Once the service is accessed, you can perform functions such as downloading (copying a file from the service) or uploading (sending a file to the service). In order to send or receive files, you must select the proper protocol (rules) for sending and receiving. These protocols include KERMIT, XMODEM, TEXT, or WORKAREA. Proper protocols are selected with commands such as X_Mit from the Communications Options menu. This hands-on exercise shows these commands.

Hands On

1. Select "X_Mit" from the Options menu. The Transmit or Receive a File window (Figure 9-13) appears.
2. Highlight "Transmit" and press <ret> **Return**.
3. Highlight "Text" as the protocol for sending and press <ret>. The status line reads "Press <do> to Transmit." (Now you would enter a filename for the computer to send. Once a filename is entered, you would press <do> **F10** to start the transmitting process.) We will not transmit a file in this exercise.
4. Press <ret> to go to the Select Mode: option.
5. Use <arrows> to select "Receive."

```
BAUD: 1200  PARITY: NONE   DATA BITS: 8   STOP BITS: 1
DATE: 10-
                     Transmit or Receive a File
Startup S
             Select Mode:          Transmit   Receive
             Protocol:             KERMIT  XMODEM  TEXT  WORKAREA
             File Name:


                         Press <do> to Transmit
                  <do><undo><arrows><search><change><halt>

   TIME: 12:52:43 PM  ELAPSED: 00:00:00  WORK USED: 0   WORK LEFT: 12,200
```

FIGURE 9-13

6. Press <ret>. Notice how the status line changes to "Press <do> to Receive." (You would now select the protocol and the filename to be received.)
7. Press <undo> **Esc** to return to the Communications Options menu. You will not be receiving a file.

Manipulating Files Within Communications

Unlike some communications packages, OA Communications provides a way to edit files without exiting to a word processor or another utility. This can be done by inserting a file into the edit work area. In fact, a file can be entered into the edit work area for editing purposes as you receive it from a remote service or computer. In the following hands-on exercise, briefly examine the commands in the Communications Options menu that allow you to manipulate a Communications file.

Hands On

1. Select "Edit" from the Communications Options menu. The Edit Workarea appears. Notice that the date and time are automatically entered. Press down <arrow> once.
2. Type [abcd] and press <do> **F10**. The Save Workarea to Text File window (Figure 9-14) appears.
3. Type [FILE] as the name of the file.
4. Press <do> to save the file. It automatically defaults to a .TXT file.
5. Press <undo> **Esc** to return to the Options menu.
6. Select "Clear" from the Options menu. A prompt asks "Clear erases your Workarea?".

```
                          Edit Workarea                    [Inserting ]
DATE: 10-12-1988  TIME: 12:49:47 PM
abcd
______________________________________________________________________


               Save Workarea to Text File

            Text File:

                       <do><undo><search>


 <undo><do><menu><search><change><format><print><status><window><edit_keys>
```

FIGURE 9-14

7. Press <do> to clear the work area and return to the Options menu.
8. Select "Load" to load a file into the work area.
9. Type [FILE] and press <do>. The file is reloaded into the work area.
10. Press <menu> **F2** to view the command choices that are part of the editing process in the Edit Command menu. These commands are similar to commands in the word processor and are described in Table 9-5.
11. Press <undo> twice to return to the Communications Options menu.

TABLE 9-5 Edit Commands

Command	*Description*
New	Clears the edit work area.
Load	Loads a text file at the end of the work area.
Save	Copies the work area, or part of it, to a text file.
Write	Copies the work area, or part of it, to a new text filename.
Merge	Copies a different text file into the work area to the current position of the cursor.
Delete	Deletes all or part of the file in the work area.
Indent	Inserts or deletes spaces along the left margin.
Format	Reformats the work area set margins.
Archive	Formats the work area and copies it to a text file or to a printer.
Quit	Returns to the Communications Options menu.

Only files with .TXT, .BAT, or .DIF extensions can be loaded into the edit work area. However, there are ways to change a file from one extension to another, load it into the work area, edit it, then change it back to its original extension. To do this, access the Communications Utilities menu with the Utilities command from the Options menu. Table 9-6 explains each command in Utilities. Practice with the following hands-on exercise.

Hands On

1. Select "Utilities" from the Communications Options menu. The Communications Utilities menu (Figure 9-15) appears.
2. Select "DOC= = >TXT" to view the command window. With this selection, a .DOC file can be used as a text file. If you select "Workarea," text is appended to the end of the work area and sends you to the edit work area.
3. Press <undo> **Esc**. Select "Crypt." With this selection, you can make a file unreadable.
4. Press <undo>. Select "Uncrypt." This selection decodes an encrypted file.
5. Press <undo>. Select "Rename." This is used to give a new name to a file.
6. Press <undo>. Select "XLATE." This selection is used to change an ASCII code into any other ASCII code. It can be used to translate characters from .TXT, .DOC, and .DIF files to a new file.

7. Press <undo>. Select "Split." This selection is used to create smaller files from one large file, while saving the large file in the original form.
8. Press <undo>. Select "Files." This selection is used to change the default modem and service files.
9. Press <undo>. Select TXT= = >DIF. This option is not available on the Publisher's Version of OA.
10. Press <undo> to return to the Utilities menu.
11. Press <undo> to return to the Communications Options menu.

TABLE 9-6 Utilities Menu Commands

Command	*Description*
DOC= = >TEXT	Converts Open Access II document files into text files.
TXT= = >DIF	Converts text files to Data Interchange Format files that can be used by the database, spreadsheet, and word-processing programs.
Crypt	Makes a file unreadable, or encrypts a file.
Uncrypt	Decrypts a file to make it readable again.
Rename	Renames a file.
XLATE	Translates individual characters in a file.
Split	Splits a text file into two smaller files.
Files	Changes the default service and modem files.

```
 [C:FILE.TXT]                                                       Inserting ]
DATE: 10-12-1           Communications Utilities Menu
abcd
                 DOC==>TXT    TXT==>DIF    Crypt       Uncrypt
                  Rename       XLATE        Split       Files

                     <do><undo><arrows><status><change>

   TIME: 01:19:29 PM  ELAPSED: 00:00:00   WORK USED: 56   WORK LEFT: 12,144
```

FIGURE 9-15

You can communicate (i.e, send and receive files) with other computers using the Communications module and appropriate communication hardware. All files received can be converted into files compatible with all OA modules.

You can perform many functions with the Communications module; its strengths lie in its ability to

- Work with many different modems
- Allow you to create a file of modem and service configurations
- Enter all ASCII transmissions into a work area for editing
- Support XON/XOFF, XMODEM, and KERMIT protocols
- Send and receive both ASCII and non-ASCII files
- Provide user control over all the functions and to save command sequences
- Support the translation and encryption of data
- Function in the Terminal mode connected to a remote service; also function in a Bulletin Board mode to autoanswer; emulate a VT100 terminal

Exiting the Communications Module

From the Communications Options menu select the Options command. This displays the Main Options menu where you can select another module or exit OA.

Hands On

1. Select "Options" from the Communications Options menu.
2. Press <do> **F10** to abandon the work area. The Main Options menu appears.
3. Select another module or return to the operating system.

Command Summary

The commands from the major menus in the Communications module are briefly described below.

Communications Options Menu

Command	Description
Terminal	Places the program in the Terminal mode for communicating with another computer.
Invoke	Initiates command sequence for connecting with another computer.
Modem	Selects a modem file.
Service	Selects a service file.
Xmit	Uploads text files, or nontext files with KERMIT or XMODEM protocols.
Receive	Downloads text files, or nontext files with KERMIT or XMODEM protocols.
Get_Log	Records all ASCII communications.
Quit	Logs off communicating with a remote computer.
Hangup	Sends the hangup commands to the modem.
Window	Controls the screen splitting between the Edit window and the Terminal window.

Edit	Transfers to the Edit mode.
Load	Loads a text file into the edit work area.
Data_Sav	Saves contents of the work area to a file.
Clear	Clears the work area.
Archive	Prints all or part of the work area to a file or a printer enabling the user to control formatting.
Print	Prints entire text file from work area to a file or a printer.
Utilities	Accesses Communications Utilities menu
Bulletin_Brd	Uses the computer as an intelligent autoanswer system. Not used in this version of OAII.
BB_Config	Selects bulletin board file. Not used with this version of OA II.
Options	Returns to the Main Options menu.

Configure Modem Menu

Format	Sets baud rate, parity, stop bits, and data bits.
Misc_Params	Sets miscellaneous parameters such as COMM port for the modem, timeouts, modem command character, etc.
Startup	Sets defaults and readies the modem for use.
Init	Activates modem once the format parameters are initialized.
Dial	Sent before a phone number is dialed.
Post_Dial	Sent after the phone number is dialed.
End_of_Line	Up to one line sequence sent at the end of each line of a modem sequence to indicate the end of a line.
Hang_Up	Hangs up the modem.
Restore	Returns the modem switches to a previous state or condition.
Break	Sends a line break or may be a user-defined sequence.

Configure Service Menu

Format	Allows setting of various formatting parameters.
Misc_Params	Sets service timeouts and other defaults pertaining to service files.
Phone_No	Allows up to three phone numbers to be set for autodialing.
Logon	Logs on to a service.
End_of_Line	Sent after each line of a service sequence.
Quit	Ends or quits the connection to a service.
1User to 8User	User-definable strings for control sequences used in Terminal mode.
Ansback	Enters a code required by some phone networks that require you to send back an answer when accessing them.
C_Filter	Removes certain characters from an incoming transmission.
X_Password	Sets or changes password to enter the service file.

Edit Command Menu

New	Clears the edit work area.
Load	Loads a text file at the end of the work area.
Save	Copies the work area, or part of it, to a text file.
Write	Copies the work area, or part of it to a new text filename.
Merge	Copies a different text file into the work area to the current position of the cursor.
Delete	Deletes all or part of the file in the work area.
Indent	Inserts or deletes spaces along the left margin.
Format	Reformats the work area set margins.
Archive	Formats the work area and also copies it to a text file or to a printer.

Quit	Returns to the Communications Options menu.

Communications Utilities Menu

DOC= = >TEXT	Converts Open Access II document files to text files.
TXT= = >DIF	Converts text files to Data Interchange Format files that can be used by the database, spreadsheet, and word-processing programs.
Crypt	Makes a file unreadable, or encrypts a file.
Uncrypt	Decrypts a file to make it readable again.
Rename	Renames a file.
XLATE	Translates individual characters in a file.
Split	Splits a text file into two smaller files.
Files	Changes the default service and modem files.

Study Questions

1. What is a modem?
2. What is a modem file?
3. What is a service file?
4. What is a control sequence?
5. What filename extension(s) must a file have in order to be loaded into the edit work area?
6. What is the purpose of the command and data modes for a modem?
7. What is a protocol? Name three protocols.
8. List and briefly describe eight modem control commands.
9. List and briefly describe six commands found in the Configure Service window.
10. What is the purpose of setting a password for a Service file?
11. Create a new modem file using the name MODEM1. Set the following modem parameters for the modem file:

    Baud Rate: 2400
    Parity: EVEN
    Data Bits: 7
    Stop Bits: 1

    Use the print screen key to create a hard copy of this window if a printer is available.
12. Set the modem miscellaneous parameters for MODEM1 as indicated; then use <prt_scr> to print a hard copy if a printer is available.

    Select COMM Port to use: COM2
    Translate Modem Character: NO
    Modem Character Command: (none)
    Modem Character Translation: (none)
    Dial Pause Character: ,
    Timeout: 200
    Character Timeout: 50
    Time Between Redial: 25

13. Create an initialization sequence for the modem file MODEM1 using the INIT command. Enter the following character sequence: (Reminder: Material to be entered is enclosed in brackets.)

    [ATS0=0
    ("OK(13)(10)")]

    In the above sequence, which part is a command to the modem and which part will be a response from the modem? Print the initialization sequence using the <prt_scr> key if a printer is available.
14. Configure a service file called SERVICE. Do not enter a password at this point. Use the Format command in the Configure Service menu to set the following parameters:

    Baud Rate: 2400
    Parity: MARK
    Data Bits: 7
    Stop Bits: 2

    Print the screen contents using the <prt_scr> key if a printer is available.
15. Access the Misc_Parameters window and change the following parameters to the values indicated.

    Xmit/Receive Protocol: KERMIT
    Local Echo: YES
    Report Errors: NO
    Number of Times to Redial: 4
    Timeout: 200
    End of Text File Character: ,

    Then print the window using the <prt_scr> key if a printer is available.
16. Create a password using "ser" as the password for the service file SERVICE. Then exit the program back to the main Options menu and reselect the service file SERVICE. You will have to enter the password to enter the file. What happens as you enter the password and why might this be desirable? What happens if the wrong password is entered?
17. For your service file, enter the phone numbers [313-555-4321] and [313-555-9876] into the Service Phone Number List.
18. Select "Edit" from the Communications Options menu.

    (a) Enter [The quick green fox jumped]. Save the file under the name FOX. Print the contents of the file to the CONSOLE or to a printer if one is available.
    (b) Clear the work area with the Clear command. Select "Load" from the Communications Options menu to reload the file FOX into the edit work area. Add [over the lazy dog] to the text already there.
    (c) Return to the beginning of the file. Use the <change> function key to search for the word "green" and replace it with [brown].
    (d) Print the contents of the file to the CONSOLE or to a printer if one is available.

Chapter 10

Data Integration

Introduction

OA allows data to be shared among modules in a variety of ways. In some cases, data can be stored in intermediate files (such as DIF or ASCII) for later use. In other cases, data may be "picked up" and moved from one module to another. Also, selected data can be directly retrieved by a module other than the one in which it was created.

The hands-on exercises throughout the chapter demonstrate several of these methods as you retrieve records from a database file, transfer them to a spreadsheet file, perform some calculations, and then use the spreadsheet file in a letter composed in the word processor.

With the two-drive system, you must change disks when transferring to each module.

Data Integration Example

Suppose that you work in the Overdue Accounts Department at a local credit bureau. Your manager says that the Billing Department would like a memorandum that alphabetically lists customers who still maintain a balance on their loan with an explanation of the data. You should calculate the average balance due and the total of all outstanding balances. Since an explanation and several new calculations are required; simply printing a report from the customer loan database is not appropriate. You'll need to integrate the database data into the spreadsheet to perform the necessary calculations and then transfer this data to the word processor and incorporate it into the memorandum to the billing department. The following hands-on exercises lead you through this process.

This exercise accesses the Database module and selects the appropriate data from the file that is to be transferred to the spreadsheet module.

Hands On

1. Select "Database" from the Options menu. This displays the Database Main menu.
2. Select "Retrieve." The Data Retrieval Methods window appears.
3. Select "Compose." The Query Composition window is displayed.
4. Type [BORROW] after the FROM clause and press <ret> **Return**. This specifies the database file to use. Since you don't need all the fields, specify the ones that are needed with the Select command.
5. Type [SELECT NAME, PHONE, MIN_PAY, BALANCE] and press <ret>.
6. Type [WHERE BALANCE>0] and press <ret>; only those records with outstanding balances will be retrieved.

```
 NAME                    PHONE                  MIN_PAY          BALANCE
>Abel, Jeffery           (436) 555-8847           62.50           500.00
>Heinz, David            (635) 555-8363          310.73          2485.80
>Nelson, James           (232) 555-2999           37.50           300.00
>Ruthoford, Tammy        (331) 555-1648          187.50          1500.00
>Varney, Keith           (818) 555-2956          500.00          4000.00









                  record #1 of 5 records.
       (repeat factor)  <arrows> <change> <menu> <print>
```

FIGURE 10-1

7. Type [ORDER NAME] to alphabetize the names; press <do> **F10**. The desired records are retrieved (Figure 10-1).

The next step is to transfer the database records to the spreadsheet where the appropriate calculations can be made. This is accomplished with the Context command as shown in the next hands-on exercise.

Hands On

1. Press <menu> **F2**. The Database Operations menu is displayed.
2. Select "Context." The Context Options menu is displayed.
3. Select "Spread_Sheet." The prompt "Model Name: (<ret> =none)" is displayed.
4. Type [SSLOAN] and press <ret> **Return**. The data is then transferred from the database to the spreadsheet. The prompt "Enter password for new model (<ret> if none):" appears.
5. Press <ret>. A blank spreadsheet grid appears. The prompt at the bottom of the screen "Import: location:" asks you for the cell location to load the incoming data.
6. Type [B2] and press <do> **F10**. The data is now loaded into the spreadsheet starting at Cell B2 and the Spreadsheet Command Selection menu is displayed.

Notice that there is not enough room in column B to display the full names of some of the customers. The next two hands-on exercises change the column width and format the column headings.

Hands On

1. Press <undo> **Esc** and use <arrows> to move the cursor to column B.
2. Press <menu> **F2** to access the Spreadsheet Command Selection menu.
3. Select "Format." The format options line appears.
4. Select "Width."
5. Type [20] as the new width of column B; press <do> **F10**.
6. Press <do> to set only one column--B--to this width.
7. Press <undo> and use <arrows> to move the cursor to column C.
8. Press <menu> to access the Spreadsheet Command Selection menu.
9. Select "Format." The format options line appears.
10. Select "Width."
11. Type [14] as the new width of column C and press <do>.
12. Press <do> to set only column C to this width.

The previous exercise changed the width of the columns so all the data will be seen. Now center the column headings PHONE, MIN_PAY, and BALANCE to improve the spreadsheet appearance.

Hands On

1. Select "Format" from the Spreadsheet Command Selection menu.
2. Select "Attributes." The Attributes menu appears where "Justification" is displayed.
3. Press <change> **F6** twice so that "C" for Center is displayed. Press <do> **F10**.
4. Type [B2:E2] as the area to apply the format attribute and press <do>.
5. Select "Insert." The prompt "Insert: Row Column" is displayed.
6. Select "Row." The prompt "Insert: Row(s) starting at:" is displayed.
7. Type [3] and press <do>. The prompt "How many Rows/Columns?:" is displayed.
8. Press <do> to accept the default of 1. This inserts a blank line between the headings and the data.

Now calculate the average balance and the total outstanding balance.

Hands On

1. Press <undo> **Esc** to exit the Spreadsheet Command Selection menu.
2. Use <arrows> to move the cursor to cell C10.
3. Type [Ave. Balance] and press <do> **F10**.

```
W1      A     |        B          |      C       |     D     |     E     |
 1
 2                   NAME              PHONE         MIN_PAY     BALANCE
 3
 4            Abel, Jeffery       (436) 555-8847       62.50      500.00
 5            Heinz, David        (635) 555-8363      310.73     2485.80
 6            Nelson, James       (232) 555-2999       37.50      300.00
 7            Ruthoford, Tammy    (331) 555-1648      187.50     1500.00
 8            Varney, Keith        (818) 555-2956      500.00     4000.00
 9
10                                Ave. Balance       1757.16
11                                        Tot. Balance           8785.80
12
13
14
15
16
17
18
R
Model C:SSLOAN               99.8%   Pointer:E11    Current:E11     LR  W:1 #0

NUM [R   2  -] +SUM(E4:E8)
       input:
```

FIGURE 10-2

4. Use <arrows> to move the cursor to cell D10.
5. Type [+MEAN(E4:E8)] and press <do>. The mean, or average, of the total balance due is calculated. The result is 1757.16.
6. Use <arrows> to move to cell D11.
7. Type [Tot. Balance] and press <do>.
8. Use <arrows> to move to cell E11.
9. Type [+SUM(E4:E8)] and press <do>. The total of all the balances column E (8785.80) is automatically calculated and entered. The screen looks like Figure 10-2.

To incorporate the spreadsheet file into the word processor, it must be transferred to a text file. The next hands-on exercise shows you how to exit the spreadsheet and transfer the file.

Hands On

1. Press <print> **F3**. The Print Command Setup window is displayed.
2. Use <arrows> to move to the "Area:" field.
3. Press <all> **F8** to include all the data. The cursor moves to the "Output device:" field.
4. Press <search> **F4** and use <arrows> to highlight "File" and then press <do> **F10**. The prompt "Output file:" appears.

5. Type [PASTDUE] and press <do>.
6. Press <do> to "print" the report to the file.
7. Press <undo> **Esc**. This displays the Spreadsheet Command Selection menu.
8. Select "Exit/Save."
9. Select "Options." The main Options menu appears.

With the Options menu on the screen, you will select the Word Processor module. Then you will incorporate the contents in the text file PASTDUE.TXT into the body of the report that has been saved in a file called MEMO.DOC. The first step is to load this report file into the word processor as follows.

Hands On

1. Select "Word Processor" from the Options menu. This displays the File Selection menu.
2. Select "Read_Old." You are prompted to enter a filename.
3. Type [MEMO] and press <do> **F10**.

The file, MEMO, is now loaded into the word processor, and the next step is to incorporate the spreadsheet data into the report.

Hands On

1. Use <arrows> to position the cursor on the blank line above the second paragraph that starts with "The minimum monthly payment . . . ."
2. Press <menu> **F2** to access the Command Selection menu.
3. Select "Copy." This command allows you to copy data from another file into the current file.
4. Press <change> **F6** to copy from another file. The prompt "Copy from which file?" appears.
5. Type [PASTDUE.TXT] and press <do> **F10** to begin the process of loading the spreadsheet data into the letter.
6. Press down <arrow> four times.
7. Press <do> to mark the beginning of the area to copy.
8. Press down <arrow> ten times.
9. Press <do> again to mark the end of the area to copy.
10. Press <do> again to start the actual copying process.
11. Press <do> to indicate position for placing the copy.
12. Press <del> **Del** eight times to reposition the headings.

Overdue Loan Company, Inc.
Fleeceum Bank Building
555 Turnip Blvd
Imbrook, MA 54690

INTER OFFICE MEMO

TO: Billing
FROM: Past Due Accounts

RE: Overdue Accounts

The following names represent those remaining customers who have outstanding balances. Please contact these people by phone as soon as possible.

NAME	PHONE	MIN_PAY	BALANCE
Abel, Jeffery	(436) 555-8847	62.50	500.00
Heinz, David	(635) 555-8363	310.73	2485.80
Nelson, James	(232) 555-2999	37.50	300.00
Ruthoford, Tammy	(331) 555-1648	187.50	1500.00
Varney, Keith	(818) 555-2956	500.00	4000.00
Ave. Min. Payment		219.16	
	Tot. Balance		8785.80

The minimum monthly payment represents 12.5% of the customer's remaining balance (10% payment plus 2.5% penalty). Also, per your request, the average minimum payment as well as the total of the outstanding balances are included.

FIGURE 10-3

The spreadsheet data has now been copied into the memorandum. The report including the figures from the spreadsheet is now complete. The following hands-on exercise shows how to print the report if you have a printer available.

Hands On

1. Press <print> **F3**. The cursor is in the Print Device field.
2. Press <search> **F4** and select the appropriate printer.
3. Press <print> to start printing the memo (Figure 10-3).

The following hands-on exercise shows how to return to the main Options menu.

Hands On

1. Press <menu> **F2** twice. This displays the Word Processor menu.
2. Select "Options." The prompt "Update changed current file "MEMO.DOC"?" appears.
3. Press <undo> **Esc**. This returns you to the Options menu.

Exercises

The following five problems provide more practice moving data from one module to another. Problems 1 through 4 deal with moving data between the Database, Spreadsheet, and Word Processor modules. If you forget how something is done, review the chapter text for instructions and explanation. The last problem uses a graph from an image file as part of the transfer process.

1. As part of your weekly duties, a memo is sent to the Purchasing Department informing them of any items that fall at or below 40 percent of the maximum in-stock number. You will retrieve the data from a database file previously created, make some modifications in a spreadsheet, and then finally transfer the data into a prepared memo template.

   DATABASE MODULE. Retrieve the data from the file called STOCK in the Database module. Select only the INVENTORY# (stock number), MAXIMUM (maximum in-stock number), and CURRENT (current number in stock) fields WHERE CURRENT< =ORDER (40% of maximum in stoc amount). This retrieves only the records that the Purchasing Department wants to see. When the records are retrieved, transfer them directly to the spreadsheet module into Cell B3 and use the model name INVENTORY. What is shown in the query composition window?

   SPREADSHEET MODULE. Once in the Spreadsheet module, enter new data at column E to calculate the number of items to order. Move cursor to cell E3 and enter the label [ORDER]. Move to cell E4 and enter the formula [+C4-D4]. Copy the formula from cell E4 to E5 and set Repeat to 5 times. Center the data in the range C3:E9. Format the entries in column E to remove the ".00." Insert a blank row at row 4. Now change the spreadsheet file to a text file using the filename ORDERFIL so that it may be included into a word processor document. Exit the spreadsheet module.

   WORD PROCESSOR MODULE. Select the Word Processor and load the file called INVENTORY. Move the cursor to the bottom of the Edit window and then press <ret> twice. Copy the file ORDERFIL.TXT into the INVENTORY file. Enter today's date at the top of the memo and print the letter to the console or to a printer if one is available.

2. As part of an advertising program, the Advertising Department is mailing a flyer with selected items to be discounted. It is hoped that these discounts will entice people to come in to shop and buy other items as well. You have a list of items in a database file called PARTS, and a letter in a word processor file DISCOUNT.DOC. Your manager has decided that the items should be discounted thirty percent. You will select the items from the database file, enter and calculate a thirty percent discount in the spreadsheet, and combine them into the letter to mail.

   DATABASE MODULE. Retrieve the data from the file called PARTS in the Database module, selecting only the ITEMNUMBER, DESCRIBE, and ITEM_PRICE fields. Sort in ascending order on the field ITEMNUMBER. What is shown in the query composition window? When the records are retrieved, transfer the data directly to the spreadsheet module using the model name ADVERTISING. Locate the model at Cell B4.

SPREADSHEET MODULE. In the Spreadsheet module, enter data at column B to calculate the thirty percent discount. Move the cursor to cell E4 and enter [DISCOUNT]. Move to cell E5 and enter the formula [+.7*D5]. Copy the formula, using relative cell reference, from cell E5 to E6 and set Repeat to 8 times. Set left justification for column B, center justification for column C, and right justification for columns D and E headings. Insert a blank row at row 5. Now output the spreadsheet to a text file named THIRTY so that it can be incorporated into a word processor document.

WORD PROCESSOR MODULE. Enter the Word Processor module. You will copy the data in the text file THIRTY into the memo DISCOUNT to be sent to the Purchasing Department. Load the text file DISCOUNT into the word processor. Move the cursor to the bottom of the first paragraph and press <ret> twice. Copy the contents of the file THIRTY.TXT (start with the column headings) into the DISCOUNT document file. Print the DISCOUNT file to the console or to a printer if one is available.

3. Data from a database file does not always need to go through the Spreadsheet module before being incorporated in a word processor document. In this exercise, you will send a memo to the Credit Manager with a list of all those customers in the file who have a credit rating other than 01. In this case, you will not use the Context command. Instead, you will create a .DIF file with the Export command.

   First, retrieve from the database file CREDIT, the NAME and BALANCE fields for all records WHERE RATING< >'01'. What is contained in the query composition window? Export that data to a .DIF file called RATING using the Export command. Exit the Database module.

   Access the Word Processor and then access the file BADDEBT.DOC. At the end of this file, insert the data from the RATING.DIF file. If you do not insert the document squarely in the file, use the Format command in the Word Processor to align the data with the rest of the letter. Also, add your name and date at the top of the memo. Print the document to the console or to a printer if one is available.

4. In this exercise, you will incorporate a graph from a spreadsheet into a word processor document. First, select the spreadsheet model EXER4.FMD. This model contains data about sales for four different sales representatives.

   Making the graph:

   (a) Press <menu> F2.
   (b) Select "Graph."
   (c) Select "Data"; this defines the data to be graphed.
   (d) Enter [B5:D8] and press <ret> Return.
   (e) Press up <arrow> once.
   (f) Highlight "Columns for data levels are:."
   (g) Press up <arrow> once.
   (h) Enter [A5:A8] for Row Label (the Sales Rep Names).
   (i) Press <ret> Return.
   (j) Enter [B3:D3] for Column Label (Months).
   (k) Press <do> F10.

(l) Select "Display."
(m) Select "Stack-Bar" as the chart type.
(n) If you have a high-resolution monitor, select "No" for transpose.
(o) Select "Bar" as the Type for each Level Name.
(p) Press <graph1> F7 to display the graph.
(q) Press <undo> Esc; then <do> F10.

Who has the most sales? What number appears at the top of the y-axis? What are the names on the x-axis?

Making the image file:

(a) Select "Output"; this creates an image file that can be included into a word processor document.
(b) Select "Normal" for Hardcopy.
(c) Select the printer you are using, or press <search> F4 for a list of output devices.
(d) Select "Image" for Output to:.
(e) Highlight "False" for Page Eject.
(f) Enter [GRAPH] as the Output name.
(g) Press <do> F10.
(h) Press <graph1> F7.
(i) Select "Exit/Save."
(j) Select "Options"; you are now back at the main Options menu.

Including a graph in a document:

(a) Select "Word_Processor."
(b) Select "Read_Old."
(c) Enter [SALESMAN.DOC].
(d) Press <do> F10.
(e) Press <End>; this takes you to the end of the body of the letter.
(f) Enter [^include(GRAPH.IMA)]. (This causes the graph to be inserted when the document is printed.)
(g) Press <print> F3.
(h) Make sure the printer is on-line.
(i) Select the appropriate printer.
(j) Move the cursor to the footer character |-#-|.
(k) Press <space> and then <ret> Return.
(l) Press <do> F10 to deselect the footer.
(m) Press <print> F3 to print the document.
(n) When printing is finished, press <undo> Esc; then select "Options" to return to the main Options menu.

Chapter 11
Programmer

Introduction
Batch
Arrange
Perform
Reset
A "Guided Tour" of Programmer
Study Questions

Introduction

The Programmer module provides a programming language that can be used to create database applications. Custom applications can be created using Open Access II-style menus, data-entry masks, and print forms. These and many other complex procedures are reduced to easy-to-use, English-like commands.

Some of the useful features that the programming language contains include

- Control structures: IF-THEN-ELSE and WHILE statements
- Structured Query Language (SQL): FROM, SELECT, WHERE, ORDER
- Variables: Strings, Numbers, Data, Booleans
- Windows: Multi-paned, Pop-up, and Overlayed

Now load and examine the Programmer module in the following hands-on exercises.

Hands On

Select "Programmer" from the Options menu. The Programmer editor appears on the screen.

The Programmer editor window is similar to the Note Pad in the pop-up Desk Accessories. They are similar because both operate on simple TXT (text) files. However, if you look at the Programmer menu, you'll notice that there are several other options that are not on the Note Pad's menu--Batch, Perform, Reset, and Arrange.

Batch

Batch is a command that enables you to perform an operation on several files at once. For example, it lets you

1. Print all your files at once with a heading printed before each one, identifying that file.

2. Perform a search and replace on all your files at once. This option is handy for changing variable names that are used in many subroutines.
3. Build, or combine, source TXT files into a single batch file with a .CND extension (for CoNDensed). A CND file is encrypted and cannot be read by anyone; however, it is still executable by the Programmer module. This feature allows you to distribute an application you've created to other people without revealing the source code.

The Batch function has been disengaged in this OA Publisher's version, and if selected, the Publisher's Error window will be displayed.

Arrange

The Arrange command lets you define the various aspects of the operating environment. Selecting the Arrange command displays the Arrangement from System Defaults window (Figure 11-1).

Hands On

1. Press <menu> **F2** to access the Programmer menu.
2. Select "Arrange" from the Programmer menu window. The Arrangement from System Defaults window is displayed. Now set some parameters that split the screen into two windows to display the program MAIN.
3. Highlight "Unframed." Press <ret> **Return**.
4. Enter [0] as the trace pane height.

```
[-- New File --]                 Programmer                     [Inserting ]
                     Arrangement from System Defaults

                   Perform Window:   Framed  Unframed
                Trace Pane Height:    6
              Trace Pane Position:   Bottom  Top
          Trace Filename Position:   None  Top  Right

             Programmer Tab Size:     3
               Main Program File:
                 Batch File Name:

         Pre-allocated Variables:      0
                 Total Variables:      0

        <do> saves arrangement; <undo> cancels changes.
       <menu> gets submenu. <edit keys> <print> <search>

    <menu><search><change><print><edit keys>  <execute> performs selection
```

FIGURE 11-1

5. Press <do> **F10**.
6. Enter [main] as the name of the Arrangement file. Press <do>.

The upper portion of this window has three prompts that enable you to control the appearance of the screen when executing Programmer files. When a Programmer application is running, any entry made or text displayed by the application is done so in the Perform window. The first prompt "Perform Window" lets you define whether this window will be Framed (have a border) or Unframed.

To help you debug Programmer applications, you can also set up a "Trace Pane," which allows you to track down the exact statement causing an error. The number of lines displayed in the "Trace Pane" is controlled by the "Trace Pane Height" prompt in the Arrangement from System Defaults window. The "Trace Pane Position" prompt lets you display the Trace Pane window at either the bottom or the top of the display screen.

Perform

The Perform option lets you run a program that you have written. Programs may be either TXT files or CND files.

Reset

The Reset option clears out any variables that remain in memory after running a Programmer file. It is a good idea to use the Reset option after running an application just in case you've forgotten to deactivate variables at the end of your program. Repeatedly leaving variables open and active in memory can cause errors to occur while running programs.

A "Guided Tour" of Programmer

A complete description of the Programmer is beyond the scope of this worktext and the courses for which it was designed to be used. For those who are curious and would like a brief overview, files have been supplied to take you on a "Guided Tour" of the Programmer. This "Guided Tour" was written by Software Products International, the developers of Open Access II, using only the Programmer tools available to you in the OA version that you have. In addition, we'll show you how to load the programs that were used to create the "Guided Tour" so you can examine the Programmer commands used to create them. Table 11-1 displays more of the commands and syntax rules applicable to the Programmer. Now execute the "Guided Tour."

TABLE 11-1 Available Programmer Functions

Programmer Functions
Flow of Control
DO <filename>
WHILE <condition>

Programmer Functions

```
        <statements>
        END WHILE
IF <condition>
        <statements>
ELSE
        <statements>
        END IF
MENU {vertical} options are <word> or <key>
        :<option>:<statements>
        :<options>:<statements>
        END MENU
KEYS <input statements>
        :<key>:<statements>
        :<key>:<statements>
        END KEYS
```

Variable Definition

```
Simple <variable> = <expression>
Database VIEW <variable> = <query>
Windows WINDOW <variable> =SIZE <x> BY <y> AT <x,y>
        [mode] [FRAMED]
or   WINDOW <variable> =TOP|BOTTOM|LEFT|RIGHT
        <expression> in <window> [mode] [FRAMED]
Printers
      PRINTER              IS <expression> [TO<expression>]
or FILE <variable>         IS <expression> [TO<expression>]
```

Activation / Deactivation

```
SCREEN <window>
        <statements>
        END SCREEN
USE <view>                 USE <view> END
PRINTER END                FILE <variable> END
```

Input / Output

```
        GET <variable>
or      OUT [TO<printer>]
or      PUT [IN<window>]

DO<command> <output only>
        SCROLL UP            SCROLL DOWN       NEWLINE
        CLEAR END LINE       CLEAR LINE        PAGE
        CLEAR END SCREEN     CLEAR SCREEN      BEEP
```

TABLE 11-1 Available Programmer Functions (continued)

Programmer Functions

```
or [<position clause.]<expression> [<formatting options>]
[<position clause>]
      AT <x,y>          TAB <x>          COLUMN <x>
      SPACE <y>         LINE <y>

[MODE<mode list>] <output only>
      <windows>         <printers>
      NORMAL            NORMAL           COLOR1..COLOR4
      ERROR             UNDERLINE        SUPERSCRIPT
      TITLE             BOLD             SUBSCRIPT
      PROMPT            ITALICS          SIZE1..SIZE3
      USR_1 ..USR_2     HIGHQUALITY

[<formatting options>]
      WIDTH <expressions>    LEFT|RIGHT|CENTERED
      FILLED                 FILLER <expression>
      GROUPING               VEIL <expression>

allowable chars (input only)
      LOWERCASE         PUNCTUATION      BLANK
      UPPERCASE         DECIMAL          NUMBERS
      WITH <mask>
```

Database Access

<u>Positioning</u>

```
FIND <view> <position>
      TOP               BOTTOM
      NEXT              BACK
      <expression>

FIND<view>WHERE<field> <relop> <expression>[AGAIN]
```

<u>Manipulation</u>

```
<command> <view>
      INSERT            DELETE
      REPLACE           NEW
      LIST              PURGE
      DISPLAY [WITH<mask>]
      ENTER [with<mask>]
      REPORT [TO<printer>] [WITH<mask>]
      RESORT [BY<field>,<field>]
      LOCK [PRIVATE|SHARED|END]
```

TABLE 11-1 Available Programmer Functions (continued)

Programmer Functions

RECORD <view> = <view> [WITH <field> = <field>]
APPEND <view> TO "File"

Database Functions
RECNO (<view>)
COUNT (<view>)
DB_EXISTS ("File","Field", <value>)
Statistical functions (<view>,"Field")

DB_SUM	DB_SUMSQUARE	DB_MIN
DB_MEAN	DB_STDEV	DB_MAX

Other Functions
ERRORS ON/OFF
DATE(<string>)
DATE(<number>, <number>, <number>)
RANDOM(<lower bound>, <upper bound>)
date_Functions(<date>)

WEEK	DAYOFWEEK	YEAR
DAY	DAYNAME	DAYOFYEAR
MONTH	MONTHNAME	

math_Function (<number>)

ABS	SQRT	EXP	
SIN	COS	ATAN	LN

string_Functions

LENGTH (<string>)	STRING (<expression>)
UCASE (<string>)	TRIM (<STRING>)
EXTRACT (<string>, <start>, <length>)	VAL (<STRING>)
POS (<pattern>, <string>)	MACRO (<filename>)
POS (<pattern>, <string>, <start>)	

Hands On

1. Press <menu> **F2**.
2. Select "Perform" from the Programmer menu. The prompt "Perform which file?" appears.
3. Type [MAIN] and press <do> **F10**. The "Guided Tour" begins. Read and follow the instructions and then press <return> here. After the "menu" command is described, a Choose Any Option window appears. With any option chosen, the demonstration continues.

In order to see how the Programmer commands were used to construct the "Guided Tour" applications, load each of the files and examine them. We'll show you how to load the MAIN.TXT file of the application. The same procedure can then be used to load and examine any of the other TXT files that serve as subroutines for the application.

Hands On

1. Press <menu> **F2**.
2. Select "Load" from the Programmer Menu. The Load Existing File window appears.
3. Type [MAIN] and press <Do> **F10**. This loads the file MAIN.TXT into the Programmer editor.

After the file MAIN.TXT is loaded, you will see several statements that say "DO xxxx" where xxx is the name of another TXT file. Each of these files were executed in turn when you ran the application MAIN. To see how each is programmed, select the Load command from the Programmer menu and enter the desired subroutine TXT filename.

In addition to using the Perform command, you can execute a TXT file that is loaded in memory by pressing <execute> Alt-F10. Now exit the Programmer module.

Hands On

1. Press <menu> **F2** to display the Programmer menu.
2. Select "Options." The Options menu returns. If you are prompted with a message that says the current file has been changed, choose "Abandon changes." With this choice nothing will be written to the disk, and you'll be able to rerun the demonstration without errors occurring.

Study Questions

1. For what purpose is the language in the Programmer module used?
2. What is the purpose of the Batch command?
3. Which command allows various aspects of the operating environment to be defined?
4. Which command allows a program created with a programmer to be run?
5. For what purpose is the Reset command used?